RACE
WITHOUT END

Other books by the author:

RAC RALLY

BRITISH GRAND PRIX

GRAND PRIX – BRITISH WINNERS

RAC RALLY ENCYCLOPEDIA

Patrick Stephens Limited, an imprint of Haynes Publishing, has published authoritative, quality books for enthusiasts for more than a quarter of a century. During that time the company has established a reputation as one of the world's leading publishers of books on aviation, maritime, military, model-making, motor cycling, motoring, motor racing, railway and railway modelling subjects. Readers or authors with suggestions for books they would like to see published are invited to write to: The Editorial Director, Patrick Stephens Limited, Sparkford, Nr Yeovil, Somerset, BA22 7JJ.

RACE
WITHOUT END

The grind behind the glamour of the SASOL Jordan Grand Prix team

MAURICE HAMILTON

Photography by Diana Burnett and Nigel Snowdon

PSL

Patrick Stephens Limited

First published in 1994

British Library Cataloguing-in-Publication Data:
A catalogue record for this book is
available from the British Library.

ISBN 1 85260 500 6

Library of Congress catalog card no. 94 76779

Patrick Stephens Limited is an imprint of Haynes Publishing,
Sparkford, Nr Yeovil, Somerset, BA22 7JJ.

Typeset by MS Filmsetting Limited, Frome, Somerset.
Printed in Great Britain by Butler & Tanner Ltd. of London and Frome.

Contents

Cast of Characters

EDDIE JORDAN	Team owner
LINDSAY HAYLETT	Team secretary
RUBENS BARRICHELLO	Driver
IVAN CAPELLI	Driver
THIERRY BOUTSEN	Driver
MARCO APICELLA	Driver
EMANUELE NASPETTI	Driver
EDDIE IRVINE	Driver
GARY ANDERSON	Chief engineer
STEVE NICHOLS	Chief designer
IAN PHILLIPS	Commercial manager
LOUISE GOODMAN	Press officer
TREVOR FOSTER	Team manager until March 1993
JOHN WALTON	Team manager
PAUL THOMPSON	Chief mechanic
TIM WRIGHT	Design and race engineer
MARK SMITH	Race engineer
ANDREW GREEN	Race engineer
BRIAN HART	Engine builder

Introduction

I make no apology for being influenced by one of the best motor sport books ever written. *The Chequered Year* by Ted Simon charted the 1970 Grand Prix season as seen through the eyes of the March team, then in its infancy. It was a compelling read because Simon took his audience behind the scenes. The story, warts and all, was a major departure from the softly, softly approach of the day when authors did not make waves and Formula 1 was deemed to be sacrosanct.

Simon had an ace card which he played at the very end. He knew he would not need to face the main characters of his plot the following year; having told the unexpurgated story, he was, I believe, literally on his bike and off on a round-the-world trip. By the time he had returned with the material for another excellent tale, the dust had settled in the F1 paddock and some other subject had filled the vacuum of moral outrage.

I did not have that line of defence available, and neither did I need it. Due credit must be paid to Jordan Grand Prix for the fact that I was not pinned against the garage wall when these words first reached print a few months ago.

It was agreed from the outset that the purpose of this book was to tell the story of a small team's struggle. That would involve recounting the hardship and the frustration as well as sharing the many moments of pleasure and *bonhomie* which are part of the daily routine at Jordan Grand Prix.

To achieve this, I would need unimpeded access to the team. This was granted with the proviso that the facts could be checked for accuracy. I was happy to accept on the understanding that, in return, my opinions – for what they were worth – would stand.

Eddie Jordan and his colleagues were as good as their word and I will always be immensely grateful for that. The absence of paranoia was a measure of the dignity, professionalism and self-assurance which permeates the team from top to bottom. I should add at this point that any errors are mine and not theirs.

Making judgements while watching from the sidelines is a dangerous game. I don't claim to have got it right every time. But I would like to think that it has been possible to convey the mood of the moment. The hard part is to describe the reasons for the struggle without turning the book into a catalogue of caveats and excuses.

One or two team members perhaps feel I have been unnecessarily harsh in places; that I have abused the trust and privilege which came with the territory. But, at the end of the day, the entire team is driven by the desire to win and the failure to do so is as much a part of the story as the moving moments which come with success.

Jordan Grand Prix was deliberately chosen, not only because of the lack of ego and pretension, but also because the requirements of operating on a tight budget would give a sharp edge to the plot. But there had to be a point to it all and, as the penultimate race of the 1993 season beckoned, it seemed that the team was destined never to finish in the top six.

The Japanese Grand Prix changed all that. I could not have wished for a more dramatic turning point. Having increasingly felt a part of the pressure which had mounted throughout the season, I must admit that the relief accompanying the result at Suzuka was not merely confined to the team.

This book would never have happened without Eddie Jordan's approval. Yet, once he had given the go-ahead, Eddie never interfered, even when moments of stress were played out before us. There was the occasional anxious glance at my notebook, but never a hint of censorship.

My thanks must also go to a number of people for their assistance, patience and understanding, particularly Ian Phillips and Louise Goodman for helping me feel at home and offering a guiding hand; Gary Anderson, for being totally honest and exceptionally tolerant in the face of sometimes inept and difficult questions on such a complex subject; Brian Hart and Jane Brace for words of wisdom and timely wit on the mysteries of engines; Trevor Foster and John Walton for explaining so much about how the team operates; Paul Thompson and his race mechanics for putting up with me hanging around doing very little while they worked so hard; Henny Collins and Chris Leese for keeping body and soul together with excellent sustenance at the motor home; Lindsay Haylett for making me a part of her already massive workload as she laboured tirelessly behind the scenes; and, of course, not forgetting the drivers, Rubens Barrichello, Ivan Capelli, Thierry Boutsen, Marco Apicella, Emanuele Naspetti and Eddie Irvine for their unstinting co-operation at all times.

Thanks are also due to Sasol – particularly Paul Kruger and Jan Krynauw – for providing encouragement and showing such vigorous enthusiasm for the book. My gratitude, also, to *Autosport*, Steve Bryan, Nick Burrows, *Carweek*, Clive Chandler, Adam Cooper, Tim Edwards, Chris Forster,

Andrew Green, Phil Howell, Dave Hudson, Marie Jordan, John Lievesley, Micky Miller, Simon Munger, Steve Nichols, Chris Rea, Gerard O'Reilly, Geraldo Rodrigues, Neil Roper, Mick Shaw, Mark Smith, Marek Sobas, Andy Stephenson, Jim Vale, Chris Walker, Ian Webb, Rick Wiltshire, Tim Wright, not forgetting Diana Burnett and Nigel Snowden for their usual excellent standard of photography, my wife Diane for her typing and support when I ran out of steam, and, last but definitely not least, Darryl Reach for offering his professional and speedy assistance when I needed it most.

Maurice Hamilton,
Rudgwick, West Sussex,
April 1994

Chapter 1

Beneath the Blarney

The best we've ever made

There is something about Eddie Jordan which makes you smile the minute you see him. To be sure, he has a slightly comical look; an expression which, at one and the same time, can suggest preoccupation and vigilance, bewilderment and cunning, mild melancholy and twinkling humour. Eddie Jordan may be small in stature but he is big on personality.

No one in Grand Prix racing underestimates him. Beneath the blarney is a fierce competitiveness, an acute awareness of money, a love of motor racing, an eye for the main chance; ideal credentials for Grand Prix racing in the '90s.

But the difference is that the Irishman brings a touch of humour and humanity to a business frequently overburdened by ego. Having only been in Formula 1 since 1991, his is a fresh outlook among the blasé. The Jordan team has already suffered good times and bad. But throughout, Eddie has always been worth listening to, even if the content is, perhaps, a touch dubious from time to time. It's the way he tells it which makes the difference.

Here is a small extract from his speech at the launch of his 1993 Formula 1 car, the Sasol Jordan Hart 193:

'It's the best car we've ever made and I can tell you that we're bullish about 1993. This year will either make us or break us – and I'll guarantee you that it will make us.'

He had said much the same 12 months before. And he would more or less repeat the line in January 1994. Yet, each time, the audience was charitable simply because they wanted it to be true.

That is the distinction between attending a press conference with a small team such as Jordan Grand Prix and listening to a polished pronouncement from a championship favourite. The underdog syndrome is as healthy in Grand Prix racing as in any other sport. Perhaps more so because of the money involved in the higher levels of Formula 1.

Nonetheless, each time, Jordan was making a serious commitment and a brave prediction. He had no choice. The launch of each new car is always seen as the start of another era but, in truth, Formula 1 never stops. The history of Grand Prix racing is littered with worthy efforts crushed by the relentless competitiveness of the sport. For all his brave talk, Eddie Jordan knew that he simply had to succeed. For all the genuine optimism about achieving regular success, 1993 would simply be about survival in this race without end.

Chapter 2

Preparing the Way

End of the honeymoon

Nothing had been left to chance. Louise Goodman, Jordan's press and public relations officer, had produced a six-page document. Every minute of the morning of Friday 15 January 1993 had been accounted for. The motor sport press and important guests visit the team *en masse* once a year; the last thing Jordan needed was an embarrassing cock-up. You only get one go at launching your new Formula 1 car. In the wake of a miserable year for the team in 1992, everything depended on this latest creation. This was the fresh start.

Actually, it was the second fresh start in two years. But Eddie Jordan did not want to dwell on that. He had already drawn heavily on the goodwill of the media during 1992, his second season in Formula 1 and a total disaster by any standard.

On reflection, having such a sparkling first year in 1991 was all very well at the time. But the next 12 months had been spent nursing the wounds inflicted by the rod created for their own backs during that debut season. No one in the team expected it to be easy to follow up fifth place in the championship at the first attempt. But neither did they anticipate the hardship and frustration which had followed.

In 1991, Jordan scored 13 points. In 1992, they earned just one. And that was scraped from the bottom of the barrel at the last race. No one said Grand Prix racing was simple. But the success and hype of 1991 had softened the skin and relaxed their defences. The harsh reality of the sport then smashed its way through to the core of hunger and determination which motivates any racing team worth its salt.

Eddie Jordan had experienced this sort of thing before in the junior formulae. But this time the fall was longer, faster and more public. It was the name of the Formula 1 game. But now, he and his 57 employees had to prove they were worthy of their place in one of the most expensive and glamorous games in town. The honeymoon period – in which the gregarious Dubliner had wooed the paddock with his chat and lack of pomposity – was definitely over. 1993, as he said in his speech, would be make or break.

Jordan's arrival had been a breath of fresh air, the little team holding its own and making a colourful contribution to the image of the business. But, in 1992, a switch to another engine manufacturer had proved catastrophic. The association ended almost before the season was through. By then the damage had been done. Another year like that in 1993 and Jordan would run out of credibility, not to mention sponsorship and goodwill. Everything depended on this new car.

Race against time

Louise circulated the press launch briefing to key members of the team. They each had specific duties to perform at Silverstone that day; the signing in of guests, organizing coffee, formal speeches, shepherding the audience to the garage below, the removal of a curtain to reveal the car in all its glory, the running of a few laps for the benefit of the cameras.

But this was literally a formality. For the engineers, it was an interruption which had to be tolerated. What the guests were seeing was the shining veneer: the window dressing. Everything looked to be in place. It was as if the car had arrived, pre-packed, that morning, received a dusting down and was now ready for the first race.

It was anything but. The opening Grand Prix in South Africa was eight weeks away. And that was eight weeks too soon. The serious work had commenced 18 months before and yet the team had to go racing in between. It meant the bulk of the operation had to be crammed into the previous eight weeks. And that seemed like eight weeks too late.

Nothing in Formula 1 is ever on time; nothing is easily programmed. It is always a rush. The relentless search for perfection means that nothing is ever completed satisfactorily. Pushing the deadline is as much a part of the game as defeating the opposition. And the launch of the Jordan-Hart 193 was no different to the first appearance of the latest Williams or the new Benetton or the 1993 McLaren. Everything associated with Formula 1 is a race against time.

Grand Prix people seem to work in the belief that tomorrow, magically, will have 25 hours within it. And for those involved, that's sometimes how it feels. As Eddie Jordan's guests adjourned upstairs for lunch, they did not know that the mechanics had worked through the night to finish the car. And, even if it was common knowledge, the fact would scarcely have caused a stir. Such a thing is almost expected. The contorted logic is that if a car is made ready with time to spare, then the team is clearly not trying hard enough.

At Jordan Grand Prix, the effort had been incessant. Drawing of the new car had begun the previous autumn as the 1992 season went into what was, for the team, its lingering death spasms. They couldn't be done with it quick enough. A scheme to use a Yamaha engine – chosen among other reasons because it cost nothing, as opposed to the £4.3 million bill which came with the off-the-shelf Ford-Cosworth engine used in 1991 – foundered almost from the moment the Japanese V12 ran for the first time.

It was all very well receiving support from a major manufacturer such as Yamaha, but the product had to be competitive. And this engine most certainly was not. The struggle to make it work plunged the entire team into a spiral of despair as the reliability problems meant little or no running which, in turn, placed the development of the chassis on hold. As the 1992 season got up and running, the Jordan-Yamaha team was already marking time at the back of the grid. It was evident from an early stage that a substitute engine needed to be found for 1993.

I know a man who can

Brian Hart is, in motor racing parlance, 'a racer'. His adrenalin is pumped, not primarily by the thought of commercial gain, but by the sound of a high-revving engine and the thrill of competition on the track. It is often said that motor racing is a drug; once in the system, it can never be expunged. Brian Hart main-lined on the sport from an early age by building a kit car – the Terrier – and racing it. Not only was he competent as an engineer, he was also a talented driver, so much so that he could compete 25 years ago as a highly acclaimed privateer in the European Formula 2 Championship, which was then the final stepping stone to Formula 1.

Engines were his first love. His business began by tuning them. Then he designed his own Formula 2 engine, won the European Championship in 1980 and, the following year, took the brave step of building a turbocharged Formula 1 engine for the Toleman team. That was the start of his association with Grand Prix racing. And, having experienced the challenge of competing at this level, Hart was reluctant to be involved with anything else.

Grand Prix racing represents the leading edge of autosport technology; it sharpens the mind, tests ingenuity and allows engineers to have the products of their thinking race against the very best in the world. When the turbo era ended in 1986, Formula 1 insiders felt it would not be long before Brian Hart returned with his own normally aspirated engine. The challenge would be irresistible for 'a racer'.

The man himself was not so sure.

'People did keep saying that I would do it,' Hart recalls, 'but I didn't really believe that we would. It finally came about because I recognized that the company needed its own product again. It's the only way you can survive at this level of racing. I bit the bullet and threw everything behind it, absolutely everything. The company funded the engine totally – and it came perilously close to breaking the company.

'From the first piece of paper to the building of the first three prototypes – all those hours and all that thought time – the engine cost us in excess of £2 million. That's a huge amount of money for a small company. But it's amazing how you can survive when your back is against the wall. All the time, we believed that if we could get the engine to a reasonable state of reliability and power, then we would have a good product. That's what drove us on.'

Hart designated his V10 the 1035 (10 cylinders, 3.5 litres) and successful bench tests confirmed his deep-rooted conviction that Brian Hart Limited could produce a competitive Formula 1 engine. But that was all very well. Now he had to find someone interested in racing it.

How many you got, Guv?

Hart's reputation for sound and sensible engineering was such that he received a call from John Barnard, design chief at Ferrari. Barnard visited Hart's small factory in Harlow, Essex, examined the engine in detail and discussed the possibility of the V10 forming the basis for a Ferrari engine. Barnard was impressed by what he saw and was interested in taking the proposal a stage further.

For Hart, this was the equivalent of Gucci calling upon the advice of a seamstress in Southall. But, given the history attached to this great team and its racing engines, the project was beached on a bedrock of pride and the inability to admit in public that the Ferrari engine department needed outside assistance.

Meanwhile, Hart had three engines with nowhere to go. Not that he was hawking them from team to team in search of a partner. Indeed, such was his natural reluctance to crow about his achievements that two members of the Jordan team – chief designer Gary Anderson and team manager Trevor Foster – were regularly visiting Hart's premises on Yamaha business without realizing the depth of his commitment to his own engine.

'I was prepared to do consultancy work for Yamaha,' says Hart. 'The Jordan team had highlighted one of the problems with the Yamaha V12 and I was willing to look into that but, as things turned out, we withdrew from the consultancy for a variety of reasons which don't really matter now.

'But the point was, at no time during their visits did either Gary or Trevor say "Oh, by the way, can we have a look at your engine?" It was never mentioned at any stage. And, for our part, we knew they were in the first year of a four-year deal with Yamaha, so therefore it never occurred to us that we could work together with the Hart engine. It wasn't until the Jordan-Yamaha situation deteriorated to the pretty desperate state it was in during August 1992 that Jordan started asking about our engine.

'Gary and Trevor came to see it – and they were surprised at what we had done. It was almost a case of "Blimey! How many have you got?"

' "Three."

' "Well, how soon can you do 14?"

'That was the way it started. We were on our way back to Grand Prix racing.'

The discussions and negotiations took three months to complete. And, irony of ironies, four days after Hart had signed with Jordan, he received a call from McLaren International, world champions six times in the previous nine years.

McLaren calling

McLaren's success had been on the back of Honda power. The slick organization of Ron Dennis's team, coupled with the brilliance of Ayrton Senna, had brought five wins in 1992. But now the team was facing an uncertain future following the withdrawal of Honda from Formula 1.

Dennis was trying everything to get his hands on the next best thing, a Renault V10. But as the days went by, it became clear he needed to look at alternative sources of supply. Had Dennis not left it so late to contact Harlow, Brian Hart's future might have taken an entirely different path, one cushioned by adequate finance but made extremely difficult by the pressure associated with a team expecting to win races as a matter of course.

There was no point dwelling on what might have been. Hart had a deal with Eddie Jordan and he was extremely pleased with it. In the short term, this was precisely the right place to be. Jordan and Hart would improve together. Each would understand the other's growing pains.

But first, Hart had to walk before he could run. Encouraging readings from a test bench and dynamometer were all very well; the 1035 had yet to be installed in a car. Put bluntly, no one yet knew whether the engine would be competitive in its working environment.

Jordan agreed to modify one of their Yamaha cars to accept the Hart; a date was set for Silverstone on Tuesday 17 November, just seven days after the weary team had stepped off a flight from the final Grand Prix of 1992 in Australia. Forget holidays at the conclusion of a punishing 16-race season; Jordan was already looking to 1993 in this race without end.

Chapter 3

Beautiful Noise

Cold reality

The day is bright and crisp, but very cold. In theory, there is a 12-week break before the first race in South Africa. But here, just about as far away as you can get from the sunshine of the Veldt, are Williams, Benetton and Jordan.

For Williams and Benetton, this is routine test work; trying modifications to the aerodynamics; evaluating changes to the computer software.

For Brian Hart, the day is much more gut-wrenchingly basic than that. His three years of graft and £2 million investment could literally go up in smoke. Small wonder that the test is being kept low key. The press has not been invited and the few photographers present, working for the Williams and Benetton sponsors, are not being encouraged to come too close.

Brian Hart has been at the Jordan factory – conveniently placed opposite the main gates to the Northamptonshire circuit – all weekend, overseeing the installation of his engine in a chassis which had previously carried the 12-cylinder Yamaha. He is pleased with the conversion and now, in the austere grey breeze-block of a pit lane garage, he watches in silence as the final assembly is completed.

After the hullabaloo of the Australian Grand Prix, this is strangely quiet. There are eight Jordan mechanics and three Hart personnel, plus a man from Zytek, manufacturers of the electronics black box governing the engine.

No one speaks. The only sound is the roar of the portable heater and the occasional clang as a spanner falls to the concrete floor. Worthwhile conversation has been exhausted. Everyone is waiting for the engine to have its say.

As if to add to the burden of expectation heaped upon Hart's shoulders, the Jordan team gear has had the word 'Yamaha' either covered over or removed. This is the new beginning. And it's all down to you, Brian.

It's a runner

The whir of the car's electrics indicates everything is ready for the engine to fire. It does. Willingly. That's the easy part.

Mauricio Gugelmin will do the driving. Eddie Jordan has not yet decided who will drive for the team in 1993 but Gugelmin has been asked to carry out this test. He is steady, experienced and, having struggled with the Jordan-Yamaha all season, is in the perfect position to comment on the Hart. Besides, he thinks he may be asked to stay with the team for a second season. There is only a slim chance of that – but Eddie Jordan is not about to alienate the Brazilian at this stage.

Gugelmin climbs on board, the engine is started once more and, at 11.05 am, a Jordan-Hart turns a wheel for the first time.

In time-honoured fashion, one slow lap is completed before returning to the garage to have the car checked over for leaks. Then a flying lap past the pits. It is the first time Brian Hart has actually heard his engine sing, free from the mufflers and silencers of the test bed. He says nothing. Nobody says anything. It's far too early.

Gugelmin comes back to the pits. An oil leak is discovered between the crankcase and the gearbox. A seal needs replacing and that is done during an early lunch break, the work interrupted only by a pause for lasagne and chips brought in polystyrene boxes from the Silverstone clubhouse.

Hart makes an attempt to eat but his preoccupied expression says everything about the importance of what is to come. The garage door is thrown open, the engine bursts into life and Gugelmin sets off again.

But not for long. There is a problem with the gearbox. Anderson ascertains it can be fixed in 30 minutes. This is very frustrating but, having been involved in racing for more than 30 years, Hart knows it is the name of the game. Thoroughbred machinery, when it works, is thrilling to watch; the best there is. But it needs coaxing and cajoling first.

Now, finally, everything is ready. Eddie Jordan, in sheepskin jacket and jeans, has arrived with Jan Krynauw, the head of communications for Sasol, the team's main sponsor and suppliers of fuel. It means even more pressure for Hart at this delicate stage.

This time, Gugelmin keeps going. Hart has restricted him to 11,500 revs (the V10 will eventually exceed 13,000 rpm, roughly twice the maximum of a family saloon) because the last thing anyone needs is a failure of some sort at this early stage. But even at 11,500 rpm, the Hart V10 sounds lusty and willing. The team stands on the pit apron, anoraks zipped to the chin, shoulders hunched as they listen to Gugelmin working his way round the back of the circuit. There is no one else on the track and they can hear almost every gearchange. It really does sound impressive.

By 4.30 pm, the day's work is done as darkness begins to close in. Twenty-five laps have been completed; the engine has worked perfectly; everyone is talking now; the mood is distinctly upbeat.

'I know Brian had set a limit,' says Gugelmin, referring to the number of engine revs, 'but I took it to eleven-seven at one stage and I could feel it really wanted to get going. It feels free; really willing.'

'It's good,' says Anderson. 'You can tell by the sound of an engine – and that sounded right to me. Stefano (Modena – one of the team's drivers in 1992) used to say that the Yamaha engine was fine. But he always felt that you could press your finger against the nose and stop the car, just like that. There was no depth to the engine power worth talking about.'

But what is impressing Anderson even more is the cooling of Hart's engine. For the past 12 months he has battled with Yamaha as they debated overheating problems, always a potential source of trouble for engine manufacturers since the majority of Grands Prix are run in punishing heat. But even on a cold day such as this – when outside cooling should not really be necessary – the Yamaha would require most of the radiator to be exposed without resorting to blanking tape.

This afternoon, the radiators have been almost blanked completely. It means Hart has done his sums right and the engine heat losses are being kept to a minimum. And, since these are 30 per cent smaller radiators than those used for the Yamaha engine, it also means that Anderson's calculations were right all along; the radiators were big enough despite Yamaha's views to the contrary. Although he does not say as much, it is doing a lot for the designer's embattled confidence.

'Y'see,' muses Anderson to no one in particular, 'Yamaha had the basic problem of not really understanding the fundamental needs of a *racing* engine. Brian understands.'

Hart, for his part, has been impressed with the speed at which the problems on the car have been cured quickly, efficiently and without fuss.

And there, you could say, the final brick in the foundation of trust between engine builder and car designer has been finally put in place. It may have only been a test car but the Jordan-Hart is now a runner in every sense.

Chapter 4

Who's Gonna Drive my Car?

A Brazilian gamble

In 1981, Eddie Jordan was struggling as an entrant in Formula 3. The seasonal review in *Autosport* said: 'Eddie tried to run the car (a Ralt-Toyota) on a professional basis but without proper resources ... a deal (with the equally financially embarrassed Scottish driver David Leslie) which did little to enhance the reputation of either party.'

In the same review, a kind word was given to a former mechanic, Gary Anderson, who had designed and built his own Formula 3 car, the Anson, but was in just as much fiscal difficulty as the man who would eventually employ him as the designer of the Jordan Formula 1 car.

While all of this was going on in Britain, a slightly built lad by the name of Rubens Goncalves Barrichello was embarking on his competition career in the São Paulo City Junior Karting Championship, 6,000 miles away in Brazil.

Eleven years later, all three would join forces, Jordan Grand Prix announcing on 26 November 1992 that Rubens Barrichello would make his Formula 1 debut with the team. Barrichello was only 20 when he signed.

His climb had indeed been meteoric. Success in various karting categories led to his first racing car proper, a Formula Ford, but history had shown that, regardless of the impressive nature of performances at home, any aspiring Brazilian world champion needs to follow the steps of Emerson Fittipaldi and Ayrton Senna by moving to the heart of the action in Europe.

Britain in winter, for all its cultural and physical anathema for any South American making the lonely pilgrimage, is nevertheless a Mecca in motor racing. The majority of Grand Prix teams are based within these shores. The technical know-how, nurtured for decades by small businesses specializing in the sport, is second to none. And the racing is both plentiful and competitive. Win in Britain and Europe and your credentials are not only impressive but also highly visible.

Barrichello's name came to prominence when he won the European Opel-Lotus Championship in 1990 and the British Formula 3 Championship the following year. Both single-seater series were recognized as being worthwhile barometers of form. Eddie Jordan, a keen observer of the junior categories and, having been a racing driver himself, a shrewd judge of talent, watched with interest as Barrichello moved into Formula 3000, widely regarded as the final stepping stone to Grand Prix racing. Barrichello's F3000 season in 1992 was competent rather than spectacular. The review by Simon Arron in *Motoring News* spoke of Barrichello's consistency, with mentions of the occasional thrusting drive but, reading between the lines, it was clear that the young Brazilian could do with another season to improve fundamental matters such as his starting technique. After all, time was on Rubens's side. No one was denying the fact that, thus far, his progress in motor racing had been impressive.

Nonetheless, Eddie Jordan took a considerable gamble when he decided that Barrichello was ready for Formula 1. The risk was that his relative lack of experience might arbitrate against him. Could he cope with the pressure which would come from all sides?

Jordan was in no doubt that he could. Jordan and Ian Phillips, Jordan's commercial manager, had been impressed – taken aback, even – when this 20-year-old calmly negotiated his own contract. He knew precisely what he wanted and the view of Jordan and Phillips was that he would bring the same calculating approach to his racing. Not to mention in excess of $2 million from Arisco, a Brazilian food company which had supported Barrichello from an early stage.

But much would depend on his team-mate. Barrichello would need to lean heavily on a more experienced driver for advice but, more important, the Number 1 would provide the yardstick against which Barrichello would be measured.

With Barrichello now on the team's books, Eddie Jordan redoubled his efforts to finalize negotiations with a lead driver: preferably on or before the launch of the new car on 15 January 1993. He had a short-list. And at the top of it was the name of a former world champion. No one, not even the most diligent gossip merchant in the motoring press, had any idea of its presence on the list of prospective candidates.

Would you believe it?

Few people had noticed Martin Brundle's Mercedes-Benz slip quietly into the Silverstone paddock on the day that Brian Hart's engine ran for the first time. Brundle and his adviser, Mike Greasley, were keen to assess Jordan's prospects for 1993 and much would depend on the new liaison with Hart.

Brundle was reasonably impressed, but against this he had to consider an offer from Ligier, a more lavishly funded French team but one with a reputation for squandered resources and a singular lack of achievement.

Brundle and Jordan knew each other well, the Englishman having enjoyed an excellent season with Eddie in 1983 when they raced against Ayrton Senna in Formula 3, Brundle beating the Brazilian on a number of occasions.

Brundle could cut through Jordan's verbal flamboyance and yet still be aware of the team's potential. Equally, Jordan reckoned he still knew how to motivate Brundle. The presence of a British driver with almost 100 Grand Prix starts to his name would generate a fair amount of coverage in the home media; his experience and speed would be the perfect match for Barrichello's youthful zest. Jordan underlined Brundle on the list. But, always, his eyes would stray wistfully to the name at the top.

Eddie Jordan never missed an opportunity to tell anyone who would listen that he had given Ayrton Senna his first run in a Formula 3 car in 1982. It was a test session; a useful means for each to assess the other with a view to a possible Formula 3 contract for 1983. In the event, Senna joined Jordan's closest rival and set the scene for a memorable dual.

They remained good friends throughout and Senna had been pleased to see Jordan finally reach Formula 1 as an entrant in 1991. By then, Senna had already won 26 Grands Prix and two championships. He was a star and it was never likely that he would drive for Jordan Grand Prix when teams such as McLaren-Honda were willing to pay in excess of $20 million for Senna's services.

And yet. And yet.

When Senna learned that Honda intended to withdraw from Grand Prix racing at the end of 1992, he knew that McLaren's power base would be temporarily eroded in every sense. Senna was testing at Silverstone in June 1992 and, at the end of his day's work, the Brazilian paid a social visit to the Jordan factory.

During conversation, Eddie Jordan sparked Senna's interest by saying that not only would the team be interested in doing a deal with Honda (the story was that they were leaving F1 only because of the gradual deterioration of their relationship with McLaren) but also Senna could have a slice of the action. Senna did not reject the idea out of hand.

It was one of the many options Senna had at his fingertips; Jordan and Phillips were under no illusions about that. But such was the Brazilian's substantial talent and attractiveness to sponsors, that it was worth clinging to the slim belief that a deal could be done.

Jordan would not be high on Senna's list of possibilities. But neither did his interest wane when, in November 1992, Eddie revealed his plans to run the Hart V10.

Senna knew and respected Brian Hart's talent as an engine builder (they had worked together when Senna drove for Toleman-Hart during his Formula 1 debut season in 1984). And here was a team which Senna could fashion to his mode of working. He alone would be seen as being responsible for lifting Jordan into the winner's circle.

It was the sort of challenge which would attract him. And the thought of working alongside Barrichello and moulding a future champion for Brazil had to be appealing. That, at least, was what Eddie Jordan and Ian Phillips kept telling themselves as the autumn of 1992 slipped into winter.

They kept Senna abreast of every development. The responses were never dismissive. And for as long as there was a glimmer of hope, Jordan would wait. If an announcement about the team's Number 1 driver could not be made at the launch of the new car on 15 January, then too bad. The thought of springing Ayrton Senna on a surprised motor sport world was worth whatever penalty came with the delayed revelation.

Photo opportunity

As 15 January approached, Ian Phillips had to field an increasing number of queries from the press as speculation mounted over the identity of the Number 1 driver. Brundle remained the favourite choice even though news had leaked out that he may have signed an option with Ligier. But Phillips would say nothing – mainly because he didn't know any more than the insatiable media. For as long as lines of communication were open – albeit infrequently used – with Senna's office in São Paulo, then the situation would remain static.

Besides, as commercial manager, Phillips had other issues to deal with. The new car was nearing completion and thought had to be given to arranging a photo shoot for the press kit. Ian consulted with Louise Goodman over the best angle. But aesthetic values were not to the fore in this discussion.

Fresh in their minds was the outrage once caused when an official Jordan photograph, published in an Italian magazine, had managed to hide the small logo of an Italian sponsor. The fax machine almost caught fire as indignation poured from the other side of the Alps. Forget the flowing lines of the car; just think about the cash flow to the bank.

The designers and engineers, meanwhile, had more pressing matters to concern them – such as actually finishing the car on time. A week before, everything had been on schedule – a fatal turn of events, as any seasoned campaigner will tell you, since it inevitably heralds an unforeseen last-minute drama of shattering proportions. The Jordan 193 was to be no exception.

Something funny going on

The electronic and electrical complexities of the modern Formula 1 car are such that the intricate wiring loom forms the main artery. Without it, there is very little which can be operated on the car. Anderson and his team had to wait while the loom was manufactured and underwent the equally lengthy installation process. Only then could the team begin to discover if there were any problems with the systems on the car.

The plan was to run the 193 briefly for the first time on Thursday in order to ensure that everything went smoothly during the official launch the following day. But that precaution seemed less and less likely as the massive operation involving the wiring loom became more apparent.

It was necessary, for instance, to bring the loom and install it in a half-finished state, simply to ensure that everything could be located as planned within the tight confines of the car. Then the loom was returned for completion by the manufacturer before the last trip back to Jordan for final assembly on Wednesday. The technician responsible, Clive Chandler, fell into bed at the Towcester Travelodge at 5 o'clock on Thursday morning. Anderson was very impressed with the workmanship involved.

Less than 30 hours to go before the launch. And there would be just enough time to run the car on Thursday afternoon. Then the starter motor broke. That was the end of that.

While Anderson put in hand the design and manufacture of a larger and stronger bevel in time to have the starter motor ready for the launch, the interim car (used to run the Hart engine for the first time in November) was taken across to Silverstone circuit on Thursday.

While one half of the team concentrated on finishing the new car, the rest worked with Anderson at the circuit as Barrichello evaluated the semi-automatic gearbox and traction control, two new developments incorporated on the 1993 car. For the first time, they tried running fully automatic on the up changes, the driver having to do nothing other than keep his foot flat to the floor.

All of this formed a noisy backdrop in the Jimmy Brown Suite above the pits as Louise put the finishing touches to the room booked for the press conference. A board carrying the names of 14 team sponsors had been placed at the rear of the platform. It looked impressive under the spotlights. But Louise was astute enough to realize that, when seated, the platform party would partially obscure the name of some of the minor sponsors. Judicious use of wiring – and the placing of indoor plants to cover the appearance of an ugly gap to the floor – raised the board and everyone's profile satisfactorily.

There was little contentment evident elsewhere in the team. A problem with the software had electronics technicians from Lucas – unfamiliar with the racing environment – poring over the car, muttering a strange language: 'stage 2 ... 34 per cent ... pressure ... 941 ... is 308 degrees, right?'

They spoke loudly to one another, as if reassuring themselves. Anderson, clipboard cradled in his arms, looked on and said nothing. But his expression failed to conceal his growing concern. The semi-automatic gearbox was not working properly at low engine revs. The problem had been tracked down to the electronics. And, for the moment, there were no solutions emanating from the boffins poking around the black boxes and the wiring.

Anderson wandered over to Brian Hart and muttered with some incredulity: 'One of them just said, "Hmmm ... there's something funny going on here!"' Hart shook his head; Anderson half-smiled.

It was clear that, for all their technical brilliance, these people were not 'racers'; pragmatic engineers who understood that, in the Formula 1 environment, things needed to be fixed NOW! Nonetheless, Anderson was more than willing to tolerate the potential frustration; he knew the Lucas engineers had been working as hard as the rest of the team and their skills were such that the operation would struggle without them. As all running ceased for the day with the advance of darkness at 4.20 pm, the official launch was less than 18 hours away.

A bit of a risk

Back at the factory, the pressure was beginning to tell. The workshop lights had been dimmed while Bryn Williams, a freelance photographer, set up the background for the press kit pictures of the new car. Three mechanics took the opportunity of the subdued light and the welcome break to doze on the work benches. Williams, having snapped the car, now needed Anderson, Hart and Barrichello for the official photograph and, to Eddie Jordan's annoyance, they were late in returning from the track.

Jordan questioned team manager Trevor Foster on the subject and the dialogue quickly degenerated into a heated discussion over other matters concerning working conditions. Given Jordan's voluble and sometimes excitable nature, this was quite normal as Foster looked after the interests of the lads on the workshop floor. It was evidence, too, that the management did not always agree with Anderson that the running of the car had to take priority. But, under the rising tension of the moment, the debate took on a distinct cutting edge.

Save for the clicking and whirring of Bryn Williams's equipment, the photographs were taken in strangely muted circumstances. Gary Anderson and Brian Hart stood behind the car and it was clear their minds were on other things.

When the posing was done, they fell into immediate discussion. It was decided, on the lessons learned at the track, that the wiring on the new car needed changing. That would take three hours at the very least.

Upstairs, Ian Phillips was digesting the unexpected news that Martin Brundle had actually signed for Ligier. This was a blow, since despite the slim hope of attracting Senna the reality was that the Englishman had been their best hope. There would doubtless be questions about this from the floor at the press conference in the morning. Phillips began to prepare his set-piece, non-committal answers.

For Trevor Foster, there was no easy solution to the problem before him. The previous week, Barrichello had signed a contract for the supply of crash helmets from Arai in Japan. Now he had broken the fastener on his sole remaining Arai helmet and, since the replacements would not arrive for a couple of days and he was due to drive the new car on the track the following morning, there was no option but to take the helmet to a specialist for repairs. That meant a trip to Nottingham. Foster would not reach home until 1 am.

While he was about it, Foster could peruse another little difficulty. The regulations for 1993 called for narrower wheels and tyres. This meant a massive work load for Goodyear, the sole supplier of Formula 1 tyres, and their schedule had not yet covered the manufacture of grooved, wet weather tyres. There were enough slick, dry weather tyres of the new specification available (and, of course, the latest Jordan had been designed to only accept the latest size), but what if it rained tomorrow?

The answer was to have grooves cut by hand in a set of slick tyres. But this took time and, in any case, such a solution would not be adequate if it rained hard. The last thing Jordan needed was to have the new car skate into the crash barrier in front of the world's press. The team consulted the evening weather forecast; it spoke of wind, cold – and rain.

It raised questions about the need actually to run the car at all; the majority of the media would be content just to see it, and half of them wouldn't know a wiring loom from a water melon. But they would recognize a good story if Jordan's great white hope from Brazil wrote the car off before the paint was barely dry.

That's assuming the team got the engine started in the first place. The element of risk seemed to rise in direct proportion to the advance of tiredness as the evening wore on.

An order was taken for sandwiches. 'It wouldn't be a new car if we didn't have last minute problems and an all-nighter,' joked a mechanic with the minimum of conviction. At the back of everyone's mind was the fundamental thought that the car upon which they were lavishing so much attention had yet to turn a wheel. And there were less than 12 hours to go.

Chapter 5

In the Public Domain

Don't look now

Friday, 15 January 1993. 10.15 am. Rain lashes the empty paddock. A vicious wind rattles the Silverstone fencing and orchestrates signs and gates as they crash to and fro. A lone car scurries through the puddles, followed by a plodding minibus carrying European journalists collected from London's Heathrow airport.

They are shepherded swiftly upstairs, ostensibly for warmth and coffee. In truth, they need to be diverted from the sight of the Jordan articulated transporter as it crosses a bridge in the distance. Inside is the new car. Yet to turn a wheel.

The engine has been run in the factory but the plan is to do one lap – just to make sure – before the official presentation.

The team has been busy since before 8 am. Anderson (slightly self-conscious in a jacket and tie) and his crew grab bacon rolls and tea while the car is rolled into the garage. Some are reading Louise Goodman's briefing. Anderson has little time for that: 'Let it happen,' he drawls, half-joking. 'It'll be all right on the day.' Everyone fervently wishes they could believe him.

It's cold and miserable as Barrichello climbs on board. There's so much that could go wrong here, it doesn't even bear thinking about. The engine blasts into life, the door is rolled open and Barrichello is given the thumbs up.

There's plenty of revs. But no forward movement. The car won't engage gear. For the briefest moment, everyone present is rooted to the spot, faces frozen with shock.

Then Anderson leans into the cockpit, disengages the button which selects neutral, and the car jerks forward. Everyone laughs, more from relief than side-splitting humour.

Barrichello swings right and splashes down the pit lane. Then he's off for one lap. Almost immediately, the Hart V10 is singing its head off, the revs rising and falling abruptly.

'The bugger!' says Hart, empathizing with the finely honed mechanical parts suddenly being thrown into urgent action. 'He's playing racing drivers – and it's still cold!'

Barrichello completes the lap and the car is quickly pulled back into the garage. Verdict? 'Okay. No problems.'

That's the end of the rehearsal – such as it is.

Wanna see my new motor?

Coffee is in huge demand upstairs. Silverstone, while being centrally located, requires a lengthy drive for most journalists. The temptation on a morning like this is to give the whole thing a miss and rely solely on a faxed copy of the press release. But, when Eddie Jordan is part of the plot, there is always a quote worth having; always humour, unconscious or otherwise.

And there remains the question of the lead driver. Besides, the warmth of feeling for the team means few absentees from the regular press corps as they sign in and receive a gift pack of motoring accessories from Unipart, one of the team's sponsors. Time was when the goodie would be of considerable value. But, in these days of recession and restraint, de-icer and a squeegee is at least practical.

Shortly after 11 am, Ian Phillips calls the press conference to order and introduces the platform party: Eddie Jordan, Gary Anderson, Brian Hart and Rubens Barrichello.

Jordan gets up to speak. And, as if by magic, the rain stops lashing against the window.

Jordan talks for nine minutes, running through the standard catch phrases outlined in the opening chapter of this book. He pays tribute to Brian Hart and the difficult job ultimately completed so successfully by Lucas. And he thanks the major sponsors: Sasol, Barclay cigarettes and Unipart. Then, tactful as ever, a word of appreciation for the press.

'We didn't see much of you last year,' he says, tongue in cheek. 'But our results will *compel* you to come back in 1993.'

The audience laughs appreciatively; the rest of the platform party wears fixed smiles.

Hart, Anderson and Barrichello have their say as they give rehearsed answers to Phillips's scripted questions. (It is considered a waste of time to attempt such a thing with Eddie Jordan. Indeed, it is considered an amazing fact that he managed to restrict himself to 'I will' at his wedding without launching into a monologue about the wonders and wisdom of marriage and its place in society today.)

11.35 am: 'There seems to be a break in the weather,' says Phillips brightly. 'I suppose it's as good a time as any to go down and see the car running.'

He is right on cue yet he manages to use a clever mixture of enthusiasm and carefully masked trepidation. It's as if the audience has been invited to see his train set. He speaks as though the car is on hand to be started at any time of the day and will purr into life and move gently away with the practised ease of a Rolls Royce.

Meanwhile the mechanics, waiting down below, have had time to think about the million and one things which could go wrong on a car they still know very little about.

Will the new starting gear continue to work? If not, it will be necessary to remove a rear wheel in order to get at the starter motor and coax the engine into life. Hardly a picture of slick efficiency, but a quick fix given the limited time available. Any moment now and 30 or 40 lenses will be probing the depths of the garage, waiting to snap the slightest glitch. God, let's get this over with and press on with the serious business. Only eight weeks to the first race, y'know.

A large Irish hand

Louise has given strict instructions. The briefing document says, in capital letters, that at this stage everyone should avoid being sidetracked for interviews and head for the garage. And there's Eddie Jordan, talking 19 to the dozen at a television camera. Louise smiles benignly, as one would with an ageing relative.

The rest, meanwhile, assemble in the garage as Rubens climbs into the car. In order to avoid a clumsy struggle with the garage door, and as a means of presenting a respectable-looking backdrop showing the team logo, a royal blue curtain has been hung across the opening. As the engine fires, and on a given signal, Jordan and Anderson whip back the curtain to reveal the Sasol Jordan Hart 193, the car on which the team's hopes will be pinned for the next 11 months on 16 race tracks around the world.

As Barrichello blips the throttle, the noise of the raucous V10 bouncing off the garage wall, the morning's proceedings have taken on a more dramatic turn.

It may be hard on the ears, but there is nothing so compelling as a racing engine, unimpeded by silencers, catalytic converters and the like, being given its head. Barrichello motors gently down a pit lane now conveniently drenched in sunlight. The plan is to have him do a couple of laps and then return to the pit lane for photographs.

So far, so good.

After just one lap, he's back. This is not on Louise's schedule. Anderson and Hart sensed a problem as they listened to the car on the back of the circuit. Rubens did not appear to be changing gear. It could be any number of things. Possibly the electronics. In which case they might have to wait until this time next week before the thing is running correctly.

Thoughts like that flick through Anderson's mind as he watches the car burble into the pit lane. Barrichello confirms there is no response from the gearchange paddles mounted behind the steering wheel spokes (the driver pulls the right-hand lever to change up and the left-hand lever to change down a gear).

Calm as you like, Anderson peers into the cockpit and spots immediately that, in all the excitement, the steering wheel – which has to be removed to allow the driver access to the cockpit – has not been replaced properly; it is only on the so-called safety position. One firm shove of a large Irish hand and the steering wheel is pushed home that final fraction on the column. Now the gearchange mechanism works perfectly and Barrichello accelerates away. The whole episode is over so quickly that it looks like a matter of routine. Louise keeps smiling broadly.

Barrichello completes three laps at speed for the benefit of the cameras, the still wet track allowing the traction control to prove its worth.

Traction control is a system of reducing wheelspin as more than 700 bhp searches for grip. Wheel sensors detect imminent loss of traction, the message being relayed to the onboard computer which briefly cuts engine power to a few of the 10 cylinders. The net result is a flat, strangulated sound which makes Brian Hart wince. For an engine specialist, it is the equivalent of listening to a tenor with laryngitis.

But few people notice since the object of the exercise is to see the car in action. And it looks neat and purposeful, the blue, cream and red colour scheme reflecting off the glistening track.

Barrichello returns to the pits and poses with Jordan and Anderson for photographers. Ian Phillips, meanwhile, grabs coffee and biscuits from the mechanics' supply at the back of the garage. 'Breakfast,' he mutters. It's just after mid-day.

Is that it?

A buffet-style hot lunch is served upstairs. Jordan, true to his vocation, remains in the bitterly cold pit lane to see through the last of the television interviews. For the media, the day has been successful. Given the relaxed nature of the team, the key personnel mingle freely and are available for questions. As the interest dies down and journalists begin to leave, Hart and Anderson are focused once more on the mammoth task which lies ahead.

'The learning curve is so steep,' muses Hart. 'There's just so much to experiment with; things like engine mapping, the fuel, the traction control – which cylinders do we cut – and so on. We've got a helluva a lot to do.'

'Yeah,' agrees Anderson, looking at his watch. 'Is that it?' he asks no one in particular. 'Can we go now?' It is a rhetorical question for he is already on his way to the door, heading for the next phase of this race without end.

Her indoors

Eddie Jordan, Rubens Barrichello, Gary Anderson, Ian Phillips, and Louise Goodman had been the public personae of Jordan Grand Prix. When the press launch was over, they returned to a factory which had not missed a beat while the window-dressing had been completed across the road. They were the representatives of a workforce which had sweated blood to have the car ready on time; each department playing an important part, no matter how small.

Charles Sunley headed a team of five in the buying office and stores, the fruits of their labours going to the machine and fabrication department. Sub-assembly and inspection was the responsibility of Don Raper; Tom Anderson leading the composite division responsible for the major part of manufacturing the chassis. All of these departments, not to mention the general well-being of the factory, was under the watchful eye of Bob Halliwell.

Upstairs, in the administration department, Richard O'Driscoll acted as financial controller and worked with one book-keeper. Louise and Ian shared a large office with Lindsay Haylett, who occupied the desk beside the connecting door to Eddie Jordan's executive office.

Lindsay's job was, in some respects, the most difficult of them all; she was responsible for keeping Eddie in check and informed as well as handling much of the day-to-day details ranging from Eddie's appointments book to invoicing, the typing of contracts and the arranging of hotel rooms at the races – a major headache in itself. She rarely got to see either her boss or the cars in operation; some would say that was a mild blessing. But Lindsay Haylett ran much of the show. Her input was incalculable, despite the inevitable jokes about being the 'her indoors' of Jordan Grand Prix.

Digging a mole

It was with more than passing interest that the team fell upon the motoring publications the following week. The reports of the launch would reflect the success or otherwise of Louise Goodman's ministrations.

Unfortunately for Jordan, the week ending 16 January 1993 had been a busy one in terms of Formula 1 news. Normally, this time of the year is quiet and the unveiling of the Jordan 193 should have been the lead story. But, in the same week, Brundle had signed for Ligier, Benetton had taken the wraps off their latest Formula 1 offering and Mitsubishi had shown their new rally car for the first time.

Autosport (weekly glossy magazine, priced £1.80) had also chosen that Thursday to publish an exclusive interview with Damon Hill, billed on the front cover as Britain's next World Champion. The Jordan story occupied page 2 of the 'Pit & Paddock' news section inside.

Motoring News had a picture of the Jordan, tucked away in the bottom right-hand corner of the front page. But the weekly newspaper (75p) had devoted a considerable amount of print on the inside pages to a story about the launch and a good interview with Gary Anderson. Too good, in fact.

Anderson, in his usual up-front, straightforward way, had made reference to the fuel consumption of the Hart V10. It was complimentary. But, for the secretive Hart, this was giving too much away to the opposition at such an early stage.

But what really bothered Hart was a reference to an engine failure which had occurred in a recent test session at the Paul Ricard circuit in the south of France. For an engine builder, a mechanical failure is a mortal wound. David Tremayne, the paper's editor, had ferreted out the rumour in his usual diligent way and then presented it, in matter of fact fashion, to Anderson during their conversation. Anderson, believing it must be common knowledge, had fallen into the trap by then confirming the story.

Hart was angry, not with Anderson since he fully appreciated the man's sincerity and direct honesty, but with the fact that Tremayne might have been tipped off. It appeared there was a mole at work within the team. Hart had his suspicions. But, whatever the source of the leak, it was unsettling, particularly as Jordan and Hart were about to embark on a serious test session at the Estoril circuit in Portugal. This could throw up all sorts of problems. The last thing Hart wanted to do was read about them the following week.

Chapter 6

The Business of Testing

Portugal in January, eh? Lucky you

London, Heathrow. Sunday, 24 January 1993. 7.15 am.

The concourse of Terminal 2 echoes to the clatter of skiing equipment and the gung-ho banter of people going on holiday. The blazer-clad members of Jordan-Hart, mingling with the shell suits and the dayglo anoraks, scarcely notice. This may be a trip to Portugal, leaving Britain on a stormy winter's morning. But it is strictly business.

Heathrow is as familiar to racing teams as Waterloo station is to southern commuters. It is a place to be got through with the minimum of fuss and, like passengers at the mercy of British Rail, regular users of London Heathrow unconsciously acquire immunization against being herded into situations characterized by delay and frustration.

This morning it is the turn of the fire alarm system to play havoc. Having checked in for the flight to Lisbon, the Jordan crew have begun to gather in the coffee shop when the bell sounds.

A public address announcement asks everyone to stand in a nearby corridor. They wait there for 15 minutes as the terminal comes to a standstill, save for officials bustling to and fro, speaking intently into portable radios. It does not take a genius to work out that flight movements will be seriously disrupted. This may be a Sunday morning but the airport is busy. The knock-on effect of the delay will be felt all day.

Sure enough, once on board the Boeing 737, passengers sit in the desperately cramped Economy Class seats for 45 minutes before the TAP aircraft is pushed back from the gate. It eventually gets into the sky one and a half hours behind schedule. The Formula 1 people take it in their stride.

Joining Jordan on the flight are members of Benetton-Ford. The difference is that Benetton can afford a test division which operates separately from the team which will attend the Grands Prix. The Benetton mechanics on this trip rarely see any racing; their job is important development work conducted away from the glamour of the main event.

For Jordan Grand Prix, there is no such luxury. The mechanics en route to Portugal, and any other test sessions on the schedule, are the same mechanics who will also undergo the rigours imposed by the 16-race calendar. But at least, at the end of it, they will be entirely familiar with the car. Too much so, in fact.

Test sessions are rehearsals in mufti. They are often lengthy and always without the hype of race weekends. Some people like them for that very reason; others miss the adrenalin associated with the urgency of a Grand Prix. But testing is work which has to be done if the team is to be adequately prepared for the season ahead.

A Grand Prix car is as highly strung as any thoroughbred. The slightest change – often measured in millimetres – to the suspension settings can alter the character of the car, changing it from a responsive and willing sprinter to an obstinate and lethal bronco.

'This test is critical for us,' says Anderson. 'We need to discover more about the gearbox. For instance, we want to try fully automatic down changes and see how that goes. At the same time, I want to learn more about how to set the car up; what happens when you try different things on the suspension, aerodynamics and so on. All of this is very important for us at this stage because it will help us decide which way we should go with the car during the first few races at least.'

Can Barrichello cope?

With the choice of the second driver still undecided, Barrichello will carry out cockpit duties. It is an onerous task and one which, although he makes no mention of it, must give Anderson cause for concern.

Feedback from the driver is everything. His word can heavily influence the road of development down which the team will eventually choose to travel. But with no Formula 1 experience to fall back on, Barrichello, for all his enthusiasm and natural ability, will be struggling to establish a performance bench mark. If the handling is poor, is this normal in a Formula 1 car? And, if it improves, is this as good as it's going to get? How will he know? If lap times are disappointing, is it him or is it the car?

The team has already witnessed the side-effect of his inexperience. During the tests at Silverstone, he complained of locking brakes. It was eventually discovered that insufficient pressure was being applied to the brake pedal early in the movement, when the car was still at speed and operating with the maximum downforce.

(In simple terms, downforce is created by the passage of air over the wings and bodywork, thus forcing the car on to the track, giving, among other things, increased stability under braking.) By braking harder, later, the car was going comparatively slower and was therefore less stable. Hence the tendency for the brakes to lock.

It was thought that Barrichello might not be comfortable in the cockpit; unable to reach the pedal properly. There was a suspicion that he might have back trouble of some sort. Already, he was into his fourth different seat, each one moulded specially to fit his diminutive build. And still the brake trouble had persisted. 'He's got to brake hard,' observed Anderson. 'I've told him to try and shove his foot through the bulkhead *immediately* he hits the pedal. He'll be okay.'

Maybe so. But it's an undeniable fact that a designer would not need to preach such fundamental values to a driver with the experience of Senna or Brundle. It is cause for mild concern about precisely what might be achieved in the days that lie ahead.

Them and us

The Iberian climate – warm, sunny, clear sky and no wind – has a soothing effect at the end of a two-hour flight which has seemed twice as long. There will be no running at the track today, so the 20-mile drive to Estoril is a leisurely one. Well, leisurely by Formula 1 standards; the hire cars – driven by crew chief John 'John Boy' Walton and Brian Hart – are conducted at a fast cruise rather than an apparent audition for the role of getaway driver in a Hollywood epic.

There are doubts that the truck will have arrived after the three-day journey from England. But it's already in place at the back of the pits, the car unloaded and equipment in position. Chief truckie, Rick Wiltshire, is already in shorts and busy washing the dust from the massive transporter. He flicks spray through the open sunroof of Walton's Fiat Tempura in response to a ribald remark about a truck driver's easy life in the sun.

Thirty-one spectators are sprinkled across a white concrete grandstand designed to accommodate several hundred. Brian Hart takes a walk along the near-deserted pit lane. Sauber, new to Formula 1 for 1993, are present and ready for action. Benetton are unloading two cars while, alongside, the presence of the Ferrari motorhome suggests the Italian team is on its way.

Away from the rest, the Williams-Renault crew have spread themselves over a number of garages, as befits a top team seen by many as favourite to win the championship. Hart peers through the door and notes with barely concealed disappointment that the Renault technicians have screened off the area in which the engines are to be worked on. But he does note the banks of monitors and telemetry equipment which will be used to receive and analyse information from the Williams cars while on the move. Such a scene would not be amiss from a back room at NASA.

Hart, along with most small teams, will rely on a couple of lap top computers and a collapsible pasting table, the computers plugged into the car when it comes to rest. It is the equivalent of comparing a calculator with an abacus: the results are much the same, it's just that they take longer to achieve. But Hart is content enough. He says the £400,000 needed to provide telemetry – and the truck to carry it – can be better spent in an operation as financially restricted as his.

In the garage next door, the Renault chef has set up enough tables and chairs to seat 35. Jordan, housed in their single garage at the opposite end of the row, will rely on fast food from wherever they can find it. Already the Formula 1 class divide is evident, even before a car has so much as turned a wheel.

Once the Jordan-Hart has been finally prepared and the engine run briefly, the car is covered over and the mechanics set off for their hotel and the luxury of a night off. If you need proof that this is business rather than a holiday trip abroad, they eschew the famous seafood of the region for a German restaurant next door.

Gastronomic pleasures come low on the list of priorities. This particular restaurant is chosen simply because it is convenient, has a round table which seats 10 – and serves litres of draught beer. The boys from Jordan-Hart make a considerable dent in the restaurant's liquid stock. They make the most of the occasion. The first really serious track work of 1993 starts tomorrow. If there is time to eat out tomorrow evening, then the test is going according to plan. And everyone present knows Formula 1 is not as straightforward as that.

In the dark

Monday, 25 January 1993. 8.30 am.

During a race weekend, mechanics will usually arrive at the track before 7 am. By then, the summer sun will be climbing, making short-sleeve shirts and shorts the order of the day. It is a matter of routine from Barcelona to Monaco to Budapest.

But today is very different. The fact that this is a pre-season test session is brought home as the headlights from the hire cars pick out the gates to the almost deserted paddock. It is like holding Wimbledon on a Monday morning in the middle of January. Nothing seems right, least of all the late sunrise. Mechanics, jackets zipped against the wind ripping across the exposed plateau, walk briskly to the garage which will be their place of work for the next few days. It is hardly a welcoming sight.

Electric cables are draped across the white-washed walls. Concrete beams with a rough finish support the asbestos sheet roof. A badly faded notice, hanging as if in temporary fashion by wire, warns against using the beam as a means of support for lifting heavy items. The advice is irrelevant; only a fool would dare to test the strength of this structure. The roller doors tremble gently in the wind. A large cylindrical urn, already on the brew, is the only heart-warming sight. But the team is oblivious to all of this. Immediately they are bending into the task of making the car ready to run. The Jordan 193, up on stands and without its wheels, is like some brightly coloured missile. It is the undisputed focus of attention.

The bodywork receives a final polish. A water heater is connected to the engine in order to warm the coolant and overcome potential problems with shrinkage when the engine is first started from cold.

A technician from Goodyear arrives to explain that the tyres available this week are, in fact, old stock. The factory is flat out making the new tyre sizes required for 1993 and this is the best they can offer. Everyone accepts the situation since the purpose of this test is not to evaluate tyres but the cars themselves.

The wheels are fitted and the car drops from the jacks. Jordan is ready to run.

Minute by minute

09.37 Roll up the front shutter; momentarily caught by surprise by clear sky and sunshine. Barrichello is the first car onto the track. The opportunity is taken to quickly sweep the garage floor. Barrichello completes two slow laps. Back to the pits to have the car checked for leaks and anything untoward.

09.50 Joined on the track by the Finnish driver, J. J. Lehto, in the Sauber. A flag above the empty grandstand opposite is almost rigid and flying parallel to the main straight. The gentle calm and embracing warmth of the day before has been dramatically usurped.

09.55 Barrichello returns to report that an oil slick and a large amount of dust is making the surface very slippery. He reckons it will take the cars half a day to gradually clean up the track. In any case, the strong following wind on the main straight means the gearing is wrong. And Anderson is aware that Hart does not wish to run his engine at maximum revs on the first day. It is decided to change the top gear ratio.

10.00 The first Williams-Renault (driven by Alain Prost) appears but only completes a few laps.

Changing the gear ratios is a comparatively slow process since this is the first time the mechanics have done it on the new car. The roller door is closed and heat seeps into the garage as the sun shines on the metal. Outside, the track is silent. In general, there is a surprising lack of activity and urgency; it sums up the frequently tedious nature of testing.

11.00 Both Williams (Prost and Damon Hill) on the track but interest focuses on the paddock; Ferrari has arrived. This is the first track appearance of their new car. As the two chassis are unloaded, it gives rival teams a chance for a close look before the cars are rolled into the garage and the area is cordoned off.

11.45 Barrichello is out once more. Consternation when the engine momentarily hits 13,280 rpm as the Jordan bounces off the bumps on the main straight. Hart does not want to exceed 12,900 rpm at this stage. Anderson muses that the engine rev-limiter is not reacting fast enough.

12.00 Red flag. The track is closed for lunch – an hour earlier than anyone had expected. No point in arguing. This is Portugal.

Having drawn information from the car's on-board computer, the technicians pore over the laptop computers and make assessments. Among other things, it is decided to change the gear ratios again.

Lunch arrives from McDonald's at a nearby shopping centre: burgers, milk shakes and Cokes. Down at Williams-Renault, they tuck into Mozzarella and tomato, pasta and, for anyone not actually working on the cars, a glass or two of white wine.

15.10 Barrichello returns to the track. But the problem of over-revving the engine is still there as he hits a particularly treacherous bump while touching 190 mph at the end of the straight. 'It's even worse than before,' says Hart. 'My heart goes every time I hear it ... '

15.30 Red flag. Track closed to allow a broken-down car to be retrieved.

15.45 Barrichello returns to the track. Hart, watching and listening by the pit wall, notes that, unlike some drivers, Rubens does not move to the right of the offending bump, the stiffly-sprung Jordan bouncing quite badly. Is this his lack of experience showing?

16.30 The new Ferrari (driven by Gerhard Berger) emerges for the first time. Almost immediately, it is evident that the handling of the red car on the bumps is 10 times worse than the Jordan. But that smidgen of consolation is quickly forgotten as Barrichello returns slowly to the pits with a potentially serious problem. The engine oil pressure has fallen to zero.

Initial diagnosis suggests it may simply be a faulty sensor. This is changed. The engine is started but Hart's personal antenna is on full alert. 'Don't like the sound of that,' he murmurs, while ordering the engine to be switched off immediately.

He unscrews the filler on top of the oil tank and sticks his nose into the opening. If things have gone wrong inside the engine, a pungent smell, reminiscent of rotten eggs, can be a tell-tale sign. He's not happy. The mechanics stand motionless by the back of the car, watching his every move and waiting for the verdict.

'Change it,' says Hart, quietly. All manner of thoughts go through his mind. An engine failure at this stage would be a disaster.

17.05 Barrichello climbs from the cockpit as the mechanics spring into action. The car is raised at the front, the better to tip the remaining fuel to the back of the tank to facilitate drainage. The wheels are removed; trays to catch the engine oil are made ready; the appropriate tools quickly gathered together. Hart's assistant, Neil Roper, uncovers a fresh engine and finalizes preparations for installation.

17.10 Much activity on the track indicates that the opening session is drawing to a close. Michael Schumacher's Benetton joins Prost as they set the fastest times of the day. Word has it that they are already four seconds faster than Barrichello's best lap time. That's a huge gap. But everyone at Jordan consoles themselves with the undeniable fact that comparisons are meaningless at this early stage.

Even so. Four seconds. That's a lot. Is it the car? It is the engine? Is it the driver? These are questions which no one voices aloud. But you can sense the beginning of niggling doubt.

17.15 Berger attempts to join the track for one last run but is turned back by a man with a red flag at the end of the pit lane. The track is closed for the day. Berger and Ferrari have been even slower than the Jordan.

In the absence of the official timing normally evident at the Grands Prix, the teams exchange information, revealing their best lap times of the day. It merely confirms what Jordan and Hart knew already; they have much work to do.

Prost, making his comeback after a year's absence from Grand Prix racing, holds an informal press conference for the half-dozen or so members of the media present (a Grand Prix would boast a press attendance of several hundred journalists).

18.55 The engine is removed from the back of the Jordan. Hart quickly discovers that a belt driving the oil pump has broken. The telemetry shows that it failed going through the last corner, a very fast right-hander, yet Barrichello was able to drive back to the pits with no oil pressure – and no drama. That, at least, is positive.

But the failure of the belt requires a rethink and a change of specification. Within minutes, Hart is on the telephone in the transporter, sending instructions back to base, liaising with his secretary, Jane Brace. This is exactly what pre-season testing is all about; the exposure of problems and, hopefully, their successful eradication. Barrichello relates his experiences in Portuguese to a South American journalist. Anderson checks his log sheet and summarizes the day's activities.

'30 laps,' he says. 'At least we did more laps than Ferrari!'

'Anyway,' says Hart, relieved that the trouble is not more serious, 'that engine was due to be changed after another nine laps in any case.'

Music drifts indoors from the ghettoblaster mounted on the back of the truck. It remains windy, the chill now blowing under the roller doors at the front. Hands of those watching the mechanics at work are dug deep in anorak pockets. The evening is beginning to drag.

21.32 'Are we ready to make a noise?' asks Hart, as the final hoses are secured and nuts tightened.

'Yeah, nearly,' says Anderson.

21.40 The brand new Hart V10 breaks into a throaty burble at the first attempt. It runs for a couple of minutes. Everything is in order. Switch off. Time to go home.

22.05 The tendency is to become immersed in your particular problems and forget there are fellow-sufferers in the pit lane. A Ferrari V12 unexpectedly bursts into song and indicates the day is not yet over in the garage next door. It is a consolation of sorts as the weary Jordan-Hart crew walk through the dark towards the waiting hire cars, a late pizza and bed. Conversation is limited simply because there is little to say. Not much has been achieved so far in this latest phase of a race without end.

Early finish, late arrival

The purple and orange of dawn breaking, for all its beauty and promise of a better day, does not actually herald much improvement for the team on Tuesday, 26 January.

A change to a larger rear wing on the Jordan increases the downforce, improving the grip and bringing the lap times down. But not by much. Williams are really getting into their stride now, Prost exploring the 1m 13s area as a matter of routine. After 27 laps, Barrichello has only managed 1m 17.45s. Not that out-and-out lap times are everything, of course. But that broad disparity is worrying.

Just before midday, it is decided to remove the engine in order to give Brian Hart the opportunity to inspect the wear and tear – if any – on the oil pump belt. There is none. Even so, Hart is not taking any chances. A redesign has been put in hand, details of changes to the pulleys faxed back to John Lievesley, another engine boffin and an important part of Hart's small team in Harlow. The revisions will be drawn up properly and forwarded to the manufacturer. The new belts will be ready in four days' time.

Barrichello goes out in the afternoon – and spins. There is total silence in the garage as the mechanics, anxious to get their hands on the car and assess the damage, wait for the Jordan to be returned on the back of a lorry. This is not what anyone needs.

Barrichello is perplexed. There is no obvious reason for the spin; he hadn't been over-stretching himself or the car. It had simply snapped sideways without warning.

Anderson discovers on Wednesday that the floor panel is flexing thanks to the layers of carbon fibre not behaving the way they should. Even a deflection of a couple of millimetres is enough to upset dramatically the aerodynamics and make the handling unpredictable.

While it explains Barrichello's sudden departure from the track, such a fundamental fault means there is no point in continuing. It is decided to curtail the test.

Some of the team members manage to catch the evening flight out of Lisbon. Hart misses the plane and is forced to wait until the next day. Thursday's mid-day flight will be cancelled, forcing him to cool his heels until the evening. It is totally exasperating; the final straw.

Meanwhile Patrick Head, the chief designer at Williams, and two of his engineers also fail to catch the last flight on Wednesday. Williams simply send a private jet to collect them. It may be Formula 1 profligacy at its best but, with so much to do, Hart admits there is something to be said for such extravagance. Thursday is a complete waste as far as he is concerned.

The test itself has not been much better. Anderson consoles himself with the thought that 20-year-old Barrichello had much to do, adapting himself to the car, the team and the circuit. The Williams-Renault has only been between 1 and 2 mph faster on the straight, so at least the wind tunnel work has been productive. But, as a final postscript, someone manages to steal the steering wheel from the Jordan as the truck crew turn their backs for a moment while loading the car for the long journey home. For all Anderson's guarded optimism, this has hardly been an auspicious start.

Chapter 7

For Old Time's Sake

The man who came back from the dead

The Martin Donnelly story has become part of Formula 1 folklore. It is a near-tragedy with a happy ending; a tale of how a racing driver managed to survive a crash which came close to killing him.

Donnelly's Lotus flew off the road when a suspension component broke during practice for the 1990 Spanish Grand Prix at Jerez. The car slammed into a metal crash barrier and disintegrated, Donnelly being flung from the wreckage at precisely the right moment: had it happened a second before, he would have left his legs behind in the still intact cockpit; had he remained on board for a fraction longer, his body would have been pulp.

As it was, his injuries were bad enough. He lay unconscious on the track, a rag doll in racing overalls, his left leg hideously contorted. It was only the swift intervention of Professor Sydney Watkins, the doctor provided by the sport's governing body to attend every Grand Prix, which saved Donnelly as he lay choking on his tongue.

Remarkably, Donnelly's major injuries were confined to his legs. His torso had barely a scratch. As soon as he regained full consciousness some weeks later, Donnelly was talking about a return to the cockpit. Visitors, seeing the emaciated form who could only speak in a hoarse whisper, doubted it. But no one was about to divert the Ulsterman from his vision; it was a goal which was driving him forward, providing the motivation and strength to endure the pain which came with the lengthy recovery.

Yer man

Eddie Jordan was among the first to call and see Donnelly at The London Hospital in Whitechapel. They may have been from opposite sides of the Irish border but such a potentially disturbing political divide did not intrude on their sport or their friendship. Donnelly had raced for Jordan in Formula

3000 and Jordan's estimation of Martin's potential as a Formula 1 star had already been confirmed during that first season of Grand Prix racing with Lotus.

Donnelly told Jordan he intended to return; Jordan offered the use of his Formula 1 car as an incentive. It was a generous gesture since few Grand Prix teams would have either the time or the inclination to disrupt their work in order to accommodate the wishes of a man who, in truth, did not have much chance of racing again, never mind performing at the sport's highest level.

But that was not the point. Donnelly had set himself a target. He knew the accident was not his fault and he wanted to prove to himself, if nobody else, that he could still drive a Formula 1 car; that he had not suffered, that he had not been beaten. It was unfinished business.

Donnelly came close to death once more when an artery in the injured leg burst unexpectedly. While he may have been saved by the speedy actions of hospital staff, the effect of the burst would be far-reaching. A thigh muscle would become stuck to the bone and prevent full movement of his left knee. Although he held hopes of successful remedial action, Donnelly's career as a Grand Prix driver was more or less over from that moment on.

But still he wanted to get his backside in a car and banish the bogey created by that mechanical failure in Spain. And Jordan was to be as good as his word.

An expensive lesson

Thursday, 4 February 1993 was set aside for Martin Donnelly. The so-called interim car would be used. Even though this was the 1992 chassis which had been altered to accept the Hart engine for that trial run the previous November, it was more than adequate for Donnelly's needs. He was not about to shatter any lap records. All he wanted to do was get his hands on the wheel, feel the unique sensation and urgent power of a Formula 1 car – and then take control of it.

Part of the deal was to allow the media to attend. After all, Donnelly was now a national hero of sorts, particularly after he had plucked many a heartstring the previous year as he walked, unaided for the first time, while going down the aisle to marry Diane McWhirter, a long-time and long-suffering girlfriend, the daughter of Donnelly's former mechanic. Now the media's story would be complete as he returned to the sort of potentially lethal machine which had almost cost him his life.

Even though the morning at Silverstone was foggy, damp and very cold, the cameramen were out in force. Martin and Diane posed by a car in the paddock but the main event – Donnelly actually driving the car – looked like being cancelled as the persistent fog threatened to prevent safety marshals, stationed around the circuit, from seeing enough of the track.

Shortly before noon, it was decided the fog had lifted sufficiently to allow a couple of laps before lunch. At the end of the run, however, one or two members of Sasol Jordan would not feel like eating.

It was a struggle for Donnelly, his leg still stiff, to climb on board. But the legacy of the accident made for good pictures even if this was the very reason why his Grand Prix career was unlikely to continue. Once snuggled into the cockpit, Donnelly had little trouble getting under way, the automatic gearbox with its clutchless changes then literally playing into his hands.

He completed one lap at reasonable speed and then began to give the car its head. All the old sensations and feelings were there; the moment held no fears for him whatsoever. He was elated.

No so, Brian Hart. As the Jordan swept into sight at the end of the second lap, blue smoke swirling from the back of the car sent a shiver down Hart's back.

It is the sight an engine builder dreads most; the signal that his handiwork may have come apart in a major way. After hundreds of miles of testing without any serious problems, suffering an engine failure on such a public occasion was excruciating. Hart felt sick to the pit of his stomach.

Donnelly pulled off at the end of the straight and waited for the rescue-truck to arrive. The cameras kept rolling as the Jordan-Hart was towed in, streaks of brown oil besmirching the rear bodywork. But, fortunately, most of the media present were not motor sport specialists and did not appreciate the gravity of the situation from Hart's point of view. It was thought this was the normal way to conclude the outing; it had been said Donnelly would do two laps and that's precisely what he had done. In any case, the press was more interested in the driver than the car which was quickly being wheeled out of sight.

'I feel absolutely gutted,' murmured Hart as the engine cover was removed to reveal the oily mess beneath. At this stage, he had no idea what had gone wrong. After all, Donnelly had only completed two laps and the engine had not been thrashed.

It was quickly discovered that an oil pipe had not been tightened properly during the installation of the engine the previous day. It was a bad case of 'finger trouble'; the motor racing euphemism for a mistake by a mechanic.

The actual engine was therefore not at fault – but, to the untutored eye, it was the Hart V10 which had failed as smoke and oil spewed on to the track. It could have been avoided had the engine been run as a precaution before the main event. Or, failing that, the standard procedure should have been adopted whereby the driver completed one lap and then returned to the pits for the routine inspection which, most certainly, would have revealed the wayward oil pipe before too much harm had been done.

So, what was the summary? Donnelly had achieved a remarkable goal and would be ever grateful to Sasol Jordan Hart for the opportunity. Jordan and his sponsors had received excellent exposure, nearly all the national newspapers carrying the story the following day.

On the debit side, Anderson had been unhappy about putting his overworked mechanics through what he termed 'a PR stunt'. And once insurance, preparation, hiring the circuit and time spent by Louise Goodman arranging the day and handling the media had been taken into account, the bill would be in excess of £20,000. But, in truth, as Brian Hart surveyed his wrecked engine and mused on the team's organization, the cost had been much higher than that.

Chapter 8

Excess Baggage

Nice man; wrong decision

The previous Sunday (31 January), Jordan had announced that Ivan Capelli would be the team's Number 1 driver. With McLaren having nominated Senna as one of their drivers, that improbable dream had finally ended for Jordan.

Capelli, an old friend of Eddie Jordan, had driven for Ian Phillips when Phillips ran the now defunct March/Leyton House team. His credentials were therefore well known and he was a likeable character; he would fit in well with the team. But was he really the man they needed?

Capelli had 92 Grands Prix to his name and, during a period of peak competitiveness with March in 1988, he had actually challenged Alain Prost for the lead of the Portuguese Grand Prix, and then led in Japan. In France two years later, he had run at the front for a considerable time and enjoyed a fleeting taste of success. But, since then, his career – and his morale – had taken a dive, the dream chance of driving for Ferrari in 1992 more or less torpedoing his reputation as the Italian went through an absolutely dismal year which was not necessarily his fault.

Phillips and Jordan felt they knew Capelli well enough to muster what was undoubtedly a great natural talent. But Hart, during conversation with a close friend who worked for Ferrari, was disturbed to hear that Capelli could only handle the car if it was set up in one particular way. If not, he was likely to quickly lose motivation.

Was this what they needed at Jordan-Hart? Was this the man capable of guiding and cajoling Rubens Barrichello in the manner that everyone had hoped? Despite the encouraging noises emanating from Jordan and Phillips, the jury would remain out for some time. Perhaps Capelli's first test at Silverstone the following Tuesday would provide some answers.

In the event, they didn't learn anything about the car, never mind the driver. Lucas had written a new programme for the electronic control box on the car – but news of this development had not be imparted to the rest of the team. As a result, nothing worked properly on the car. Capelli, on another cold and wet day, managed just 14 laps; slow ones at that.

A bit of a shock

Matters did not improve the following week when the team returned to Estoril for another test. A whole day was lost when new gearbox control units failed to work for no obvious reason.

Gary Anderson received an unexpected clue in the form of a static shock from the car. It was discovered that the Lucas computer had been plugged into mains which had not been earthed. The passage of more than 200 volts through the chassis eventually wrecked the control boxes on the car and made it necessary to have someone fly from England to put matters right.

Barrichello and Capelli eventually got going. Capelli completed a considerable number of laps but it was immediately apparent that he was tiring very quickly on a punishing circuit which seeks out any weaknesses in a driver's fitness. He was not pushing the car hard and there was the first inkling that he did not seem prepared to commit himself in the whole-hearted manner the team desperately needed.

Barrichello could lap comfortably in the 1m 16s bracket (Williams, by now, were into the 1m 12s region) but venturing into the 1m 15s (his best lap was 1m 15.5s) appeared to require a lot of effort from the young Brazilian. When he made a number of driving errors, it seemed he might be trying too hard.

At the end of four days, there was not much satisfaction to be had. Progress had been constantly interrupted by niggling problems. Such diversions are to be expected when running a new car, but with the start of the season less than a month away, time was running out.

Despite the mood of manufactured optimism, there was an underlying feeling that the package – engine, chassis and drivers – was not gelling as well as it should. But nobody would say as much. They simply had to do well in 1993 and that's all there was to it.

Further test sessions followed at Silverstone. Anderson was happier with progress, the automatic gearbox in particular working well after 380 miles. But such was the need to have both cars finish the first race in South Africa – home of Sasol, the team's principal sponsor – that the less-efficient but tried and proven sequential gearchange used in 1992 would be brought along as a back-up with provision to fit the system in an emergency, just in case the automatic gearbox gave trouble.

All of this, of course, meant extra freight – and more headaches for Trevor Foster as he supervised the packing in readiness for the trip.

Packed and ready to go

The South African Grand Prix was scheduled for Sunday 14 March, with the freight due to leave Heathrow the previous weekend. On Tuesday 2 March, the process had begun, Foster keeping a careful eye on the heavy duty packing cases (known as 'packhorses'), ensuring only essential items were stowed.

The Formula One Constructors' Association (the company which collectively handles affairs for the teams) would pay for the shipment of two cars and 5,000 kg (about 5 tons) of freight. The rest would be down to the team. And, if Jordan Grand Prix did not score any points in the first half of the season, they would have to pay for all shipment at future long-haul races. The cut-off point was 10th place in the championship. Jordan, with one point scored in 1992, was on the financial bubble, hovering on the edge of massive expenditure.

As things stood, they would be paying $22 for every 1 kg over the FOCA subsidized limit; they expected to take 7,500 kg in total at the very least. But that was chickenfeed compared to the likes of Williams and McLaren, who would each carry between 18,000 and 20,000 kg to these so-called 'flyaway races'.

'The difficulty,' said Foster, 'is knowing what to take and what to leave at home. We are under particular pressure because of racing on Sasol's home ground; you don't want to have to turn round and say you can't do this or you can't do that because you have left something important behind just to save on freight.

'On top of that, this freight will be going on to Brazil – so we have got to think of that race as well and cover all eventualities. It's a case of keeping an eye on the mechanics; given half a chance, they will put everything in the packhorses – "just in case"!'

Each packhorse must be marked with its precise weight in order to avoid disputes with the freight company and to facilitate loading on to one of the two jumbo freighters hired by FOCA for the trip. Each car has a protective panel fitted to the underside, with sponge-covered side pieces shielding the car's sidepods. The front and rear wings are removed but wheels remain in place in order to roll the car on to a pallet for loading. A special cover offers final protection, and the fitting of aircraft-style straps allows the trussed-up car to be moved easily by fork-lift trucks. Meanwhile, other details such as team gear are taken care of during the final fortnight. Anderson finds that, despite the provision of detail measurements of his imposing frame, the Japanese manufactured uniform is too tight a fit, a turn of events which causes him to note sardonically that his crew can design and build a new car on time but a simple matter such as clothing arrives late.

That is the least of his worries as he oversees the production of the third car in readiness for South Africa. (This, in fact, will be raced by Ivan Capelli with Barrichello taking chassis 02 and the first car, 01, acting as the spare car).

Across the road at Silverstone, last-minute preparations are carried out. Benetton, Williams and McLaren are joined by the Jordan team for a final run in bitterly cold conditions. Damon Hill, his nose red and teeth chattering, poses on the steps of the Williams transporter for a publicity photograph which will do little to flatter him. Down at McLaren, speculation is mounting over whether or not Senna will actually race for the team. But whether he chooses to or not, it's too late for Jordan. They have their drivers in place and right now they are going through final checks with the automatic gearbox.

As Barrichello pounds round the track, Capelli jumps up and down in a vain attempt to keep warm. His mind is on other things. It is imperative that he catches the evening flight to Milan; he's getting married the next day. Talk about adding to the pressure as the start of the season beckons.

The sound of racing engines echoing through the roof lights of the Jordan factory lifts the tempo another notch as activity intensifies. All of this – the packing, the finalizing of details, the urgency of late testing – gives the unmistakable feeling that winter is over, the preliminaries are done with and the race proper is about to begin. For everyone concerned, the moment cannot come quick enough.

Now the rumours and speculation will be put to the test. Jordan and Hart are about to discover the true value of their labours in a very competitive business.

'I reckon,' says Anderson, 'we'll qualify middle of the grid – 14th, 15th – something like that.'

His forecast will turn out to be reasonably accurate. But it will not come close to predicting the frustration to be experienced in the months that lie ahead.

Chapter 9

Off to Africa

A bit of a blur

By Thursday morning, five of the pictures had been stolen. On the one hand, it was flattering that a poster depicting the Sasol Jordan Hart should be such an attraction to the South African race fans. On the other, it was four days before the Grand Prix and the last thing Sasol needed was to have valuable publicity material removed from the bridges spanning the road to the Kyalami circuit.

By Thursday, Gary Anderson might have noticed their absence. Two days before, he was happily oblivious to most things in and around Johannesburg after celebrating his 42nd birthday on the overnight flight from London.

Brian Hart had started the process by ordering a bottle of champagne. The small gathering at the back of the Boeing 747 quickly expanded into something more serious as the British Airways steward fuelled the celebration with another bottle. Racing people, bored with the tedium of flying, can sniff the source of potential revelry from 100 yards. Somewhere over North Africa, the steward probably regretted his largesse as the party, joined by representatives from rival teams, threatened to get out of hand. But, by then, Anderson was beyond caring. He had never known a flight go so swiftly or so smoothly.

The next day, Tuesday, 9 March, was a blur in every sense. With barely time to check in to their hotel, key members of the team were whisked by helicopter to the first of many press conferences as Sasol made full use of a dramatic promotional tool in a country enamoured with Grand Prix racing.

The first South African Grand Prix had been held in 1934, the subsequent history of the race peppered with financial and political worries as well as constant changes of venue. The original Kyalami circuit had been built in the 1960s but seemed to have been lost for ever when the rand hit rock bottom against the dollar in 1985 and the land was sold two years later. But such was the enthusiasm for the Grand Prix that the race was revived in 1992, albeit on a new track which utilized a small part of the old Kyalami circuit.

Much of the atmosphere had gone, the cramped layout being a poor compromise after the broad expanses of the former circuit. Nonetheless, the pit and paddock facilities were regarded as first class and no one was complaining about leaving Britain in March for the agreeable climate of the Veldt in late summer. And, for Sasol, the promotion of a top rate international event on their doorstep was nothing short of a godsend.

A big slice of a small cake

According to the official Jordan press hand-out, Sasol leads the world in the conversion of coal and gas into liquid fuels and petrochemicals, a fact which no one in the industry would dispute. But what the business found difficult to understand was precisely why a leading South African company with more than 20,000 shareholders should want to get involved with Grand Prix racing – and with a small team run by a former bank clerk from Dublin.

'For a start,' says Paul Kruger, managing director of Sasol Limited, 'we export to 120 countries, so the connection with a global sport such as Formula 1 is obvious. We are dealing in the commercial rather than the consumer market and we believe that an association with Grand Prix racing helps the perception of how serious we are. To be seen in F1 is good and, on top of that, we have gained a lot from technical feedback. It has been an excellent move so far.'

So far meant one year in 1992, bouncing along the bottom as Jordan wrestled unsuccessfully with the Yamaha engine. Although the results disappointed Sasol, Eddie Jordan had explained from the start that his team was still finding its feet. He used much of his personal charm to get the point across, of course, but it was clear that Sasol were comfortable with the association.

If Sasol had wanted instant success, that would have meant a link with the likes of McLaren or Williams. It would also have meant a small amount of exposure on the car for the equivalent amount of money spent with Jordan, plus the acceptance that they would be one of many small fishes swimming around the large team's corporate sponsorship pool.

Gaining major exposure with the championship leaders would have cost Sasol an increase, to use the anaesthetizing language of big-team sponsor-ship co-ordinators, in 'investment'. Far better to spend less and have a larger slice of the cake at somewhere like Jordan; have your name written large on the side of the cars; be the so-called title sponsor and not merely another name in a list of clients.

So far, this had cost Sasol an estimated £4 million. Having found their feet in Formula 1, they wanted more enduring success. 'We expect to score points fairly regularly in 1993 – and then be close to the top three in

1994,' said Kruger.

It seemed a reasonable request at this stage of the season when genuine optimism had yet to be crushed by punishing and relentless reality. And, for this race in particular, the pressure to produce some form of worthwhile result was being applied to the team and their main sponsor right from the start.

Earning some ink

Much of the pressure was self-inflicted through necessity. Louise Goodman had organized a busy schedule of public relations appearances for Eddie Jordan and the drivers, starting with a 6 am appointment with a television breakfast show on Wednesday. Capelli had taken part in a fashion shoot for *The Star* newspaper – all of which had been filmed by the South African Broadcasting Company – and both drivers had been heavily involved with radio and television interviews and photo sessions.

By Friday, the first of two days of practice, the success of the campaign was evident. Both *The Star* and *The Citizen* ran Grand Prix supplements with their morning editions, and both made reference to Sasol.

'This weekend,' said *The Star*, 'the eyes of the world will be on South Africa.'

'Sasol ... currently our country's only real identification in the heady world of Formula 1 ...' wrote *The Citizen*.

There were colour pictures of the Jordan and portraits of both drivers; the team colours of blue, turquoise and red were easily identified. Now the locals knew who to look for since, in many respects, Sasol Jordan was 'their' team. And that applied the pressure one more turn as car 14 (Barrichello) and car 15 (Capelli) joined 24 others for the first of 80 official practice sessions to be held around the world between now and the final race in Australia on 7 November.

The schedule would be the same at each Grand Prix. Practice and qualifying would be held on Friday and Saturday (Thursday and Saturday at Monaco) with the race on Sunday. Each lap during the morning practice sessions (known as 'free practice') would be recorded but the lap times would not count towards grid positions.

That was reserved for qualifying in the afternoons when each driver's progress would be monitored as usual, the driver's quickest lap over the two qualifying sessions then determining his grid position, the fastest starting from the front (pole position) with the slowest driver at the rear. On Sunday morning, there would be a 30-minute warm-up to allow the teams to make final adjustments for the race. Simple enough.

For 1993, however, the sport's governing body had managed to confuse everyone by reducing the length of the practice periods – supposedly in the interests of economy. Instead of free practice on the morning lasting for 90 minutes, it would run for just half that time, a swingeing cut back which would seriously affect a team's ability to tune their cars to the circuit.

The indisputable fact was that the professional and well-prepared teams, particularly those with experience of the circuit in question, would manage better than others. How, then, would Jordan fare as Barrichello, a novice, struggled to learn not only the circuit but also the routine necessary for efficient management of time spent on the track during practice?

Capelli at least had plenty of experience and much would depend on his ability to tune into his new team and pass on what information he could. As the sun beat down from a cloudless sky, this was very much a venture into the unknown as the season literally roared into life.

A reasonable start

The first session ended with Capelli 16th and Barrichello 17th; not brilliant but, so the thinking went, reasonable enough to allow for improvement when qualifying began in the afternoon.

Capelli, raring to go, parked his Jordan at the exit of the pit lane, waiting for the signal for the first qualifying session to commence. It was an encouraging sign for the team; the Italian was clearly feeling confident. That soon changed.

As luck would have it, trouble with a hydraulic pump, followed soon after by a faulty voltage regulator, meant his session was seriously disrupted; his rhythm shattered. Twenty-first out of 26 was a disappointing way to begin the association. But there was always tomorrow.

Barrichello was much happier. It was difficult to judge whether this was to do with a respectable 15th place, or the fact that he was faster than Capelli – a psychological advantage for any driver regardless of the troubles afflicting his team-mate. In any case, Barrichello was confident he could go faster on Saturday since the run on his first set of tyres (each driver is limited to two sets during qualifying) was spoiled by a puncture. And he was still learning the track, discovering where he could gain a tenth of a second here and a fraction there. All told, the team was reasonably satisfied.

The mood continued into final qualifying on Saturday afternoon, Barrichello improving his time to take 14th place on the grid for his first Grand Prix – a respectable achievement by any standard. He also did a reasonable job concealing his satisfaction over beating the more seasoned Capelli in a personal battle which, on this occasion, had not been disrupted by unforeseen technical problems for the Italian.

Changes made to the suspension and aerodynamics on Capelli's car for final qualifying had proved unsatisfactory. It was a gamble which failed to pay off and meant he had he wasted his first set of tyres. The car was returned to its original specification and, by the time Capelli was ready to rejoin at the end of the session, the circuit was busy in the last-minute dash to improve grid positions. Capelli could not get a clear lap. Eighteenth place was hardly an auspicious start.

Nonetheless, he knew all about how to handle himself and his car during the course of a 190-mile Grand Prix, something which would be a novelty to

Barrichello. Experience would pay handsomely in the hot conditions, particularly during a race in which many drivers could be expected to retire due to mechanical problems caused by the relatively untried nature of their cars.

Eddie Jordan and his team did not expect to win. Neither did they anticipate grabbing any headlines. But the hope was that they might steal a point or two through reliability, just by being there at the end and finishing in the top six.

Ten points would be awarded to the winner, ranging down to a single point for sixth place. One point would be as good as a win for Sasol Jordan Hart at this stage. After all, it was the sum total of their efforts after an entire season in 1992.

Surely they could improve on that? Indeed, they *had* to do better. The smiling expectancy on the faces of the Sasol guests arriving in the paddock on Sunday morning made that very clear.

Stabbing in the dark

A hazy sun made race morning bearable, sponsors and their guests enjoyed the agreeable climate as they took coffee at tables and chairs laid out in the tarmac paddock behind the pits.

The mechanics had been at work from an early hour in preparation for the 30-minute warm-up at 9.30 am. This would give the teams a last chance to run in race trim, with a full load of fuel on board. The object would be to fine-tune the handling of the cars to suit the extra weight – an additional 260 lb over and above what the driver had experienced during qualifying when running with a minimum amount of fuel.

Decisions would have to be made concerning tyre-wear. How often should they stop and change tyres? And when? Would it be possible to run non-stop, balancing the loss of increased performance from a fresh set of tyres with the time gained by not having to enter the pit lane, come to a standstill and accelerate out again? There was much for Anderson and his drivers to consider.

In the event, they learnt next to nothing. Barrichello's car developed an oil leak, a fault which could have been corrected easily had a young mechanic, in a moment of overenthusiastic zeal upon seeing smoke swirling from the back of the car, not blown fire extinguisher powder in all directions, rendering the car inoperable, at least while the remainder of the session was spent clearing up the mess.

On such occasions, the spare car can be brought into play. But the rules – again chasing minimal cost savings – said the spare car could not be used during the two days of practice, only on race day. This was another new regulation, one which caused much inconvenience since, in the past, teams had placed heavy reliance on the spare car as a time-saving back-up while race cars were being worked on during practice. Anderson had to force himself to adjust his thinking – so much so that he forgot, since this was now race day, he was allowed to use the spare. As a result, Barrichello only managed half the number of laps completed by his rivals.

Capelli was even worse off. He had completed just two laps at reasonable speed when the Jordan suddenly stopped for no obvious reason and stranded Capelli on the far side of the circuit. He returned to the pits to report that the engine had simply cut out. When the car was eventually returned to the pits on the back of a tow truck, the engine fired at the first attempt by Capelli's mechanics and revved quite happily. There was no hint of trouble.

This was the worst possible scenario since the team did not have any clues, particularly as the data stowed on the on-board computer had been wiped out. There was absolutely nothing for Brian Hart to go on. The engine may be running sweetly now, but who was to say the problem might not recur five minutes into the race?

A faulty rectifier regulator was subsequently found to be the cause of the trouble. But, at the time, there was no alternative but to change all the electrical components on the car. The only good thing to be said was that, with four hours until the start of the Grand Prix (the minimum allowed between the warm-up and the race in order to cater for emergencies such as this), the work could be completed on time.

But this was scarcely a brilliant start to the day; the team was no further on than before. Anderson and his engineers, Mark Smith and Andrew Green, were stabbing in the dark when it came to working on a definitive campaign for the race.

Eddie Jordan and Ian Phillips did their best to put a brave face on the dilemma as the Sasol guests stood at the back of the garage, still smiling, still expectant.

Now, here's the plan

There was a serious collision of sound when kilted pipers marching down the pit lane battled to be heard against the urgent bark of the Hart V10 and the shriek of a 12-cylinder Lamborghini in the garage next door. The resulting cacophony merely heightened the tension as the start of the first Grand Prix for nearly five months drew close. Barrichello and Anderson, oblivious to the noise, were examining every possible scenario regarding tyre wear. With little or no evidence to work on, Anderson had to call upon 20 years of experience in order to brief the novice. 'What we'll have to do,' said Anderson, his Ulster accent even stronger as it competed with the background commotion, 'is show you a sign saying 'tyres' at around the 25 lap mark. That's when we reckon you might need to stop. When you see that, get on the radio and tell us how you are getting on, how you feel the tyres are holding out. If you think you can keep going without stopping, then do that.

'Meanwhile, we will be keeping an eye on the lap times of the cars around you. If your times are dropping off and they're going quicker because they've got fresh tyres, then we'll tell you to come in. Okay?'

Barrichello nodded. For a 20-year-old about to embark on the trip of a relatively small lifetime, he was remarkably calm. On the surface at least. It was impossible to tell what was going on in his head and in his stomach. But you could guess.

No one remains unmoved by the potent mixture of exhilaration and tension which accompanies the 30 minutes leading to the start of a Grand Prix. Least of all, your first Grand Prix. His priority would simply be to finish the race. Easier said than done given the controlled mayhem which was about to erupt as 25 drivers dived headlong into the first corner.

Barrichello was about to be acquainted with those potential perils sooner than he thought.

Knocked off early

Near the front of the grid sat Damon Hill, whose singular advantage over Barrichello was that he had at his disposal one of the most competitive cars in the field – the Williams-Renault. But, in terms of Grand Prix experience, Hill was also a comparative beginner. That became evident when he spun in front of everyone at about 160 mph as the field poured into the first series of corners. Barrichello, having made an excellent start and passed at least three cars, backed off when confronted by the sight of the wayward Williams and dropped to 14th place again. But at least he survived that first lap.

So did Capelli, a reasonable start bringing the second Jordan into 16th position. The team heaved a momentary sigh of relief. Then, after just two laps, Capelli disappeared.

The television pictures showed a badly damaged Jordan smouldering on the grass. The cockpit was empty and a bemused Capelli was seen standing not far from the wreckage. He would explain later that the car had understeered unexpectedly, failed to take the corner, got on to the grass and then spun mightily into the barrier.

Understeer is described in the racing text books as the car wanting to plough straight on rather than respond to the steering and take the corner. It is a common complaint with a highly tuned racing car, particularly when running in close company at the beginning of a race. Nothing was said but the obvious shortfall in genuine sympathy from the team suggested that a man of Capelli's experience should have been able to cope. It was the sort of error one would have expected from a novice in his first Grand Prix.

Barrichello was showing no signs of nerves. Retirements and accidents elsewhere had moved him into a very handy seventh place by the end of lap 31. There were 41 laps left, and even if Barrichello simply maintained his pace without overtaking anyone, a championship point or two would be on the cards, given that the law of averages said that at least one of the six cars ahead would run into trouble.

Then Barrichello disappeared. The gearbox had failed; his car was parked by the side of the track. There was a mouthing of expletives in the Jordan pit.

Think about tomorrow

It was no consolation to learn that Christian Fittipaldi, who had been behind Barrichello throughout, went on to finish fourth for Minardi, a team with even less resources than Jordan. Indeed, this made Barrichello's retirement even harder to bear. But at least he had driven cleanly and with maturity. This had given the team great hope for the rest of the season. That was the theme of the upbeat post-race press release.

The reality was that too many niggling things had gone wrong. Barrichello's retirement had been due to a stud breaking inside the gearbox, a complete surprise since this type of stud had been used throughout 1992 and during winter testing.

Anderson would subsequently change the stud material (and not have a moment's bother for the rest of the season) but, at the time, the failure lent weight to the theory that the potential problem might have been highlighted had the team been able to complete a full race distance during testing.

Such routine work was a matter of course for the likes of Williams and McLaren. But the simulation of a race, although very desirable for the reasons just witnessed so publicly and painfully, was simply not possible for small teams with limited resources. But that did not ease the frustration. If anything, it contributed further to the momentary sense of futility.

None of this was helped by the sight of a filthy and seriously damaged Jordan being winched off the back of a lorry once the race had finished. Capelli was generously being given the benefit of the doubt. But there could be no disguising the fact that the team management was worried. As chassis 03 lay sadly on the garage floor, the engine cover, which somehow had been badly smashed, was tossed to one side. Alert as ever to a commercial opportunity, Ian Phillips kicked the broken piece of bodywork with his foot.

'Do we sell it?' he asked Jordan. (It has long been a habit of the teams to raise beer money for the mechanics by selling redundant items to the race fans. Such activity reaches its peak at the end of the season when team uniforms, no matter how oily and sweaty, fetch a fair price from souvenir hunters. But it's not often that a team has anything to offer the outside world after the first race.)

Jordan stared at the tattered piece of carbon fibre which seemed to sum up his weekend.

'May as well,' he said. 'There's little else we can do with it. Get rid of it.' And, with that, he walked away to think about the next race.

Chapter 10

Local Difficulty

The road to São Paulo

The road from Guarulhos airport gives fair warning of what lies in store. The dual carriageway is rutted and in need of repair, the slick surface lethal in the grey drizzle, the verges filthy and unkempt. For most of its length, the main road to the centre of São Paulo runs alongside a brown river, the appalling colour highlighted by rich green vegetation running rampant in the warmth.

The air reeks with fumes spewing from cars running on alcohol-based fuel. The abiding smell is as if boot polish and day-old cat food are being brewed together in the sprawling industrial areas alongside. The chaotic traffic is not helped by a beaten up car, on its roof in the fast lane and seemingly left there for the rest of the day.

It is 10.30 am on Thursday, 25 March. The Varig 747 from Heathrow landed in the gloom three hours before but the pace of travel has been almost strangled as São Paulo goes about its normal business.

Now the sun is easing through the smog but to turn on the blower in the hire car is to risk suffocation. There is nothing for it but to endure the clammy warmth, be patient and study either the river on one side or the ramshackle buildings on the other.

The million dollar world of Formula 1 has come to Brazil; nowhere is it more apparent that Grand Prix racing makes an incongruous bedfellow with massive international debt and poverty.

Guilty consciences – if they exist – are assuaged immediately upon entry to the Transamerica, a marble palace by local standards; a comfortable, nothing unusual, western-style hotel on the scale of Formula 1 values. Inside are familiar faces, conducting the business of motor racing as if the dilapidated world outside the front door does not exist.

The latest rumour says Ivan Capelli is to be replaced. Ian Phillips is in the large foyer, wandering among the maroon-suited bell boys and massive pot plants, waiting for Eddie Jordan to arrive from the airport.

Phillips has come in advance to tie up a sponsorship deal with Empax, a packaging company handling most of the coffee in Brazil. It's a one-off deal for this race, an arrangement which will just about cover the cost of the team's hotel bill. There won't be much change from £10,000. Every little contribution helps.

We have every confidence

But, of more pressing concern at this moment is the increasing number of questions concerning Capelli. Phillips has reiterated the team's belief in Ivan. But he wants to brief Jordan. And quickly. The media is roaming the hotel in search of any story which will make a useful preview piece before track activity gets under way tomorrow, Friday.

Jordan is duly apprised and then makes clear his whole-hearted support for Capelli. What do they expect, these people? Jordan is hardly going to say that Capelli will be sacked if he fails to deliver. Such a macho approach may catch the attention of one or two hard-nosed drivers but, for someone of Capelli's Latin sensitivity, it would tip the Italian into even deeper despair.

'You can't judge him on one race,' explains Jordan. 'We have every confidence in Ivan. Things didn't go his way in South Africa and he had a bit of bad luck, that's all.'

It is sincere enough. But it smacks of a football club chairman giving his manager a vote of confidence on the day before the inevitable sacking.

A torrid morning

Friday morning redefines the meaning of bad luck as far as Ivan Capelli is concerned. He completes just one lap before a failed pressure relief valve causes the automatic gearbox to jam in neutral and brings the Jordan to a halt out on the circuit. It is a measure of Capelli's misfortune that a similar problem for Barrichello results in his gearbox sticking in gear, thus allowing the Brazilian to motor slowly to the pits for repairs.

With use of the spare car forbidden, Capelli has no option but to cool his heels. And what makes the morning drag even more is the fact that, in the face of protest, the sport's governing body has reverted to the more familiar timetable of allowing an hour and a half for free practice rather than the 45 minute session introduced in South Africa. But now each driver is limited to 23 laps within the 90 minutes. That means there is no rush; Capelli reckons chance would be a fine thing.

Yet, with half an hour to go, the mood in the Jordan garage is fraught. Capelli has one lap to his name while Barrichello is in 25th place. Alain Prost, meanwhile, has completed 17 useful and trouble-free laps in the Williams as he sets the fastest time so far with a lap of 1m 18.4s. Barrichello has struggled to record a 1m 47s with the hobbled car.

The Jordan is so far off the pace that Barrichello's friends and fans clustering around the timing monitor know it has nothing to do with the local hero. With 10 minutes remaining, Barrichello returns and improves to 1m 22.4s. It's a step in the right direction – but only worth 23rd place so far. Capelli, of course, is bottom of the list.

The Italian, having been unable to return to the pits from the far side of the circuit – indeed, seeing no point in doing so – eventually hitches a ride with a course car. As he walks disconsolately into the back of the Jordan garage, he bumps into Ian Phillips.

'Got a nice sun tan, Ivan?' quips Capelli's former boss. Not many people could take such a liberty with a driver after a singularly useless practice session; it is Phillips's way of lightening the gloom which threatens to envelope the hapless driver. Capelli manages a wan smile.

'A torrid morning,' mutters Brian Hart. It is the last thing he needs, particularly after an evening at the bar of the hotel, easing back the local brew.

'The man came over with an unopened bottle and five glasses on a tray. We knew then that it meant trouble ... ' Hart manages to raise a half smile. It's hard to tell the exact cause of his headache this morning. There is not much levity in evidence in the garage.

'Typical, isn't it?' says an exasperated Trevor Foster. 'We've had these constant hydraulic leaks. Normally the unions never break but, this morning, one goes. So we replace it. Then another one goes! You wouldn't credit it.'

Adding to the all-round pressure on Eddie Jordan is another rumour, this time concerning Foster. The story is that he has been approached by Lotus. Such a move would be a major blow to Jordan since he has worked with Foster for several years and trusts his judgement and ability implicitly.

The team manager is responsible for tying up the many routine details without which the team simply could not operate. Indeed, Eddie Jordan is not necessarily aware of *how* everything works; all he needs to know is that it does. Remove Foster and you take away the man who lubricates the complex machinery necessary to have the team ready to perform at each race.

But familiarity breeds contempt and, for some months now, Foster has been frustrated by Jordan's refusal to budge on certain issues. It usually boils down to money: Foster says it needs to be spent; Jordan says he can't afford it.

Suddenly an offer comes from Lotus in Norfolk and the grass in East Anglia suddenly looks greener than the fields of Northamptonshire. Jordan is doing all he can to persuade Foster that, at the end of the day, things will be no different with Lotus, a team in an infinitely more precarious financial state than Jordan. But Eddie is fighting a losing battle. And the run of failures on the track is not helping anyone. It seems things couldn't possibly get worse. But they do.

The myriad problems in the morning have prevented experimentation with the suspension set-up. A combination of logical analysis and guess-work is employed on Barrichello's car as he sets off on his opening qualifying run. The first set of tyres will be at their best for a couple of laps and Barrichello manages a respectable time.

The improvisation has been reasonably accurate and further adjust-ments are made before the second and final set of tyres is put in place. Barrichello sets off – and doesn't come back. The engine has failed. Hart is mortified.

Meanwhile, with no experience to draw on from the morning practice session, Capelli adopts the suspension and aerodynamic settings arrived at by Barrichello. It does not suit his driving style in the slightest, the Jordan understeering excessively and preventing Capelli from committing himself. On top of which, his speed through the radar trap is low.

Capelli is getting nowhere and it shows in his lethargic demeanour. This is not the moment to remind everyone of the Ferrari engineer's observation that Capelli can only motivate himself if the car is set up exactly to his liking. And this car is far from it.

The list of qualifying times makes dismal reading: Barrichello, 17th; Capelli, 26th – and last. At this rate of going, with only 25 cars allowed to start the race, Capelli will be the single non-qualifier unless he improves tomorrow.

Outside, it is humid and overcast. Inside the cluttered and cramped garage, the mood is equally leaden. The optimism of the new car launch at Silverstone in January really does feel two months and 6,000 miles in the past.

Down and out

Having dug a hole the previous day, Capelli looks prepared to jump into it as Saturday's practice gets under way. There is no urgency to his actions each time the car pulls into the pits; he is going through the motions. Feeling that there may be a fault inherent with his car, it has been arranged that he is allocated the spare car for the day (this is permitted by the regulations). He tries his own ideas with the set-up. But the spare car feels no better and the discovery batters his already bruised confidence.

By contrast, Barrichello is positive in his discussions with Anderson. Free from any serious mechanical hindrances this morning, Barrichello puts the 90-minute session to good use. The car feels much better than yesterday; he is confident of a more competitive time when qualifying begins. This is good news for the growing cluster of Barrichello supporters – a goodly proportion of whom are striking young women – who have managed to find their way into the pits. They may be a hindrance in some respects but their cheerful presence helps lift the mood as the team begins to climb out of the mire.

Eddie Jordan appears in shorts, but without the blue ankle socks he had been sporting earlier in the day. Louise Goodman nods in approval.

'I'm glad you've done that,' she says, only half-joking. 'Wearing shorts and socks like that made you look like an old man.'

Jordan could reasonably claim to feel like an old man in the light of recent events but, as ever, he puts an upbeat slant on everything.

'Better this morning,' he says, stabbing his finger at Barrichello's time on the monitor. Then he has to search down the list for Capelli. He's 23rd. Jordan makes no comment.

There is even less to say once the final qualifying session has finished. Barrichello has qualified in 14th place, a respectable effort from the team and the driver given the time lost the previous day. But Capelli is 26th and last.

A Sasol Jordan Hart has failed to qualify for the Brazilian Grand Prix. Even in his worst dreams, Eddie Jordan had not expected this. It is a complete disaster.

Capelli is a beaten man – and looks it as he sits slumped in a chair. He had made further changes to the car and, while his lap time had been improved by almost two seconds, it was not enough. He tried hard but simply could not get to grips with the car.

Brian Hart is examining the screen of his lap-top computer. A trace of Capelli's best lap shows where time has been lost as he failed to make best use of the engine revs thanks to changing gear too early on the long climb towards the pits. Elsewhere, he has been over-revving the engine. These are the classic signs of growing desperation; a man not at one with his car.

Failing to qualify amounts to public humiliation. Even if you scrape on to the back of the grid, there is always the chance that luck might run your way in the race. But now Capelli will be unemployed tomorrow. There is nothing more he can contribute to the team's weekend. Usually cheerful and relaxed, Capelli suddenly looks very much alone in comparison to the confident Barrichello, surrounded by his excited supporters and family. Having their boy qualify in the middle of the grid for his first Grand Prix in Brazil is cause for minor celebration.

There is much to talk about and Barrichello, as soon as his debrief with the engineers is finished, leaves the circuit and heads for the family home, just a couple of streets away. Here, a temporary studio has been established to cater for the proliferation of Brazilian radio and television companies who either did not qualify for – or, more likely, could not afford to pay for – a broadcasting pass giving access to the pits and paddock.

Capelli prepares to fly home and does not attend a dinner hosted in the evening by Eddie Jordan and Sasol for the British media. Capelli, for all his natural charm, would have hated it.

Louise has booked a long table in Foga De Chao, a timbered *churrascaria* filled with the smell of roast and babbling conversation. It suits Jordan's warm and friendly style perfectly and helps relax Barrichello as he arrives, accompanied by his father, Rubens Snr, and his general helper and the commercial manager of Barrichello Racing, Geraldo Rodrigues.

Jordan draws an analogy with the familiar tale of feeling older as policemen appear to look like schoolboys.

'Racing drivers seem to get younger each year,' says Jordan, nodding at Barrichello. 'But this is ridiculous. I now discover that Rubens's *father* is younger than me!'

Ian Phillips recalls his first visit to Interlagos early in 1971, when reporting a Formula 2 race for *Autosport*. He entertains the table with amusing anecdotes of the absurd extracurricular activities in those laidback days, involving future stars such as James Hunt.

Barrichello is fascinated by it all. 'I wasn't born then,' he explains. Phillips, a young at heart 42, is momentarily silenced by the implication of such a straightforward statement. Jordan does not miss the opportunity to loudly repeat the fact to anyone who may have failed to appreciate it.

The table is joined by Gary Anderson and Brian Hart, direct from the circuit. The dinner guests – in truth, more interested in the fierce battle between Prost, Senna and Hill at the front of the grid – ask politely about Jordan's chances.

Optimism being the life-blood of the business, there is hope for tomorrow, the pumped-up enthusiasm displacing the disappointment of Friday. Poor Capelli is hardly mentioned. Everyone's hopes at Jordan-Hart clearly rest on the shoulders of the polite 20-year-old as he leaves at 9.30 pm, ready for bed.

A tiny fragment of metal

Jordan and Phillips are at work from an early hour on Sunday, canvassing their rivals to have the grid extended to 26 cars. There is some support for this – although the teams concerned would never dare think about it, let alone mention the fact that a bad run of luck and mechanical failures could place them in exactly the same position one day – but there is not the necessary unanimity. As Jordan reluctantly accepts the unsuccessful outcome of his endeavour, the unfortunate situation is given added poignancy by the ghostly spectre of Capelli's flameproof overalls, looming over the temporary office from a hanger slung high on the flimsy partition.

On the far side of the wall, Chris Leese and Henny Collins prepare lunch. The circumstances are incongruous in the extreme as the team's caterers, battling with ancient gas burners balanced on a folding table, wear earplugs as a defence against a roaring Hart V10 no more than five metres away.

The scene is repeated along the pit lane, these 'flyaway races' being very much a case of make do. The struggle merely heightens the appreciation of the motor homes which will form the team headquarters when the races move to Europe. But, in the meantime, the battle with the Bolognese sauce continues.

It seems to be in a good cause. Barrichello has claimed 12th fastest time in the warm-up and, as he heads for the starting grid and a warm welcome from the rowdy grandstands, he has genuine hopes of attending to the unfinished business commenced in South Africa two weeks ago. But will the car be up to the job?

Once again, Barrichello avoids a potentially hazardous skirmish as other drivers spin at the first corner. He completes the first lap in 13th place. Rubens moves up on lap 2 and seems comfortable enough as he settles down with a group of four cars battling for ninth place.

Then, without warning, the gearbox stops selecting gears. This time a tiny metal fragment has caught in the pressure relief valve. The valve will be redesigned as a matter of urgency. But that doesn't help anyone at this precise moment.

Barrichello parks on the far side of the circuit and walks slowly and disconsolately across the grass, massive sympathy rolling down from the grandstand towering above him. He could easily leg it home from here; probably wishes he could. But the local media is waiting en masse back in the pits.

Rubens explains how the car had felt good and how he had been sitting back, conserving his tyres and preparing to attack later in the race. Then he lost all the gears. Once again, the potential of the car and driver had been shown quite clearly.

Such details are ignored by the Brazilian media as they switch back to the race. Barrichello has been let down by his car; simple as that. And now Ayrton Senna is on the point of winning the Brazilian Grand Prix – for Brazil. Who needs to know about Jordan's problems? The post-race press release comes straight to the point, Eddie Jordan commenting that nothing seems to have gone right. And now his hand has been forced by Team Lotus announcing that Trevor Foster will be joining them. Jordan acknowledges the fact, paying tribute to Foster's devotion to the team and wishing him well for the future.

Jordan announces that he will promote John Walton to the role of team manager. It is a good solution since Walton has been acquainted with Eddie Jordan for even longer than Foster; 'John Boy' knows exactly what he is letting himself in for.

Jordan leaves immediately for the Transamerica Hotel, showers and grabs a sandwich before dashing back to Guarulhos airport. The rutted road had not promised much on the way in, but events during the past three days had been rougher than anyone could have imagined.

Chapter 11

Filling His Boots

Goodbye Ivan

Jordan Grand Prix and Ivan Capelli agreed to part company the following Friday.

Phillips and Capelli had talked as friends in the immediate aftermath of Brazil. It had been a difficult conversation for both sides. Capelli knew that if he gave up after just two races, then in the light of his unsuccessful season with Ferrari in 1992, this would be viewed as the final confirmation that he could no longer hack it as a Grand Prix driver.

Deep down, he knew that was not the case. So did Phillips. But events had conspired against him and his confidence was in tatters. Capelli admitted he had been over-driving; forcing the car instead of running with it; generally trying too hard. There was, too, the feeling that the car was nervous, difficult to drive. But he wasn't really in the position to complain about that.

Phillips suggested the best solution would be to take time off, give the matter some thought and perhaps look for a decent drive in the Italian touring car series – just to establish whether or not he still *enjoyed* his racing.

As things stood, he plainly did not enjoy any of it and Phillips could only sympathize. He liked Capelli – as did almost everyone who had come into contact with him – but there was no alternative.

It was agreed that the official reason given would be the failure of one of Capelli's backers to produce the sponsorship originally promised; in any case, Ivan had not been comfortable from the outset with the fact that he was a paying driver and he was thus allowed to save a small amount of face as the partnership was dissolved at such an early stage.

This was all very well. But it left the team in a difficult state as they prepared for the first race of the hectic European season, starting two weeks after Brazil at Donington Park in England. Jordan needed to do well at home and now they were without a Number 1 driver.

Jordan considered Mika Hakkinen, a very promising 24-year-old under contract to McLaren. Hakkinen was on stand-by as a third driver, waiting for any breakdown in the continuing discussions between McLaren and Ayrton Senna, the Brazilian literally negotiating from race to race in an attempt to force the team's sponsors into submitting to his financial demands. So far, he was succeeding and Hakkinen was sitting on the sidelines. But Jordan soon abandoned discussion when it threatened to become complicated and bogged down with Ron Dennis, McLaren's managing director and prime motivator.

There had to be a quicker and easier way. Besides, they really needed an experienced driver to give Rubens a guiding hand.

Hello Thierry

Thierry Boutsen's Formula 1 career had almost come to a halt. A stylish and quick driver, he had never been able to recapture the form shown with Williams in 1989 and 1990 when he won three Grands Prix. Since then, a spell with Ligier had done little for him and, having tasted success with a top team, the hunger to do well did not seem as urgent and vital as before.

Why put everything on the line to move the recalcitrant Ligier from 19th to 15th on the grid? Ten years before, Boutsen would have thrown caution to the wind. But racing maturity had altered the Belgian's perspective; it is the way of most drivers whose commitments have since embraced a wife and children. Giving everything on the track for the chance of victory with a top team was one thing; doing it to achieve very little merely exacerbated the risk factor and highlighted the new-found priorities at home.

Unable to land a decent Formula 1 drive for 1993, Boutsen was in the United States, checking out the Indycar scene which had recently become the much publicized haunt of Nigel Mansell, the reigning Formula 1 World Champion. Jordan had spoken to Boutsen earlier. The money on offer was not grand by Formula 1 standards. Neither, for that matter, was the team. Boutsen wanted to think about it.

Phillips was getting desperate now. With a week to go before the next race, he eventually tracked down Boutsen in the Caribbean, where he was on holiday. They talked some more. The deal was more or less agreed.

Then came word that Boutsen had decided not to go ahead. There was no reason given. It was Tuesday, just two days before the action began at Donington. Jordan Grand Prix came close to panic.

Inbetween trying to reach Boutsen, Phillips tried to contact other prospective candidates. Thierry had flown back to his home in Monte Carlo and he had either inadvertently failed to replace the telephone receiver properly on the hook, or he was refusing to take calls. Unable to make contact, Phillips remembered that Keke Rosberg, the 1982 World Champion, lived in the same apartment block. A call to Rosberg had the Finn running up the stairs to advise Boutsen about his state of incommunicado and the desperate plight at Jordan. Lindsay Haylett had placed Boutsen's number on the automatic redial of her telephone and had been trying for hours on end. She was as surprised as anyone when he suddenly answered.

No, he definitely did not want to drive.

Eddie Jordan spoke to him at length. Then Ian Phillips tried. Finally, late on Tuesday, agreement was reached. It was a close call in every sense.

Boutsen flew to England for a brief run in the car at Silverstone. Being over 6 ft tall, Boutsen could not get comfortable in the cockpit, something which Anderson had foreseen and passed on to the management before the contract had been finalized. Boutsen's hands hit his thighs when he tried to put full lock on the steering. Under normal circumstances, the high gearing of the steering means that the driver has to apply very little lock. But, in the event of the car sliding or getting into difficulties, the steering correction necessary – opposite lock – would be difficult, not to mention dangerous, because of the limitations imposed by the cramped cockpit.

There were no obvious solutions. If the back of the seat was cut away, Boutsen would not recline so much. That would help his reach, but it would mean he would be sitting too tall, his helmet receiving a buffeting from the airstream as well as partially blocking the air intake to the engine.

Pushing the steering further away would help – but that was impossible because his knees were in the way. People may talk about the Formula 1 cockpit being a snug fit, suggesting cosy, close comfort. It is often anything but, particularly for a tall driver whom the designer did not have in mind when he began to draw the car.

There was little time for Boutsen to brood on the problem. Because Donington had never been used for a world championship Grand Prix before, an extra acclimatization practice session had been arranged for the next day, Thursday, 8 April. Boutsen would be pitched into battle immediately.

Enthused by his new environment, and pleased to be back in Formula 1 after thinking that perhaps the moment had passed, Boutsen was complimentary about the Jordan. 'It's a good chassis with a lot of potential,' he said. 'Plenty of downforce.'

That pleased Gary Anderson. Since Barrichello could not make comparisons with any other Formula 1 car, and Capelli had been struggling with his own problems, it was comforting to receive such confirmation from a driver who had raced with the likes of Benetton and Williams.

The feeling was that the right choice of driver had been made. There was talk of building a new chassis to accommodate Boutsen's long legs and arms. Eddie Jordan bridled at the additional cost involved but, that aside, the team was adapting quickly to the unexpected change.

But such was the eleventh hour of the deal that the representative from Sparco, the company manufacturing Jordan's flameproof overalls, had already been called in to prepare driving suits for David Coulthard, Emanuele Naspetti and Boutsen. By Wednesday morning, the photograph of Capelli on the wall of the team's motor home had already been replaced by Boutsen's official portrait. Goodbye Ivan; hello Thierry. Nothing ever stands still in F1.

Chapter 12

Pointless Brilliance

Wheatie's dream

The race at Donington had been a welcome addition to the calendar. Owned by Tom Wheatcroft, a bluff and jovial builder worth millions, this circuit had been his hobby; an expensive one, but his hobby nonetheless.

It had been Wheatcroft's ambition to stage a Grand Prix and break into the British monopoly held by Silverstone and, latterly, Brands Hatch. But, with each country supposedly limited to one Grand Prix a year (Italy being the exception), and Silverstone having ousted Brands Hatch by making a long-term commitment to the British Grand Prix, Wheatcroft had little chance of realizing his dream.

His opportunity came when a race, scheduled for a new circuit in Japan, was cancelled at short notice. Wheatcroft declared his willingness to fill the breach, even if it meant working flat out to bring his track and facilities to the standard required by the sport's ruling body, the FIA.

The other drawback was that the race meeting, to be known as the European Grand Prix, would be held over the Easter weekend; a good thing if the weather was kind but bad news if the holiday forecast followed its traditional unpleasant pattern.

The financial commitment necessary to attend the British Grand Prix in July (£110 for admission and a grandstand seat) was barely acceptable once a year but there were doubts that spectators could afford to double their expenditure, regardless of the wide-spread enthusiasm for Grand Prix racing in the United Kingdom. Everyone was delighted for 'Wheatie', but few believed his race would be a financial success.

Wheatcroft's company worked wonders. The result was not perfect but, for once, Formula 1 people seemed prepared to make allowances. After all, a trip up the M1 to Leicestershire was infinitely preferable to slogging all the way to Japan and back.

The garages were rather cramped by Formula 1 standards, but if anything Brazil had been worse. And, because of limitations to the paddock layout, the motor homes could not be placed in their usual positions directly behind the pits. Instead, they were off to one side, the devious route back and forth breaking the pattern of continuity as surely as if commuters had been forced to take an unfamiliar diversion on the way to work.

This was the opening race of the European season and yet there was something missing. The strange environment was diluting the usual first day of term feeling as the motor home crews, and faces not seen on the long-haul flyaway races, got together after a long winter.

On top of which, the weather on Friday was miserable, rain damping the ambience and killing the bonhomie which comes with wandering through a shimmering paddock.

In the Jordan motor home, however, the mood was sunny. Barrichello had finished the first qualifying session in eighth place, an excellent result due to preliminary tests carried out at Silverstone, thus saving valuable time during practice at Donington, plus Barrichello's knowledge of the circuit, and the fact that he and the team had chosen the right moment to record his best lap just before the rain intensified.

Boutsen was 19th, more than two seconds slower than his young teammate. The discrepancy did not cause undue concern since Boutsen was still feeling his way, Barrichello had the advantage of a new rear wing, and Boutsen's car had been fitted with a manual gearbox in the interest of reliability following the problems in Brazil and South Africa.

Eddie Jordan, deeply disappointed by the performance of his team in the first two races, had demanded that the semi-automatic gearbox be abandoned until it was reliable. Anderson argued that the semi-automatic system itself was not always at fault; the problems in South Africa had been caused by the gearbox internals and not the electro-hydraulics.

A compromise was reached whereby Barrichello would keep the semi-automatic while Boutsen's car, plus the spare, would have the manual selection on the righthand side of the cockpit. The irony was that Boutsen, with his restricted arm movements, desperately needed the semi-automatic gearbox with its selectors mounted behind the steering wheel spokes.

Anderson, meanwhile, had been searching for the cause of the trouble. It was felt the valve control block might be suffering unduly from vibrations from the engine. A new mounting point, cushioned by rubber bushes, had been found beneath the gearbox.

By the time final qualifying had finished on Saturday, he was convinced this had been the right move; the gearbox had worked perfectly throughout. And Barrichello was 12th on the grid! Things were looking up.

'I've had no problems with the car at all,' beamed Rubens. 'Twelfth on the grid is fantastic for me but, to be honest, I'm a bit disappointed with myself. I was trying too hard and made a small mistake during my quickest lap so, obviously, I feel I could have gone even quicker. I'm not sure if I could have beaten Herbert's Lotus in 11th place. But we're definitely going in the right direction now.'

And, with that, he was immediately engulfed by South American journalists, seizing on the fact that the youngster was just over a second slower than the much-vaunted Ayrton Senna in fourth place.

The weather had been as good as could be expected in April; sunny skies and moderate, pleasant heat. Naturally, all the drivers had improved their times in the dry conditions but, at the end of the day, Boutsen was still in 19th place – and disappointed to be there.

The discomfort of the cockpit had been more telling as the car cornered faster, the bumps and the G-forces dealing out a battering and a bruising, Boutsen more or less a passenger since he was unable to grab the car by the scruff of the neck.

A smaller steering wheel had been fitted and the steering column moved up. A heel rest on the floor had been modified, as had the position of the onboard fire extinguisher located beneath the driver's legs. These changes amounted to no more than a millimetre or two. Boutsen could see that Anderson was doing everything he could; in return, the team was impressed that Thierry – a former winner, after all – was not whingeing about his plight. Steps would be taken to somehow improve his seating position when the car was returned to the factory on Monday. In the meantime, Boutsen would have to get through 76 laps of this fairly tortuous circuit.

There were mixed feelings about the forecast of rain for Sunday. No driver genuinely likes racing in the wet but Barrichello knew it would bring some advantages. The Jordan did not have the so-called active suspension used by the leading teams, a system which improved the handling of the car, particularly in quick corners.

Donington did not have too many fast bends and the rain had reduced the benefit of active suspension even further, particularly on acceleration out of the corners, where the Lucas traction control system on the Jordan was now as good as any. Also, in the dry, the Williams could make full use of the healthy performance advantage produced by the Renault V10 whereas, in the wet, the inability to transmit all that power to the road would even the score and play into Jordan's hands.

The theory was confirmed on race morning when, on a wet track, Barrichello was seventh fastest in the warm-up. Suddenly, the cold, damp and thoroughly miserable day didn't seem quite so bad after all.

A stunning start

The rain would come and go. There was no clear indication of what to expect once the race got under way at 2 pm. This presented the teams with a major headache since a Grand Prix car is sensitive enough to be set up for either the wet or the dry conditions. But not both. A compromise is literally that, the car being not particularly good in either circumstance. So a gamble must be made, with the compromise tending to favour either a wet or a dry track.

Anderson and Barrichello felt that the rain would stop eventually and the track would dry out. But allowances had to be made for the circuit being very wet in the early stages. Barrichello chose to favour the dry set-up with the aerodynamics, giving more straight-line speed rather than loads of downforce and grip which would have provided a surer footing in the slippery conditions.

To deal with the latter, he would have to rely on his speedy reactions, coupled with adjustments made to the set-up of the rear suspension. In the event, it would turn out to be an excellent balance between the two choices. He went to the starting grid feeling that inner surge of confidence which makes the difference between a winning drive and a mediocre one.

Right from the green light, he was on the attack. Barrichello takes up the story:

'The start was fantastic for me. Things had started to go well when one of the Saubers, which had been a couple of rows ahead of me, had some sort of problem on the grid and had to start the race from the pit lane.

'I passed Herbert and the Benetton of Patrese on the run to Redgate, the first corner. The next car, the Ferrari of Gerhard Berger, was just far enough ahead to allow me to take the corner exactly as I wanted without being impeded. So, I came out of Redgate very quickly and I was able to pass Berger going down the hill towards Old Hairpin. There was no time to register that I had just overtaken a Ferrari!

'Halfway round the lap, I saw that two cars ahead of me had crashed into each other and the second Ferrari of Jean Alesi was running a little bit wide to avoid them.

'I grabbed my chance going into the next corner – but Alesi is always difficult because he brakes so very late! I was braking late too because I didn't want to miss an opportunity like this. My car went a bit sideways and I thought I was going to hit the side of Michael Schumacher's Benetton, which was just in front of us. Fortunately, he saw me and went a little bit wide – and I was able to overtake him, no problem. I was fourth!

'I couldn't believe it. For sure, there was a bit of luck involved, but that's what racing is all about. I really committed myself and tried very hard. If you had asked me on Saturday to pay £1,000 and that would let me be sixth at the end of the first lap, I would have paid you. And here I was fourth, with just Senna, Prost and Hill ahead of me.'

The television and radio commentators, struggling to keep pace with the furious activity as Senna drove the lap of his life and snatched the lead in brilliant style, called the order as the cars, the drivers difficult to identify in the murk, kicked up the spray on their way past the pits: 'McLaren ... Williams ... Williams ... and a Jordan!'

Such moments of glory for a lesser light are usually brief as the heavyweight opposition gets into its stride and recovers composure. But, on a day like this, Barrichello was in his element. Alesi was applying pressure but Rubens was staying cool despite the menacing presence of the red car.

After 10 laps, with no change in the order, it was clear that pit stop strategy would play a significant part in the outcome as the rain eased. With Barrichello never having made a tyre change before, the Jordan team would surely be swept aside by their more experienced rivals.

Barrichello had his thumb on the radio button, constantly in touch with Anderson as they discussed the possibilities. The track was showing signs of drying out and when Hill dived into the pits for slick tyres at the end of lap 17, it was the signal everyone had been waiting for.

These were anxious moments for the Jordan crew. Sure, they had practised the tyre change routine time and again but there is no substitute for the pressure and urgency of the race itself. The slightest hitch could cost Barrichello a couple of places. And, with the boy doing so incredibly well, woe betide the hapless mechanic who fumbles and throws away Barrichello's brilliant efforts so far.

Even in his most optimistic moments – of which there are many – Eddie Jordan would concede that it is rare to see one of his cars nudging the top three at such an early stage in a Grand Prix. You could dig lumps out of the tension as Rubens pointed the Jordan into the now busy pit lane at the end of his 18th lap. Eyes down, lads. Here he comes!

Check your oil, Sir?

It is common for a novice driver, in his enthusiasm and anxiety, to overshoot his pit. Barrichello stopped inch-perfect, the throttle blipping, air hammers chattering their staccato tune, nuts removed in an instant, fresh wheels in place and driven home, jacks dropped, the signal to go, full revs, a touch of wheelspin, and away. Perfect!

The mechanics, their confidence bolstered, were ready to tackle anything now. Which was just as well because Barrichello would be back a few times more.

Was this the end of the big moment for Barrichello and Jordan? Rubens felt that might be the case.

'I thought, after the pit stop, maybe I would be eighth or ninth, something like that. So, okay, no problem; let's keep trying and see if we can make up any places. I couldn't believe it when I had only dropped to fifth.'

Five laps later and it began to rain again. But, whereas the Williams drivers were quick to change back to grooved tyres, it was significant that Senna, the race leader and an acknowledged wet weather expert, joined Barrichello in reserving his judgement even though the going with slick tyres was becoming more treacherous by the lap.

The argument was that time could be wasted by changing tyres – only to have the rain ease off. But there seemed little likelihood of that as the spray intensified. Barrichello and Senna eventually came in for wet tyres on lap 28, neither losing their place in the process. And, almost immediately, the rain stopped.

Sod it!

Seven laps later and everyone had returned to slicks, the Jordan team continuing to work like clockwork. Barrichello was still fourth.

Unbelievably, the rain returned once more and Barrichello was back for wet weather tyres on lap 38. The mechanics barely had time to catch their breath, particularly as Boutsen, up to 11th at one stage, was virtually mirroring his team-mate's tactics.

It was almost no surprise when the rain eased yet again but, this time, Barrichello decided to out-guess the weather. While the leaders (except Senna, who had bravely remained on slick tyres throughout the last little shower) stopped for dry tyres, Barrichello pressed on with his grooved tyres, hoping that the rain would return – in which case he would have saved himself two pit stops.

The gamble back-fired badly because, not only did he eventually feel that the wet weather rubber was overheating too much on the dry surface, he stopped for slicks and, the very second he raced back on to the track, the heavens opened. One lap later and he was back again, along with everyone else, for grooved tyres. Anderson had wanted him to stay out all along; the mistimed pit stop was purely down to Barrichello's inexperience.

But the net result of this unequalled chaos was a continuing fourth place for Sasol Jordan Hart; an extraordinary state of affairs to match the fickle weather. And still Rubens pressed on, his lap times quick and consistent as he revelled in the handling of the car in these conditions.

With six laps to go, he moved into third place when Hill made a late pit stop as the weather continued to prevaricate. Not only was Rubens Barrichello about to score points in only his third Grand Prix, he had a chance of visiting the rostrum as well.

It was almost an irrelevance that Boutsen, desperately uncomfortable, had been forced to give up the unequal struggle nine laps before when the throttle began to stick open. The mechanics braced themselves in case Rubens had to make one last tyre change. Indeed, Anderson thought that might be the case when the radio crackled into life once more.

But this time the voice at the other end had a completely different tone. Gone was the high-pitched, youthful call fed by surging adrenalin; this was the sound of disbelief mixed with crushing disappointment.

The engine had gone dead and the Jordan was on the grass, parked, out of the race.

The entire team was devastated. So, to a lesser degree, was the majority of the pit lane, always glad to see a fresh face in the points; happy for any small team receiving an unexpected reward; pleased for Eddie Jordan.

Barrichello reported that a lap earlier, the fuel pressure warning light had come on. That became the official reason for the retirement of car 14 after 70 glorious laps. The dreaded unreliability factor had struck again. But why?

An empty feeling

Perhaps the electronics were at fault. Maybe the final gallons had not been picked up by the fuel pump. It could be any number of things. It seemed unlikely that the car had run out of fuel because, in a wet race, with the engine not being used to the maximum, there is usually petrol to spare at the finish.

But, unbelievably, when the car was eventually returned to the garage, the tank was found to be empty. At first there were suspicions that, for some reason, the fuel consumption had been far greater than expected. Much to the chagrin of Sasol, tests were carried out comparing consumption with Shell fuel. The Sasol product was not quite as economic, but not enough to make a difference.

There was the thought that an electrical sensor fitted in the engine airbox – a form of choke for cold setting –- might have contributed. But, in the end, investigations would point to the painful fact that the full amount of fuel set aside for the race had not actually been put in the tank.

It was human error. And a desperate one at that.

Gutted

Eddie Jordan, his hands dug deep in the pockets of his blue waterproof, the hood pulled over his head, made his lonely way back to the motor home. There was no need to ask how he felt because it was written all over his face.

The team had performed brilliantly under the sustained pressure of the pit stops. Apart from one misjudgement, the tyre-change tactics had been perfect. The car had been super-competitive. Barrichello had been sensational. And then this.

'Gutted,' he mumbled, and walked slowly on.

Not long after, Barrichello followed the same route. He was limping, the result of cramp imposed by his longest period yet in the cockpit of a racing car. Although disappointed, he was still elated by the strength of his performance. Every few steps brought more condolences and words of encouragement from all corners of the paddock. When he reached the motor home, his entry was greeted by a spontaneous burst of applause driven by sympathy and respect.

As the rain lashed against the canvas of the motor home awning, Hart and Anderson opened a bottle of wine and reviewed the whirlwind events of the previous couple of hours. There was no point in being theatrical and upset; what was done was done.

Just as important was the fact that the car had performed. More important, the gearbox, now on a full automatic change going up through the gears, had not produced a single problem during more than 2,000 gearchanges. Anderson was very pleased – and relieved – about that.

'Well,' said Ian Phillips, chirpy as ever, 'too bad about the bloody result. Never mind, this puts Jordan Grand Prix back on the map. In just one race, we have wiped out all the disappointment of 1992. Here's to Imola and the next race. Cheers!'

He had no trouble in finding any takers. There are times when it is a comfort to.be in a business which barely pauses for breath and hardly allows a backward glance; a race without end.

Chapter 13

Counting the Cost

Loads of Lire

Gary Anderson had seen it all before. It was a lengthy case of post-race euphoria. Almost two weeks had passed since Donington and Anderson was now focusing his mind on the technical problems presented here at Imola, scene of the San Marino Grand Prix in three days time.

As he stood outside the Jordan motor home and poured a coffee, Anderson caught sight of Rubens Barrichello in the midst of a clutch of journalists. The talk was about Donington; Rubens was still elated. His confidence high, Barrichello was raring to go. There was unfinished business – so let's get on with it. Yeah, I reckon I could do it.

Anderson had no complaint with that; better to have a bullish young driver than one weighed down with self-doubt or dulled by mediocre experience. But he had been around long enough to know that the cruel, fast-moving nature of Formula 1 has no respect for yesterday.

Barrichello may still be the man of the moment. But that moment ends as soon as practice gets under way for the next race. Unless, of course, the momentum continues and the names of Barrichello and Jordan are on everyone's lips once more. Anderson was too much of a realist for that.

'He'll probably come down to earth with a bit of a bump tomorrow,' said Anderson with a grin which suggested that experience can cushion the fall.

Experience can also remove much of the hassle associated with simply getting to and from the races. Earlier that morning, Eddie Jordan and Ian Phillips had arrived on the packed flight from Heathrow. Remembering the limitations of Bologna's Marconi airport, Phillips had used his Italian contacts to have a car waiting at the door, thus neatly side-stepping the scrum around the hire car office which took 40 minutes to disperse.

Time was of the essence here; many of the team's backers were Italian and there was much pumping of flesh and massaging of sponsorship to be done this weekend. This was territory which Jordan and Phillips enjoyed treading.

Phillips has never been coy about the role of sponsorship in Grand Prix racing.

'We're all whores at heart,' he once told *The Observer* newspaper. 'There's not a square inch of the car that isn't for sale – at the right price, of course.'

The hierarchy at McLaren International, with their self-contained marketing department, presentation studio and lexicon of business-speak, probably winced at such a bald statement of fact. A documentary about McLaren, screened on BBC 2 later in the year, would devote an entire 30 minutes to the intense marketing men targeting, stalking, fussing, preparing, investigating, liaising, presenting, cajoling, flattering and, ultimately, congratulating a prospective sponsor for his wisdom in joining McLaren. The identification, mounted on the back of the car's rear view mirrors, was barely visible. The over-acted drama had Phillips – and most of the paddock – falling about.

But the truth was that, for all the apparent disingenuous dramatization, such attention to fine detail was precisely why McLaren won races and how, in a kind of Catch 22 situation, they could raise the money to run a marketing department in the first place.

That sort of thing may encourage grand talk of global brand awareness, synergy and positioning in the market place. But what it really means is the use of Grand Prix racing to promote a company's name or product. It is commonsense stuff driven by the basic tenet that everyone likes to be associated with success.

Small teams have to operate by seat of the pants intuition, an eye for the sponsorship deal, and up-front personality. And, in the latter category, Jordan Grand Prix score heavily. Phillips and Jordan could, by no means, be described as anonymous men in grey suits mouthing platitudes on behalf of their employer. If Jordan feels a deal can be done on first acquaintance at the dinner table, then why not? So long as the price is right ...

Of course, when the occasion demands it, the Jordan team can be – has to be – totally professional in their methods. The negotiation with Sasol had been conducted in the manner which a petrochemical conglomerate would expect. It was the same with Barclay, the cigarette brand owned by British American Tobacco. And Unipart, the British-based international automotive parts and accessories company.

Further down the scale, relationships with the small companies are of a more personal nature; in many cases, the deals are done simply because the owner/managing director is a Formula 1 fan and this is a means of breaching the stout barrier defending the inner sanctum of the sport. And, not surprisingly, given the country's abiding passion for motor racing, many are of Italian origin.

Identification on the nose wings for Perar Ball Valves represented a manufacturer of ball valves for the gas industry, the Milan-based company since expanding worldwide into the oil, petrochemical and water processing industries.

The arrangement with OZ Wheels is of a more practical nature since the Italian company supplies Jordan with alloy wheels, a deal worth in excess of £60,000 when servicing and repairs are taken into account. Osama produce writing instruments and the Italian company is expanding into the European market.

Butan Gas, also Italian, was looking for ways to promote its own line of camping and leisure gas tools. Uliveto sell two million bottles of mineral water each day; prominent identification on the sides of the cars cost the Italian company £430,000 for 1993. Both these companies, as sponsors of 25-year-old Emanuele Naspetti, used their association with Formula 1 to produce a package deal aimed at fostering young Italian drivers. Jordan, in turn, chose the Imola weekend to announce that Naspetti would act as the team's test driver in 1993, a mutually agreeable deal for all sides.

Diavia makes automobile air conditioning for leading motor manufacturers such as Ferrari, Fiat, Renault and Peugeot; Fiamm employs 2,500 people to make batteries and industrial power packs in Italy, France, Austria and the USA; Compact, a Japanese business consultancy, had exclusive rights to Jordan Grand Prix clothing in Japan; Keeley Group holdings is a South African company represented on the Jordan by identification for Keeley Granite, a quarrying business, and by Keeley Air, a private jet and helicopter company operating out of Johannesburg and London.

The 1993 Jordan letter-heading carried a list of more than 20 sponsors and trade associates, some of whose names did not appear on the car.

'We have deals with companies which do not require that,' explained Phillips. 'For instance, we have an arrangement with Cascina Castlet, an Italian wine company. They do not want to pay to be on the car but we have their name on our notepaper and we endorse their products and do a photo shoot for them. In return, they supply us with wine.

'Over a season, when you take into account receptions at the factory and, of course, entertaining over three days at each race, that mounts up. We would have to buy wine anyway, so if this saves expense in return for a photograph, then it makes sense for Jordan, and everyone is happy.'

It cost Eddie Jordan in excess of £10 million to run the team in 1993. The bulk of the expenditure – about £3 million – went on designing and building five cars, the first being the most expensive (around £800,000) since it took into account the cost of models, moulds, tooling and wind tunnel work.

The deal with Brian Hart meant an outlay of over £2 million for the supply of engines, a large proportion of the budget which, ironically, big teams do not have to face since their arrangements with major manufacturers such as Renault and Peugeot mean the engines are supplied free.

Salaries and wages account for another large chunk of the budget, as does the supply of tyres from Goodyear, Jordan using in excess of 1,300 tyres – at

$600 each – during the season. There would be free tyres available if a Jordan finished in the top three at any race, provided the car and the team carried Goodyear identification.

Jordan and Phillips were only too happy to oblige the American company but the real aim of their ministrations is to cover all of the costs by selling space on the cars. There is no rate card as such since it invites under-cutting by rival teams. Journalists continually face a stone wall when enquiring about the costs involved. Eddie Jordan's reply, when asked by *Autosport* to price the space on the sidepods of his car, was typically evasive.

'I can say the sidepod costs anything,' explained Jordan. 'It doesn't matter. What is important is what you can make that money do for you. If you are looking for a world class awareness programme, then it is going to cost a certain amount of money.'

Certainly, awareness through television exposure forms the main plank of any approach to potential sponsors interested in promoting their trademarks. Fancy viewership figures are bandied about but the undeniable fact is that, in 1993, more than 10,000 hours of Grand Prix racing were broadcast to 102 countries. The exposure gained on television beats traditional advertising campaigns hands down. The sponsorship money spent on Formula 1 is small beer by comparison.

But it helps to keep the likes of Jordan Grand Prix afloat. The quid pro quo is that the team must then carry that identification into range of the television and photo camera lenses. Jordan had won an excellent amount of coverage at Donington. Now the sponsors were looking for a repeat at Imola.

The proxy prix

The title *Gran Premio di San Marino* is largely irrelevant since the race is held in Italy. The adoption of the race on behalf of the nearby republic was a fancy piece of footwork which enabled the Italians to hold two Grands Prix – one at Monza (the Italian Grand Prix) and one at Imola (the San Marino Grand Prix) – at a time when the ruling body had been insistent that each country should have just one Grand Prix each year.

The political manoeuvring is no longer of any interest. What mattered is that Imola actually has a place on the calendar; it remains one of the most popular races. The atmosphere is fed by the devotion of the *tifosi* to Ferrari, the fans at Imola being just as vocal but less intimidating than their counterparts at Monza. The natural beauty and friendliness of the Emilia region adds the final touch as exquisite pasta is washed down by the local *vino*. In all, Imola usually is a good place to be in April.

The drivers enjoy it too since the circuit, rising steeply in parts and falling dramatically in others, is a perfect mixture of fast and slow corners; something they can get their teeth into and feel a deep sense of satisfaction when the car is working well.

Much depends on a lusty engine since Imola has a long, curving straight which starts just before the pits and disappears into the trees, sweeping its way to a second gear left-hander at Tosa. You can stand in the pits and listen to the cars disappear, the engines singing their hearts out on maximum revs for a long period of time. They sound glorious on a warm, spring afternoon.

For an engine builder, such an experience is good and bad; the equivalent of making exquisite love while knowing the roof could collapse any second.

Love hurts

Brian Hart was approaching another important technical milestone. Recognizing the importance of engine power at Imola, he had chosen to introduce the latest version of his V10. He would say little about what he had actually done but it was clear that it was enough to allow the engine to be revved even higher than before.

Now the Hart could work to 13,200 rpm. And it would do it within earshot of the entire pit lane. It was all very well Hart and his team carrying out their research on a dynamometer back at the factory and then perhaps having the engine run briefly during a test session. This would be the stiffest examination imaginable.

Hart worked out that the engine would be flat out for 19 seconds from the moment it accelerated out of the corner before the pits until the driver hit the brakes at around 200 mph on the approach to Tosa. That's a long time in any engineer's book.

The blunt reality was that the pragmatic nature of the driver would have him keep his foot jammed to the floor without worrying in the least about the violent forces somehow being contained within the block of metal behind his shoulders.

Each of the 10 pistons would have a force of approximately 5 tons acting upon it, almost continually. The piston surface would have to withstand temperatures ranging between 250 and 300°C – that's three times boiling point. And, each minute, the equivalent of 110 gallons of water would be pumped around the engine.

If that explosive fury succeeded in making an unplanned exit, the failure would be spectacular, messy and very public. Small wonder that Brian Hart was preoccupied when practice began for the San Marino Grand Prix on Friday, 23 April.

Hart reckoned that each of the 40 valves in the V10 would open and shut at least three-quarters of a million times during one morning practice session alone. That assumed, of course, that the car would not be stuck in the garage while some problem or other was sorted out.

The valves duly did their work without hindrance of any kind, Barrichello and Boutsen working solidly as they tried to find the best set-up for the 3.1-mile track.

Boutsen now had the satisfaction of working with Tim Wright, an engineer with whom the Belgian had been associated while racing sports cars for Peugeot. Wright, also a former engineer with McLaren, had been brought in to ease Anderson's massive work load and allow the designer to concentrate on wind tunnel work and other important matters inbetween the races. It was felt Wright could contribute much to the technical side of the team; his arrival was seen as a positive move.

It was significant that Wright and Boutsen should spend Saturday morning concentrating on the race set-up rather than chasing the sprint format which would see the ultimate quick lap during final qualifying later in the day. Such brave thinking was usually the domain of top teams, confident that they would be on or near the front of the grid no matter what.

Boutsen declared himself happy with the morning's work, saying the car felt nicely balanced with a full load of fuel. That was all very well, but to take advantage of it, he would need to be further up the grid than the 19th place earned during qualifying the previous day. In the event, final qualifying offered no improvement because even though Boutsen went half a second quicker (despite problems with the gear selection), the drivers around him also went faster and he finished qualifying still in 19th place.

Barrichello, three-tenths of a second short of seventh on the grid, would start from 13th place, slightly disappointed after he, too, had trouble with the gear selection.

But Brian Hart was happy – and very relieved. The engine had performed perfectly, both drivers speaking in glowing terms about the increase in performance.

To prove it, Barrichello had been third fastest (200.01 mph) through the speed trap at the end of the long straight. Hart knew that this information would be made available on the Olivetti/TAG-Heuer timing sheets presented to each team. The point would not be missed by the sport's *cognoscenti*. Now, all the team had to do was back it up by scoring some points the following day.

Balancing the books

Eddie Jordan was in relaxed mood on Sunday morning. A full cooked breakfast at the motor home, washed down by a cup of decent tea, set him up for the day as the Italian sponsors came and went, each apparently happy with their particular lot.

Jordan had been looking at his cash flow and, for the first time in a long time, it made reasonable reading. Outstanding sums stretching back to 1991 concerning engine bills (with Cosworth) and tyre supply, plus a catalogue of other debts, had finally been cleared.

Jordan still owed money elsewhere, including £650,000 on the factory, built in 1990/91 but now worth more than £2 million. Capelli's departure meant the loss of a potential $750,000 in sponsorship. Boutsen had not brought any backing; indeed, Jordan was paying him £75,000 towards expenses, but nothing else. It was a tiny fee by F1 standards.

All told, the situation – in Grand Prix terms – was reasonable. As Jordan pointed out: 'Not many teams are in this position.'

But, at the back of his mind was the thought that things might change if his team did not deliver on the track. And, already this morning, matters had taken a turn for the worse.

Hardly got started

Rain 15 minutes into the warm-up had virtually cut the work time in half, on top of which Barrichello's running had been compromised by a wrong choice of gear ratios. After being seventh in the warm-up at Donington, he was languishing in 20th place here, two ahead of Boutsen. Eddie Jordan did not like the look of it.

His worst fears were confirmed seconds after the start of the race. A car left the road and, in the momentary confusion which followed, Barrichello touched Fittipaldi's Minardi and punctured the left-rear tyre on the Jordan. Barrichello limped round the remainder of the lap and finally reached the pits – where he was joined by Boutsen.

Thierry had gone no more than 300 metres when the Jordan refused to select a gear. Once in the pits, there was little that could be done. The car was wheeled away.

It was discovered that an oil seal on the hydraulic pump had failed – and not for the first time this weekend. It was a mystery because there had not been a problem during 3,000 miles of running. To have three fail without warning during one weekend pointed to a fundamental fault somewhere.

'When the first one went,' said Anderson, 'we thought it might have been an assembly problem. But, when the second failed, we were in trouble but we didn't react quickly enough. It was only happening just as the engine was switched off and there was a surge of back pressure in the system. The third failure had occurred when Thierry switched off his engine as he came on to the starting grid for the statutory 15-minute countdown. And, of course, we didn't know it had happened.'

All being well, Barrichello would not need to switch off his engine until the end of the race. He had rejoined at the back of the field but, on lap 18, he spun off. The engine was still running – but the car was stuck in a gravel trap. The weekend was over for Sasol Jordan Hart after half an hour of not very impressive racing.

'Well, he was going for it, trying hard,' said Phillips, putting a brave face on Barrichello's spin. 'He spun off but, in a way, it was fortunate he did it in a situation like that and not when he was running in the top six. You can accept that when he had absolutely nothing to lose. At least he's learned something from it.'

'Yeah,' nodded Anderson with a knowing look. 'His lap times were very quick but it's brought him back to earth with a bit of a bump after Donington. I've seen it before and I'll probably see it again.

Chapter 14

The Engineer Said

Talk torque

Motor racing can be a baffling business – even to those who understand its technicalities. Or most of them, anyway. The first day's practice for the Spanish Grand Prix was a case in point; it drove the engineers to distraction.

Race engineers are the secondary link between the driver and his machine. The primary input comes from what the driver feels and how he copes when the car is at speed. The analysis of that and, hopefully, suitable improvements in performance, is the laborious result of subsequent detailed conversations between the driver and his engineer.

For most of the time, engineers are like father figures, towering over the drivers as they sit in the cockpit, often struggling to translate into words precisely how the car is behaving. Eye to eye contact can only be comfortably maintained if the engineer stands in front of the car, but a few paces back and in the driver's vision. That is easy enough these days thanks to remote radio links. But it wasn't always so.

Time was when the engineer had to lean into the cockpit and either roar at the driver's crash helmet or press his ear against the open visor slot. And even then, half of the conversation would be drowned by the racket as Grand Prix racing went about its business.

Then came radio communication in the late 1970s, a godsend although, initially, this was restricted by the need for the engineer to plug physically into the car, usually at some point near the back of the cockpit. All the driver experienced then was a dismembered voice in his helmet and trouser-leg bottoms to one side. But at least they could communicate in a more relaxed and civilized manner.

By 1993, however, state-of-the-art radios were as vital as tyres and fuel; every team had them.

A rack at the rear of the Jordan garage carried headsets and receivers for every member of the team, the units remaining on trickle charge until removed and clipped to a waistband, ready for action. Although conversation would be mainly limited to the drivers and their respective engineers, the mechanics and management personnel could listen in, keep abreast of the latest developments and leap swiftly into action when necessary.

But, as things would turn out in Barcelona on Friday, 6 May, headsets would not really be necessary. The low-key start to the Spanish weekend meant normal conversation could be carried on, almost without hindrance.

Barcelona's heritage

This was only the third time the Montmelo circuit had acted as host to the Spanish Grand Prix, although in truth Barcelona was no stranger to Formula 1. The Grand Prix had been held five times at the turn of the '50s on the streets of Pedralbes, cars blasting down Avenida del Generalissimo Franco in the western suburbs.

But the race is best remembered, for reasons good and bad, following a move in the late '60s to Montjuich Park, a breathtaking series of roads in a park high above the city.

The 1975 Spanish Grand Prix ended in tragedy when a car flew off the road and killed four onlookers standing in a prohibited area. That was the end of Montjuich, the race then moving back to Jarama, outside Madrid, and on to Jerez in the south of the country.

It was the advent of the Olympics, and the accompanying improvements to the Barcelona infrastructure, which prompted the building of the Circuit de Catalunya at Montmelo in 1991.

As modern race tracks go, the Montmelo circuit is reasonable. Which is to say, not too boring and with an acceptable mixture of corners. But to compare it with, say, Montjuich, would be to mention Aintree and a local gymkhana in the same breath.

Nonetheless, the race teams like it. The facilities are second to none, the garages large and airy, the pit lane wide and safe. And when practice got under way, the track itself was to prove favourable.

What now?

'Not bad,' said Rubens Barrichello after a handful of laps. 'In the high speed corners, the car is very good. There is a little understeer in the medium speed corners, but I'm not really pushing hard yet; the track is still very dirty. It's the best first practice I've had with the car; it's got a good balance although we have a little too much understeer in the low speed corners.

Gary Anderson is listening, nodding and noting Barrichello's comments on a clip board. Every detail is recorded, no matter how insignificant. What may seem a trifling matter now may turn out to be a vital clue when the overall picture emerges later in the day, or in the weekend. Quite simply, each time the car turns a wheel, the engineer writes about it.

'Is it touching?' asks Anderson, referring to the bottom of the car grinding on the bumps. 'Not much, maybe a little bit on the bumps. Perhaps that's giving the understeer?'

'We'll look at the front to see if it's on the packer,' says Anderson, a statement which doubles as an instruction to the mechanics to check the travel of the front suspension. Anderson also asks Paul Thompson, the chief mechanic, to have the tyre pressures measured.

Barrichello, meanwhile, watches the progress of his rivals thanks to a portable timing monitor, which has been placed on the front of the cockpit. The screen shows little evidence of any progress by Thierry Boutsen in the other Jordan-Hart.

The Belgian is sitting patiently in the car. He managed just one lap before a fault in the hydraulic system prevented the selection of gears. He's been at rest for 41 minutes while the rest of the pit lane gets down to serious work.

There is no outward sign of frustration; no sense of desperation from the management or the pit crew. The feeling is that this fault has occurred, it's a bloody nuisance but they know how to fix it. It just takes time, that's all. There's nothing more anyone can do.

Boutsen eventually returns to the track and strings together four reasonably quick laps. He is of much the same opinion as his team-mate.

'The quick corners are okay,' he tells Tim Wright. 'But there's understeer in the middle of the slow corners and then oversteer coming out. I can live with the understeer. But I want to sort out the oversteer. And make a note, Tim; I want to adjust the position of the seat belt.'

Boutsen has been given a new car, one which has been prepared with his lanky frame in mind. He says it's more comfortable than before. It's still not perfect but at least he can feel a part of the car now and understand better what it is doing.

While the brake temperatures and tyre pressures are checked, Wright suggests softening the springing at the rear of the car. Then he tells Boutsen about the changes being tried by Barrichello and Anderson; does he want to follow that same path? Boutsen thinks for a few seconds.

'No, let's try the rear springs first,' he says.

But Barrichello, breathing hard after a quick lap, seems to be on the right track.

'That's better,' he tells Anderson. 'But we still need to get rid of the understeer because I think it will be worse when we put on new tyres. How many laps have I got left?' Anderson consults the clip board and checks off the number completed against the maximum of 23 allowed during free practice.

'You've got six left. So, that means one slow lap out of the pits, four quick ones and then one back to the pits. Okay?'

Barrichello examines the screen.

'Yeah, okay. I just want to wait and see what time Fittipaldi does on his next lap. Then I'll go.'

Despite the mechanical problems experienced by Jordan during the four races held so far, it is clear that they are on a par with the Minardi team in terms of race performances. Fittipaldi's fourth place in South Africa still rankles and Rubens is keener than ever to beat his Brazilian neighbour. Fittipaldi's Minardi-Ford covers the 2.95 miles in 1m 24.7s. Barrichello's best so far has been 1m 25.4s. Not good enough. Not good enough by a long way.

Barrichello sets off. 1m 38s. On the next lap, he is held up by a slower car. Then 1m 25.4s again. The timing shows that he has crossed the finish line faster than ever before as he starts the next lap. The split time shows the first third of the lap to be his best so far. This looks good.

Then the car stops. Bloody hell. What now?

And the session is over.

Rubens has spun without harm but, worse still, the car has gone into neutral. New gearbox software has been programmed to select neutral when the engine revs fall below 1,000 rpm. But did the spin cause this to happen? Or did he lock the rear wheels under braking seconds before and cause the revs to die momentarily? Which came first?

The Jordan has barely touched the pit lane floor after being lifted from the breakdown truck before computers are plugged in and down-loaded in search of a clue. These troubles aside, the verdict on the cars is reasonable. We should be okay during qualifying this afternoon.

Really?

Not so fast!

Motor racing is about to play one of its ethereal tricks for which even the most sophisticated technology in the world has no immediate answer.

The track conditions change for no accountable reason during the two-hour break between the end of free practice and the start of qualifying. All the previous work – the changes measured in millimetres in search of fractions of a second – are rendered almost useless by a devious turn of nature. It affects all of the teams equally, of course. But some react faster than others. And Jordan is not particularly swift off the mark.

'We're losing a lot of time – too much oversteer now coming out of the slow corners and the balance of the car generally is not good,' says Barrichello.

The ride height (the level of the bottom of the car above the ground) is lowered, tyre pressures and temperatures checked. Because of the changing track conditions, the rubber is not generating enough heat to allow the tyres to work at their maximum. It is discovered eventually that there is nothing to be gained from fitting a fresh set (the usual method of finding more 'time') since it takes at least half a lap to 'scrub' the new tyres and work them to the desired temperature and, even then, there is little to be gained.

All of this is serving to disrupt the planned attack by both drivers.

At the end of the session, Boutsen is 17th; Barrichello 18th. Hardly an encouraging start.

The drivers huddle in impromptu conference around the foldaway tables in the back of the garage, Anderson and Wright discussing the findings on the lap top computers with Andrew Green and Mark Smith, the engineers who have played an important part in helping Anderson design various aspects of this car.

'The track lost grip in the afternoon and we didn't react to it,' says Anderson. 'The changes we made didn't help; in effect, we managed to shoot ourselves in the foot.

'I'm pissed off, y'know?' he says, stating the obvious. 'We didn't react more quickly to what was going on; that's the trouble. But we've learned a few things and we'll make changes for tomorrow; running the front of the car lower and stiffer; put more camber on the left front tyre – we've noticed that the outside shoulder is wearing more and the wheel has been "tucking in" as Rubens turned into the corners.

'We're also going to try running more downforce on Rubens's car. Thierry tried a bigger rear wing this afternoon – he says it made the car feel better in the high speed corners – so we'll try that on Rubens's car tomorrow.'

Tomorrow. There's always tomorrow. The fact that the same sort of anguished conversation is taking place in the garages next door is of little consolation.

In the Sauber enclave, the mysteries of this business are hitting home as the Swiss-based team settles into their first season of Formula 1.

'We don't understand,' says the Sauber public relations man, half joking, half in despair. 'We are slower than when we came testing here in the winter – and that was when we supposedly knew nothing about what we were doing!'

Williams have actually been slower in qualifying than they had been during free practice. But the difference is, they are still first and third fastest on the time sheet. The Jordans are almost five seconds a lap slower. It's a depressing thought. Still, there's always tomorrow.

What's it all about?

Tomorrow starts off on a promising note; Boutsen is 10th at the end of free practice; Barrichello, 17th. Both drivers have gone much quicker than Friday – but, then, so has everyone else. What further tricks has this curious circuit got in store?

It is decided not to attempt to out-guess fate; the cars are left as they are for final qualifying without recourse to further subtle tuning.

Both drivers go quicker still – and march steadily backwards. At the end of the day, Barrichello is 17th and Boutsen 21st. And the Williams pair are still at the front. Two days of effort. For what?

'This track is different every time you go out,' says Barrichello in exasperation. 'I tell you, my car felt good this morning, really good. With fresh tyres on, I was sure I could do a good time in qualifying. Then it starts to oversteer and I reckon that cost me half a second a lap. But, really, it was too big a gamble to start changing the car again in the middle of a qualifying session. I just had to go for it and make the best of it. Seventeenth is very disappointing for me.'

Boutsen is almost philosophical, blaming too much temperature with his first set tyres and a busy track when he tried unsuccessfully to go quicker on his second set.

There is further consultation with the computers on the foldaway table. In a quiet corner, Brian Hart is studying the readings from the on-board sensors. There may be only two-tenths of a second between the Jordan drivers but Hart can see interesting pointers as he overlays the graphs of one driver on top of the other.

The speed and revs-per-minute charts show Barrichello is getting his foot on the throttle earlier than Boutsen at the exit of each corner and therefore reaching maximum speed sooner. Whatever happened to the potential and downforce Boutsen had referred to after his first test with the Jordan prior to Donington? Is this disappointing performance due to a problem with Boutsen's car? Or is it youthful exuberance and natural speed on Barrichello's part? Or is Boutsen just slowing down?

No one is saying. But opinions are being formed just as surely as Boutsen is coming to realize that the Jordan-Hart 193 is not likely to be one of the best cars he has ever driven.

Uncomfortable reality

Such matters are not mentioned that evening in a smart downtown restaurant as Louise Goodman celebrates her 30th birthday with Eddie Jordan, Ian Phillips and a party of friends from the media. The level of conversation rises and the tone falls in direct proportion to the consumption of a very fine local wine, making this an increasingly rowdy table in comparison with a more sober meeting of minds as Bernie Ecclestone, Flavio Briatore and Tom Walkinshaw, three of the sport's leading lights, dine nearby.

Jordan feigns respectability throughout; in truth, his mischievous mind is provoking much of the lively banter. At least it provides a diversion from the uncomfortable reality of this visit to Barcelona.

Back at the circuit, the frustrating day's work is drawing to a close for the beleaguered mechanics. The rear quarter of the starting grid for tomorrow's race is not where they expected to be. And there seems little hope for any improvement.

It's not as if they can point the finger at certain failures or problems, claim to have found a fix and then face the new day with fresh hope. Sasol Jordan Hart is in the dark in every sense as Anderson and his mechanics head back to their hotel in the dank gloom of late evening.

Chapter 15

Progress, of Sorts

More steam

It's not much better on Sunday morning as drizzle threatens to disrupt the warm-up and frustrate plans to try different set-ups on the cars. Thankfully, after just one lap on wet-weather tyres, Barrichello decides the track is dry enough to switch to slicks.

It is a busy 30 minutes – and there is a catalogue of minor irritants as the drivers discuss their findings with Anderson and Wright.

Barrichello: 'I've still got understeer in the slow-speed corners. I'm right on the limit in the high-speed corners – but it's okay. I think I'm going to need some sponge in the back of my seat because the car is bouncing around a lot and it's going to hurt during the race.'

Boutsen: 'More grip in the slow corners but it's oversteering a lot – and if I attack, the car tries to spin. Also, it changed gear once on its own, going down the hill. I backed off and it went into neutral. Also, the car doesn't slow down when I back off. There seems to be some sort of problem with the throttle, like it's sticking. It is slow to come back when I lift (my foot) off (the throttle pedal).'

All of this is solemnly noted down. What now?

Boutsen stares at the floor with a preoccupied look which suggests, 'What am I doing here, coping with these sort of problems? Who needs *this*?'

Barrichello, bright eyed and with sweat trickling down his left cheek, takes a swig from a bottle of specially prepared 'sustigen' which looks like lemon-barley water. With youth on his side, all of this is a challenge; a bit of fun.

'Anyway,' Barrichello says to Anderson, 'what we need is more revs.'

Anderson agrees.

During the session, Barrichello had run close behind Martin Brundle's Ligier on the straight, the effect of this so-called 'tow' as the French car cut

Above *Team owner Eddie Jordan.*

Jordan: An inside view

Below left *Chief Engineer and designer Gary Anderson*
Below right *Driver Rubens Barrichello.*

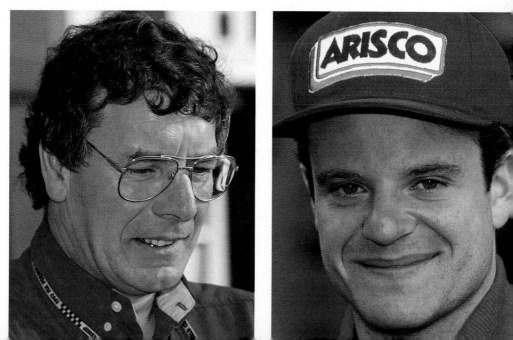

Driver Eddie Irvine with Commercial Manager Ian Phillips.

Chief Designer Steve Nichols discusses the gearchange mechanism with mechanic Nick Burrows.

Above *Thierry Boutsen examines lap times while his mechanic Nick Burrows (**right**) and Brian Hart peep over his shoulders.*

Below left *Team Manager John Walton.*

Below right *Design and Race Engineer Tim Wright.*

Above left *Rubens Barrichello and his father, Rubens Snr, after an energetic media soccer match playing for the F1 photographers at Monza.*

Far left *Driver Emanuele Naspetti.*

Left *Driver Ivan Capelli.*

Above *Driver Marco Apicella.*

Above right *'Her indoors.' Lindsay Haylett keeps Eddie Jordan on the straight and narrow while masterminding the team's logistics.*

Right *Louise Goodman contents herself with an early morning coffee while Ian Phillips tucks into a full works breakfast on race day at Monza.*

*Quiet men behind the scenes. Mark Smith (**left**) and Andrew Green: key members of the engineering team.*

The travelling team pose for a group photograph prior to the final race of the 1993 season in Australia.

Henny Collins and Chris Leese, fortifying body and soul.

Eddie Irvine tells author Maurice Hamilton how it is during practice in Australia.

Top *The imposing entrance to Jordan Grand Prix, opened in 1992.*

Above *The drawing office – and not a drawing-board in sight. Jordan, in common with top F1 teams, use CAD-CAM technology.*

Left *A Hart V10 engine is offered up to the rear of a Jordan 193 at the factory.*

Top right *Eddie Jordan and John Walton in the boss's office.*

Above right *Cosmopolitan colours on the workshop walls.*

Right *Jordan is one of the few F1 teams to boast a gymnasium in the factory. Louise Goodman takes a more relaxed approach, while Paul Warren of the factory staff gets on with the business.*

Above *Who's next? Off-the-factory-wall humour reflects the constant driver changes throughout the summer of 1993. The start of 1994 proved to show little improvement.*

Below *Brian Hart's V10: the power behind the team.*

Right *A print out of Rubens Barrichello's fastest lap during the final qualifying session for the 1993 San Marino Grand Prix at Imola. The graph shows engine revs (in red) and the throttle opening (in blue). The lap (bottom of graph) begins at 0 (start-finish line). Barrichello's foot is already flat on the throttle pedal from the exit of the previous corner (section 16 – top line) and remains there until he hits the brakes for Tosa corner (section 2 – top line, and on circuit diagram). At 19 seconds, this is one of the longest periods of full throttle work on any circuit. Imola was also notable for Hart's latest engine revving at more than 13,000 rpm. On only four occasions do the engine revs briefly fall below 7,000 rpm – the absolute maximum rev limit on a family saloon car.*

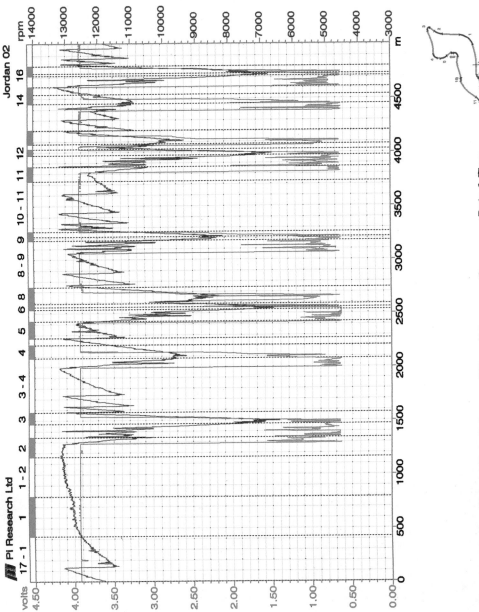

Jordan 02

PI Research Ltd

Channel	Lap Time	Data Set	Filter	Driver	Car	Date & Time
Throttle	1:25.19	<277:001:004>		RUBENS	193-14	24 Apr 93 12:29
Engine Speed	1:25.19	<277:001:004>	0.100	RUBENS	193-14	24 Apr 93 12:29

Above *'What's it all mean?' Mark Smith (**left**), Andrew Green and Gary Anderson study the computer readouts during a test session at Silverstone.*

Below *High-flying environment. The Jordan garage during a test at Barcelona.*

Above right *Curtain call. Gary Anderson (**left**), Brian Hart and Eddie Jordan pose with Rubens Barrichello during the launch of the 193 at Silverstone.*

Right *Full exposure. Rubens Barrichello prepares to give the Jordan 194 its first run at Silverstone.*

Far right *Celebrity status in South Africa. Barrichello, at the age of 20, comes to terms with being a star at his first Grand Prix.*

Top *Clive Chandler checks the wiring on the Jordan 193 during its race debut in South Africa.*

Above *Not a good start. Ivan Capelli's wrecked car at Kyalami.*

Left *Now you see him. Ivan Capelli makes a rare appearance during his final effort to settle in with the Jordan team in Brazil.*

Right *Chris Leese makes do with the primitive cooking conditions at the back of the garage in Brazil.*

Below *Mark Blundell's Ligier is sandwiched between the Jordans of Capelli and Barrichello during practice at Interlagos.*

Bottom *Red light district. Barrichello coped brilliantly with the treacherous British weather during the European Grand Prix at Donington.*

Above *Gary Anderson (**left**), wearing team travel gear after his flight to Italy, holds an informal discussion with Eddie Jordan (**centre**) and Tim Wright in the paddock at Imola.*

Below *Clearly defined. The neat lines of the sponsor-bedecked Sasol Jordan 193.*

Top right *Up against it. Thierry Boutsen shaves the wall while working hard at Barcelona.*

Middle right *In their element. The Jordan transporters in the paddock at Barcelona.*

Below right *Spanish Relay. Boutsen's hobbled car is returned to the pits at Barcelona.*

Above *The ludicrously cramped working conditions at Monaco. With no room available for the transporters in the paddock on the harbour, Jordan are forced to use a multi-storey car park.*

Below left *Making the best of it. Mark Smith loads his computer from the onboard telemetry on Barrichello's car in the pit lane at Monaco.*

Below right *Barrichello leads the Lotus of Johnny Herbert through the hairpin outside the Loews Hotel at Monaco.*

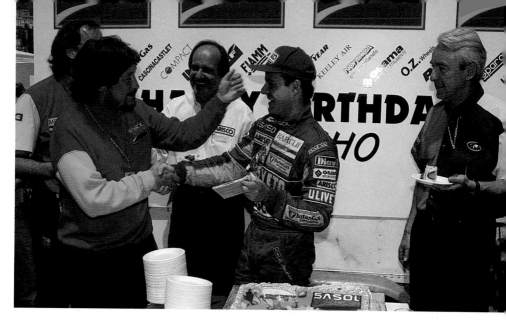

Above *Coming of age. Chris Rea presents Rubens Barrichello with his special CD at Monaco. Barrichello Snr (**white shirt**) and team owner Gerard Larrousse (**right**) share the same birthday.*

Below left *Filling the frame. Thierry Boutsen gets in close during practice at Monaco.*

Below right *The grind and the glamour. Barrichello leads the eventual winner Ayrton Senna (McLaren) through the Loews Hairpin at Monaco.*

Above *Future Past. Barrichello sweeps past a relic of the past on Ile Notre Dame during the Canadian Grand Prix.*

Below *Service halt. The makeshift catering arrangements at the back of the pits in Canada.*

Top right *Midfield mob. Barrichello heads the Larrousse-Lamborghinis of Comas and Alliot, Fittipaldi's Minardi and Warwick's Footwork during the opening stages of the Canadian Grand Prix.*

Middle right *A desperate end. Barrichello struggles home in France and Eddie Jordan is $2 million out of pocket.*

Below right *Preparations continue in the late afternoon sunshine at Magny-Cours.*

Above left *Barrichello and Boutsen greet their public prior to the French Grand Prix.*

Above right *Breaking area. A minor problem with the brake caliper cost the team dearly in France.*

Below *Fittipaldi and Barrichello: healthy rivalry.*

Above left *Truck stop. Ian Webb, Rick Wiltshire and Gerard O'Reilly take a quick break at the back of the garage at Silverstone.*

Above right *How the other half lives. Chris Rea is interviewed in the Jordan enclosure at Silverstone.*

Below *Made to measure. Barrichello's car undergoes a routine check when the car is weighed and measured during practice at Hockenheim.*

*Thierry Boutsen (**right**) tells Niki Lauda about his troubles in Germany.*

Barrichello gives the signal to start at Hockenheim.

All over in a minute. Barrichello's three-wheeled Jordan, parked alongside an abandoned Sauber in Hungary.

The Jordan motorhome; source of sustenance and comfort in Hungary.

Above left *Drivers' parade at the Hungaroring.*

Left *Now here's the bad news. John Walton (**left**), Gary Anderson and Eddie Jordan watch the monitors at the pit wall in Hungary.*

Below left *Thierry Boutsen: discomfort in the cockpit.*

Above *Cutting it fine. Barrichello on the limit in Hungary.*

Below *Rick Wiltshire takes care of the fuel bowsers in the paddock at Spa.*

Far left *Thierry Boutsen made a sad exit at Spa.*

Left *Best lap of his life. Barrichello discusses progress at Spa.*

Below left far *Mayhem at the first chicane at Monza. Barrichello (**top right**) is already having his own accident after being struck from behind.*

Right *The Big Breakfast. Chris Leese takes charge of the barbecue.*

Below left *Barrichello, watched over by his father, tells the local journalists about his day in Portugal.*

Below right *Preparing for action. Barrichello pulls his helmet over his flameproof balaclava.*

*Serious discussion in the motor home in Portugal as (**left to right**) Gary Anderson, Rubens Barrichello, Mark Smith, Emanuele Naspetti, Tim Wright and Andrew Green analyze performances during practice.*

Supper time at Estoril.

Barrichello never put a wheel out of place during his first visit to Monaco.

Eddie Irvine tells Tim Wright about a quick lap in Japan.

Above left *Irvine leads Hill during a dramatic race at Suzuka.*

Above right *All the fun of the fair. Irvine was sensational during the wet stages of the Japanese Grand Prix.*

Below *Ayrton Senna, the eventual winner in Australia, shows Barrichello how to deal with the streets of Adelaide.*

through the air allowing the Jordan-Hart to reach its top speed much easier than normal. The Hart V10 had been running at maximum revs, bouncing off the electronic rev-limiter designed to stop the engine from screaming its head off and doing irreparable damage. Even so, the urgent *rat-tat-tat-tat* sound of the limiter in action had Hart cringing as the two cars rushed past the pits.

Now he is examining Barrichello's engine with a bore-scope, the flexible telescope with a tiny light probing deep into the combustion chamber, Hart's eagle eye searching for signs of imminent failure. There aren't any. That's satisfying at least.

Hart straightens his back to find Anderson and Barrichello waiting, keen to know if they can rev the engine even higher than before; perhaps another 50 to 100 rpm. Rubens desperately needs a bit more performance if he is to have any hope of overtaking the many cars ahead of him on the grid.

Hart, conservative at the best of times due to the limited budget at his disposal, is clearly not keen on the idea. But, having been a racing driver himself, Hart fully sympathizes with Barrichello's call for more speed.

'Look,' he says. 'If we'd scored a point of two, I'd say let's go for it. But we must finish a race. My feeling is that it's too risky to try something like that. Anyway, Gary, I gave you more revs at the last race! So, I'll leave this decision to you ... '

Hart is smiling. Anderson says nothing. He empathizes with Rubens but he knows precisely what Hart is getting at. There has been gathering pressure from one or two of Jordan's sponsors to have his cars finish a race and Eddie has been relaying those thoughts in typically direct fashion to his management team. Anderson has borne the brunt of it.

Anderson and Hart examine the gear ratio charts mapped out on an IBM lap-top computer.

'The risk is,' says Hart, 'if Rubens gets into a scrap, running close behind someone, he could be sitting at high revs for a long time. If we don't finish this race, it's not going to help anyone. We must have a solid foundation to build on.

'Anyway,' he adds, 'more revs means we will be burning more fuel and that means more weight.'

Anderson knows that as well as anyone. It is decided to play safe. The top speed *per se* will not be affected. It will simply take longer to reach that point. A decision is made to change the fifth and sixth gear ratios in an effort to ease the problem slightly. Unfortunately, there has not been time to try these ratios during practice so this will be something of an unknown quantity.

Now it is Hart's turn to say nothing. Gathering in his mind is the suspicion that the team is suffering from a lack of detail planning. John Walton is still finding his feet; Anderson has a huge amount on his plate and, besides, Gary's natural instinct is to err on the side of caution. He is not a man to take unnecessary risks; never has been and never will. You either trust his judgement or you don't. Hart accepts that. But the plain fact is that time should have been found to run these ratios before.

It is almost as if the team is continuing to suffer from the unconscious malaise brought about by their desperate struggle 12 months before with Yamaha; a period when it wasn't worth planning anything because the engine would blow up after five minutes in any case.

Indeed, the Jordan crew had noted with wry amusement that a brand new Yamaha engine – now entrusted to the Tyrrell team – had failed spectacularly after just five minutes running the previous morning. But that did not ease their particular problems this weekend.

And now there seemed little chance of the rain returning to at least throw some form of variable into a race which did not hold much promise for Sasol Jordan Hart.

Questions at the bar

Barcelona airport, Sunday evening.

Andrew Green has £96 in his pocket and the Jordan team is helping relieve their engineer of his financial burden at the bar while waiting for the London flight to be called. Brian Hart has been running a book since the start of the season, each participant attempting to predict the finishing order. Green has finally scored this weekend by correctly forecasting Alain Prost, Ayrton Senna and Michael Schumacher in the first three places, thus scooping the kitty which has been accumulating over the past few races.

No one had placed a Jordan in the top six for the Spanish Grand Prix – a reasonable enough assumption – but it had been closer than anyone had dared hope after such a difficult two days of practice.

Barrichello had made a good start and held 14th place for 26 laps before gradually moving forward as those in front began to run into trouble.

Rubens had run in close company with Johnny Herbert's Lotus but, as he had predicted, the Jordan simply did not have enough power to get by on the straight. Even so, with 15 laps to go, Barrichello was ninth and keeping ahead of Mark Blundell's Ligier-Renault.

Then a flap on the left-hand front wing broke and the Jordan hurtled into the pits for a new nose. The delay cost over a minute and dropped Barrichello to 12th place, where he eventually finished, just behind Boutsen.

Thierry had been troubled throughout by a continuation of the sticking throttle problem experienced during the warm-up. Hart had recommended a stiffer throttle spring but Boutsen, not in favour of a strong return on the throttle pedal, had not accepted the advice. It had made life difficult. But at least he had finished, learning more about the car in the process.

As the beers are rapidly quaffed, it is a relief to have had two cars last the distance for the first time this season. And Hart is quietly satisfied on a day when Ferrari, Ford, Ilmor and Renault all suffered engine failures.

But it could have been better. Blundell, behind Barrichello until the pit stop, had eventually finished seventh, having relinquished sixth place to

Berger's Ferrari only in the final few laps. There could have been a point in that for Rubens. *And* he had been in front of Fittipaldi all the way but now Christian had finished ahead of him.

Questions are being asked about that broken nose flap. There is a suggestion that a similar failure had occurred during testing. If so, why was nothing done about it?

In any case, why choose to waste so much time by replacing the nose? Why not simply remove the broken flap and send Rubens on his way, leaving him to drive around the ensuing handling problem and perhaps be in a better position at the end? It would have been a gamble, right enough, but were the team tactics suspect? Was the management weak?

Anderson is adamant that is not the case. The problem, he says, is a lack of testing. Miles on the track would have rooted out the problem before it surfaced during a race weekend. Anderson lays the blame at Eddie Jordan's door for failing to spend the money where it is needed. Jordan says they have not got a bottomless budget. In any case, this does not answer the criticism of poor tactics during the pit stop.

These were potential cracks in the team structure which the press release – with Eddie Jordan speaking bravely about this being a good starting point from which to move steadily forward – would not paper over if you could read between the lines.

With Monaco next on the calendar, strong management and astute tactical thinking would be more vital than ever.

Chapter 16

Never Mind the Width

Insult and battery

'Monaco is shit.'

That muttered curse is frequently heard among the workers as they battle through the *glitterati* meandering in their path.

Generous words have been written and eulogies gushed about the magnificence of Monte Carlo. It is known with good reason as the jewel in the Grand Prix crown.

But, for the people who have to work there for five days in May, it is the dross of the season, the unacceptable face of rampant commercialism at the expense of common sense, a nonsense of a place to go motor racing. It is ... well, as the man said.

Phil Hill, the 1961 World Champion, said that if the Monaco Grand Prix had no history and you suggested running a race there for the first time, you would be considered to be mad and out of touch with reality. Hill said that in 1966.

Three decades on and Grand Prix racing has advanced beyond anything Hill ever knew when using his exquisite skills at the wheel. And still we go to Monte Carlo and race the latest Formula 1 cars on more or less the same streets which the American driver used to conduct his infinitely less sophisticated Ferrari.

But that's largely the drivers' problem. The teams have their own difficulties when it comes to conducting their business in such anachronistic surroundings.

In terms of simple logistics, it is a nightmare; a sweat; a pain in the backside. The fact is that the paddock and the pits are about half a mile apart. And, by Sunday morning, it seems five times that distance.

True, the teams have been spoiled elsewhere. Modern pit complexes allow the transporters to be backed up to the rear doors for easy unloading into spacious, secure garages which become home for the weekend. Barcelona two weeks before had been an excellent example.

At Monaco, nothing but the exorbitant costs are permanent. Only in recent years have the teams been given lockable huts at the back of the pits. But, in general, fetch and carry is the rule.

For a lesser team such as Jordan, not blessed with the privilege of being allowed to park their transporters in the cramped paddock on the quayside, the humping and moving becomes an even more laborious process as they shuttle back and forth between the pits and a car park at the back of the harbour. This is tricky enough when the track is not in use and the roads are open; it is a major obstacle race when the track is closed.

Privilege comes to the motor homes, too. Arranged cheek by jowl at the front of the quayside, some have a better position than others, the best views affording a splendid panorama of magnificent vessels of every description riding expensively at anchor.

For Jordan in 1993, the best profile to be had was the bright red paintwork of the Dallara motor home, crammed alongside. They may as well have been in Monza as Monaco.

But this was Monte Carlo nonetheless. For all its shortcomings as a place of serious work, the Principality possesses a grandeur without equal on the motor racing calendar. And, for all the restrictions imposed by the narrow streets on the progress of a modern Formula 1 car, nowhere is it possible to stand so close to the action.

The senses are assaulted and battered by the sound of urgent performance straining to be unleashed and kept barely under control. The speed at close quarters is breathtaking; the noise, bouncing off the rock face on either side of the harbour, is unbearable.

It may not be the true picture of Formula 1 at full stretch but it is a spectacle nonetheless. It is Grand Prix racing on parade. It is the place to be. Provided you are not attempting to work in the midst of this frenzied clamour. Never mind the width, just feel the quality.

Dinner money

Social activities outweigh basic graft. The evenings are an endless round of functions, dinners and 'do drop down to the boat for drinks'.

To accommodate a season's socializing packed into one weekend – not to mention lining the Principality's pockets even further – the Monaco Grand Prix stretches over five days instead of four, practice starting on Thursday, leaving Friday free.

Friday evening was earmarked for a dinner, traditionally hosted by Marlboro, one of the sport's major sponsors. It promised to be a grand affair and Eddie Jordan saw it as a useful place to entertain his guests. Staying in the Loews Hotel were Mr and Mrs Paul Kruger, the managing director of Sasol, and Mr and Mrs Peter Norton, managing director of Sasol's European operation.

The Marlboro dinner would show motor sport in full grandeur but first Jordan had to overcome one or two obstacles. Tables were in short supply, and there was the potential embarrassment of having to explain away his presence to Barclay, a Marlboro brand rival and one of Jordan's sponsors.

In typical fashion, Jordan talked his way round both problems, finally playing his ace card by securing a table on the understanding that he persuade the rock star, Chris Rea, to perform at the dinner.

It was easier said than done because Rea, a motor racing fanatic, had come to Monaco to escape the pressures of his business. Rea's relaxation comes from racing a Ferrari and a Lotus in British club events, a cosy little world more interested in springs and dampers than songs and superstars. The alliance between Rea and Jordan had been a natural one, Rea merging easily with the relaxed environment even though he had to put up with Eddie's penchant for namedropping, as and when the mood took him. Which was often.

Rea, devoid of the outrageous clothes and outlandish comportment exhibited by many of his ilk, liked nothing more than to stand quietly in the background and drink in a different kind of music as the cars sped by. And there was no better place to do that than at Monaco in May.

In the merde

There had not been much to see on Thursday morning. After just 25 minutes of free practice, the loudspeakers, doing valiant battle with the relentless cacophony, had blasted the bad news.

'*Numero quatorze, Rubens Barrichello, arrêté Ste Devote. Pilote rentre à pieds aux stands.*'

The news that Barrichello had stopped at Ste Devote, the first corner after the pits, and was returning on foot, had been barely audible. But the Jordan team had got the gist of the message.

As far as they could ascertain, the car was not damaged – which was good and bad. Good for obvious reasons, since contact with anything solid at Monaco invariably means major repair work to the car. Bad, because the track was not blocked and practice would therefore continue without stopping, thus preventing the team from retrieving their car.

With so much to do – and with Barrichello having so much to learn at Monaco – this was a disaster.

The throttle had jammed open and just as Anderson and Barrichello were pondering their atrocious luck, the pendulum swung the other way as Ayrton Senna crashed heavily at the very same corner.

Now the track *was* blocked. The session was stopped. But that was not the end of the story for Jordan. By the time Barrichello's car had been returned and the trouble sorted out, rain had begun to fall. It would continue for the remainder of the 90-minute free practice session.

Barrichello was actually fifth fastest when the rain was at its height – a fine achievement in such tricky circumstances – but, in the overall scheme of things, the team had learned next to nothing.

Barrichello was 22nd on the list. Boutsen, also in trouble with a sticking throttle, was 25th fastest, and next to last.

As the mechanics toiled in the cramped pit lane, the supposed glamour of the location was far from their minds. They felt they were in the *merde* in every sense.

That's the way to do it

Just as swiftly, the mood changed once more. During the first qualifying session, Barrichello followed his fellow countryman Senna for a couple of laps, the young Brazilian receiving a non-crash course on the intricacies of this unique place from the man who had won at Monaco five times.

It was reflected in Rubens's time; 12th fastest on the provisional grid. And he felt there was more to come. With Boutsen improving to 18th, Eddie Jordan and his party could stride into the Marlboro dinner with a fair amount of pride and satisfaction.

Not a mark on her

The track had remained damp during Thursday's qualifying. On Saturday afternoon it was bone dry, the weather perfect. And then the serious business began. As Barrichello and Boutsen pushed their cars as hard as they dared, the tight confines of the circuit exposed the dreaded understeer as the Jordans showed a reluctance to negotiate the slow corners, of which there is an abundance at Monaco.

Even so, Barrichello took 16th place on the grid, just ahead of Fittipaldi. He had every reason to be pleased on this, his first visit to such a daunting circuit. And there was not a mark on his car, which was more than could be said for several drivers as heaps of wreckage were returned to the paddock on the back of breakdown trucks. Monaco punishes even the slightest mistake in a disproportionately severe manner.

Boutsen had made no errors. But neither had he been very quick. Twentythird fastest, he was at least in a race where a failure to qualify is never more cruelly exposed.

Given his team's disappointing season so far, Eddie Jordan considered himself to be in reasonable shape. And the Monaco Grand Prix – all 78 laps of it – is one of those races which does not necessarily go to the fleet of foot.

Family planning

Louise Goodman had been busy. There seemed to be sponsors and their guests at every turn; dinners and functions at all hours. But the one ceremony she was anxious not to let pass without notice was Rubens Barrichello's 21st birthday. It is one thing to celebrate your coming of age. But quite another to do it as a Grand Prix driver. At Monaco. On race day.

Barrichello had no idea of what was in store as he walked to the drivers' briefing. There had been the anticipated congratulations from those who knew about the significance of 23 May 1993 in his young life. And that, he thought, was more or less the end of the matter.

While Rubens sat down in the control tower with 24 other drivers to listen to the Clerk of the Course, there was frantic activity by the Jordan motor home on the far side of the harbour.

Louise had organized the production of a large board, conveniently decorated with the sponsors' names and wishing Rubens a happy birthday. But now she found there was nowhere to place it as a suitable backdrop when it came to the cutting of a massive cake.

For all the intense competitiveness among the teams on the track, there exists a sincere camaraderie among the backroom workers, particularly the motor home crews. The Footwork team, parked near Jordan, offered the use of a small trailer which was quickly wheeled into place to act as mount for Louise's board.

Meanwhile, the *pièce d'résistance* was being readied. Chris Rea had gone to the trouble of assembling his band and cutting a disc with a special recording of *Happy Birthday*, sung in a Latin rhythm.

As Barrichello emerged from the drivers' briefing, the song burst forth from the public address system. And, across the harbour, on a huge illuminated scoreboard mounted on the rock face, birthday greetings were relayed to the stunned Brazilian.

Now everyone knew. He could barely go a couple of paces along the pit lane without someone shaking his hand.

Heading for what ought to have been the sanctuary of the motor home, Rubens was overwhelmed by the reception waiting for him there. Joining the party were his father – who was also celebrating his birthday – the sponsors, the team, the media, team owner Gerard Larrousse (another birthday on 23 May) and Chris Rea, ready with a copy of the record.

Naturally, Eddie Jordan made a speech, cleverly taking the opportunity to involve Sasol by presenting Mrs Kruger with a bunch of flowers in recognition of her birthday the day before. It was a genuinely happy occasion in splendid surroundings.

Now to see what 21-year-old Rubens Goncalves Barrichello would make of his first race in this extraordinary place.

Foot work

It took Barrichello a while to come back to earth and concentrate on the job in hand. There was so much to remember, if only because Monaco presented problems not experienced anywhere else. And those difficulties came in various guises – as Rubens and Geraldo Rodrigues had found to their cost on the first day of practice.

Geraldo's role in Barrichello's affairs could best be described as an easing of the way in order to allow the driver to concentrate fully on his job. That included such mundane matters as carrying Barrichello's helmet, balaclava and gloves and having them ready for use at all times; just another minor worry which Rubens did not need to concern himself with.

In the normal course of events, Barrichello would put on his overalls, socks and driving boots in the motor home and then walk to the garage, where Geraldo would be waiting. A straightforward procedure which was re-enacted at Monaco.

Barrichello had duly arrived in the pits on the first day of practice. When it came time to climb on board the car, he collected his helmet, balaclava and gloves from Rodrigues and prepared for action. Then he noticed his feet.

Because of the distance involved, he had decided against wearing his thin-soled driving boots, preferring trainers instead. A breakdown in communications meant the driving boots were still in the motor home, half a mile away.

They would be closing the track any minute. Given the tight restrictions of the footwell in the Jordan, Barrichello could not even contemplate wearing his bulky trainers. There was nothing for it but to dispatch the trusty Geraldo.

It made for quite a sight, the stocky little Brazilian jumping on board a scooter and running the gauntlet of the mob in the pit lane, then on to the track and into the paddock for a dash along the quayside. By the time he had returned, the paddock gates were shut, the track closed.

Geraldo had to abandon ship and battle through the crowd as he crossed foot-bridges and worked his way beneath grandstands and along temporary gang-planks spanning the water. Then a sprint of sorts along the pit road. In all, a sweaty and harrowing journey just to collect a pair of boots; a 20-minute job which would have taken a tenth of that time anywhere else.

They didn't make the same mistake again, Rubens and Geraldo, certainly not as the 3.30 start time approached on Sunday afternoon.

Finishing touches

Survival would be the objective.

Forget about wheel-to-wheel racing; the aim was to stay out of trouble, keep going and pick up places as the punishing nature of the street circuit extracted its dues. The rate of attrition through mechanical failures had been high in the past and, as if to prove the point, Boutsen's rear suspension broke before he was even halfway round the first lap.

But Barrichello had completed that lap in 13th place; handy enough at the beginning of a race which would last the best part of two hours.

Rubens never put a foot wrong despite pressure from Zanardi's Lotus and the worry that his tyres might not last the distance. A pit stop at Monaco spells disaster since the process is time-consuming and the performance advantage gained by fresh rubber nullified by the difficulty in overtaking on this circuit. So Barrichello did not push hard in the early stages, preferring instead to conserve his tyres and save them from unnecessary stress when the car was heavy with fuel. But the first signs that his efforts might be in vain came just before three-quarters distance.

Having worked his way into a very encouraging sixth place, Barrichello was overtaken by, of all people, Christian Fittipaldi. Clearly, the Minardi was being kinder to its tyres, a fact confirmed not long after when Herbert's Lotus pushed Barrichello down to eighth.

'I thought I was looking good,' Rubens said later. 'But when Christian started to push me, the tyres started to go. It was really bad. At one stage I thought I would crash because I could hardly hold the car at all. There was nothing else for it but to come in and change tyres. We should have stopped 10 laps earlier.'

Note the 'we'. Was this poor tactics again? Anderson, increasingly sensitive to criticism and pointing to questionable management by Williams, bridled at the very suggestion. Certainly, the team had been caught out by excessive wear on the inside shoulders of the tyres, a fact which might have been spotted had Barrichello not been stranded out on the circuit with a problem halfway through the warm-up on race morning.

But that was pure speculation. Barrichello went on to finish ninth and, once again, he brought his car back to the pits with not a single mark on it; a fine achievement for a 21-year-old on his first visit.

That made two finishes in succession. All well and good. But with six races down and ten to go, the team ought to have scored points by now.

Fittipaldi and Minardi had done it again by finishing fifth. It merely accentuated the absence of Jordan's name from the growing list of point-scoring teams.

And it increased the frustration of having to try and pack up in the midst of the chaotic scene as the world descended from the rock face and stumbled mindlessly into the pit lane, now open to all and sundry. There was not even the consolation of a beer and a bit of a laugh. The way it used to be.

'That's the trouble with Monaco,' mused Anderson. 'It's no fun any more. The fun at least allowed you to put up with the aggravation. Now it's just aggro. Nothing else.'

'Yeah,' chimed a sympathizer. 'Monaco is ... Monaco.' After five days spent attempting to work in this place, expletives were superfluous.

Chapter 17

All at Sea

Desert island risks

Jordan Grand Prix finally won a race; they left the top teams dead in the water.

It came as no surprise. In fact, it was a matter of honour since Jordan had won this event twice before. The mechanics' annual raft race is not a matter to be taken lightly.

The genesis of this sporting occasion goes back to 1988 and, ironically, it involves Ian Phillips, then team manager at Leyton House March. Phillips had arrived late that year and was surprised and partially appalled to open the local paper and find a picture of his truck drivers aboard a home-made raft. At least, he observed, they had the decency to place some Leyton House advertising on the craft as it made its way across the magnificent rectangular lake bordering the race track on Ile Notre Dame.

The man-made island, seemingly cast adrift from the city of Montreal, was constructed in the St Lawrence river with the intention of providing a novel setting for Expo '68. Plans to capitalize further on the location, once the exhibition had finished, came to very little, the crumbling pavilions and futuristic structures still dotting the bleak, flat landscape.

If little else, it was the perfect location for a motor race. The communication network was in place and no one would complain about the noise. Furthermore, the island had been used to accommodate a massive rowing lake for the 1976 Olympic Games. It was this which formed the backdrop when the race track was opened two years later.

So here was this vast stretch of water, lying vacant, as it were. Someone, probably the worse for drink, suggested building a boat and attempting to cross the lake. Leyton House had taken up the challenge. Before they knew it, the mechanics had a race on their hands.

The rules are as uncomplicated as the methods of construction. The boats must be made from materials found in the paddock and, given that the Canadian Grand Prix is a so-called 'fly away' race, packing cases and boxes are in plentiful supply. Purpose-made marine items are strictly forbidden.

Given that ingenuity and manual dexterity are a mechanic's stock in trade, the raft race provides a challenging outlet for his talents. And, with each race, the lessons learned are filed, ready for use the following year.

Shipping hazards

Paul Thompson took charge of designing Jordan's 1993 boat, the chief mechanic using the motor racing maximum of going for simplicity, lightness and speed.

Plywood from a packing case was shaped into the form of an impressive-looking two-seater canoe. Foam, normally used for the seat in the racing car, was moulded to make two floats, suspended on outriggers. Even the paddles were fashioned from wood and ply found in the garage. The boat was painted in Jordan blue and, ever mindful of the photo opportunity, the sponsors' logos prominently displayed. This was a serious effort.

Not so, the Jordan B team. In the true spirit of the occasion, a second 'vessel' was made from plastic bins which, under more normal circumstances, would be used to carry spare parts. Buoyancy would be provided by Sasol oil drums lashed in a dubious manner to the thing which Thompson, in a moment of rash enthusiasm, referred to as a boat.

The three-man crew, brave souls all, duly appeared in Viking gear topped off with helmets and beards made from foam rubber. They were at a disadvantage from the start since one crew member would work his passage, not by rowing, but by beating a makeshift drum and waving an axe. If the intention was to scare the opposition witless, then judging by the gales of laughter they had failed gloriously.

There were 17 entries in all, the object being to row the breadth of the lake, change crews and return.

It was pushing the bounds of optimism somewhat when the Jordan B team dispatched three men to the far side. On the signal to start, the Viking marauders splashed fully 10 yards before sinking with great dignity in the face of outrageous remarks from the shore.

But Thompson and Andrew Green, the outbound A team, were long gone, the Jordan craft cutting an impressive dash through the deep blue water. On the turn, Nick Burrows and Andy Stephenson, mechanics assigned to Boutsen's car but also known as 'the angry brothers', jumped on board and maintained the lead under pressure from the Goodyear boat and a challenge from the Benetton team.

By now, the shore was packed, the spectators – many drivers among them – hurling abuse, fruit and eggs in a good-humoured attempt to prevent a Jordan hat-trick. It was of no use. Burrows and Stephenson were determined that their team should win this race at least, the immaculate canoe skimming successfully past the flotsam and jetsam of an abandoned Viking invasion.

Brakeless and bewildered

All of this took place on Thursday afternoon, a relaxed period in keeping with the Canadian Grand Prix itself. After Monaco, the gentle warmth and relative calm of Montreal in June makes a welcome change from the frenzy and pomp of the Côte d'Azur. In between, however, Jordan had been busy.

Unusually, there had been two free weekends between the races rather than one. A test session with Boutsen at the Paul Ricard circuit in the south of France, and one at Silverstone, had led to the finalization of changes to the aerodynamics, front suspension, gearbox and traction control; all of these evident on the cars in Montreal. It was, said Anderson, a step in the right direction but, typically, other events would frustrate progress once practice had begun on Friday.

For a start, it was damp, overcast and muggy. With the circuit scarcely in use from one year to the next, the drivers always find the track surface dusty and dirty, thus rendering it useless for the purposes of serious running and experiments with the set-ups on the cars.

But Jordan had other troubles; typical motor racing troubles.

Automotive Products, manufacturers of Lockheed and Borg & Beck products, supplied the Jordan team and many of their rivals. AP, vastly experienced and thoroughly reliable, had produced revised seals on the brake calipers and these had been tested successfully on the Jordan at Paul Ricard. AP had no hesitation in recommending their use for the Canadian Grand Prix and, equally, Jordan saw no reason to decline.

After a handful of laps, Barrichello was in the pits, complaining of serious brake trouble. The mechanics removed the four red-hot calipers and replaced them in 11 minutes while someone was dispatched to find Steve Bryan. As AP's man on the spot, Bryan is rarely bothered by technical problems. But, when things do go wrong, the team usually wants to know the answer immediately.

Bryan set to work. Using the top of a packing case as a temporary bench, he quickly discovered that the pistons inside the calipers had failed to push the brake pads on to the discs each time the driver hit the brake pedal. They would work on the first application of brakes, after which the pistons would remain stuck inside the caliper.

The new seals were immediately suspected but, in truth, there was no obvious reason for this. The revised calipers had worked perfectly during exhaustive tests. And, typically, they would continue to work perfectly at a subsequent test held after the Canadian race. But, in the meantime, it was back to the old specification, all of which had upset Jordan's practice routine even further.

They ended the day 16th (Barrichello) and 25th (Boutsen), a catalogue of minor problems on the slippery track making the building of boats seem an easier option than coaxing a Grand Prix car to work at its optimum.

On Saturday, there were mixed fortunes. Both drivers ran strongly during free practice in the morning but, when the ambient temperature rose in the afternoon, Barrichello could not repeat his earlier time. Nonetheless, he was 14th. Again.

For Boutsen, 24th place was something of a mystery. The morning had been spent working with a full load of fuel in anticipation of the race. The car felt good. When the tank was drained to almost empty for qualifying, the car felt terrible. Thierry actually went slower than he had in the morning. Never let it be said that Grand Prix racing is easily understood.

These were somewhat confusing messages for Anderson and his technical team. In general, both drivers had enthused about the latest developments to the cars, particularly the front ride-height control, Barrichello saying it was 'a big, big improvement'. But this was not being reflected in the grid positions.

Quite what the race held in store, no one could be sure. At least the weather forecast promised a brilliant day.

Private parts

It was almost too good. As the thermometer headed towards 30°C, the rowing lake shimmered in the heat, the flags above the pits flicking gently in the breeze.

Down below, the teams did their best to find comfort in the small motor homes, rented for the weekend and parked neatly in line behind the garages. With the team personnel crammed on top of each other, this was no place for modesty.

As Barrichello stripped down to his underpants and prepared to don his overalls, Louise Goodman didn't bat an eyelid as she sat close by with Ian Phillips and planned the catering arrangements for the forthcoming French and British Grands Prix.

Barrichello handed each item of clothing to Geraldo Rodrigues, Eddie Jordan interrupting an interview with a bemused Japanese journalist to pass a ribald remark about his driver going so far as to actually carry identification for Arisco on his underwear. This was personal sponsorship taken to the extreme. Except that Jordan didn't quite put it that way.

As lunchtime approached, the atmosphere was relaxed, almost sublime. Sandwiches and salad were consumed on the picnic benches outside, Henny Collins overseeing her culinary manor from the motor home door. A few feet away, the mechanics sat in a row by the side of the lake. The only similarity between this and Monaco three weeks before was the close proximity of water. But, once engines were fired and business got under way, the surge of adrenalin and expectation was as excitingly familiar as ever.

Uninspired

Boutsen, after an uninspiring race at the back of the field, finished 12th. Barrichello, up to 12th place after 11 laps, stopped when the engine died without warning. It was a very disappointing result.

Jordan had not scored a single point so far and what made the situation even more critical was the fact that the next race in France would mark the half-way point in the season. If Jordan did not finish in the top six there, they would fail to qualify for travel subsidies to the long-haul races, the cut-off point being 10th place in the league table. Jordan were currently 11th. One point for sixth place might do it.

There was another three-week break between Canada and France. Gary Anderson did not need telling that there was much work to be done, but a lack of finance would not permit it. It was frustrating because the potential of the Jordan-Hart 193 was in there somewhere; it was simply a matter of nailing it down.

Easier said than done as the season marched on in this race without end.

The way we were

The Jordan team immediately threw themselves into a comprehensive test session on their return to Silverstone. Three cars were made ready and the services of Emanuele Naspetti as test driver were finally brought into play.

Significantly, Thierry Boutsen was not present at first and Naspetti was given the Belgian's car. Anderson, intensely loyal to his drivers, would make no comment.

But it was clear that certain elements in the team wanted to see how Naspetti would fare, particularly after Boutsen's disappointing performance in Montreal.

Few conclusions were reached as Naspetti did little to show he was any faster than Boutsen. But, when the suspension and aerodynamic settings from Barrichello's car were duplicated on Boutsen's, Naspetti suddenly went two seconds a lap quicker, a massive improvement.

That was not to say, of course, that the settings would have been right for Boutsen's style of driving. But it did prove that the effort expended while Boutsen tested at Paul Ricard (immediately after Monaco) had largely been a waste of time. Unless the car is being taken to its limit, the team will learn very little.

The three days at Silverstone were productive. Williams, McLaren, Benetton, Footwork, Tyrrell and Lotus joined Jordan for what would be the final dress rehearsal before the British Grand Prix in two weeks' time.

The media was there in force and Jordan had arranged to have the motor home present; nothing was spared. Chris Rea turned up; Ian Phillips was busy talking to prospective sponsors for 1994; it was a Grand Prix meeting without the minute-by-minute regimentation. Bar one hour off for lunch, the track was open all day for the teams to do as they pleased.

'It turned out to be one of the best test sessions we've ever had,' said John Walton. 'We went right back to basics.'

'Yes,' agreed Gary Anderson. 'We got through a lot of work and learned a bit. Things had to be tried and either put to use or put in the bin. Most of them went in the bin. But you've got to evaluate that sort of stuff, particularly as we are going to race at Silverstone in two weeks. There were things on the car which weren't really doing what we expected them to. So, we were really trying to get back to where we were and start from there.'

That translated into the undeniable fact that the team had made little progress in terms of decreased lap times at a track they knew better than any other. In a perfect world, a team should progress and the lap times should improve, if only by a few tenths of a second every now and then.

Jordan had been standing still and the danger was the competition would leave them behind; a potentially disastrous state of affairs for a team with no points on the board.

And in the background was the nagging worry about Thierry Boutsen. Naspetti had found Thierry's car too stiffly sprung, too nervous; not necessarily a crime in itself. But Boutsen had arrived for the last day and it had taken a considerable effort by the Belgian to beat Naspetti's lap time.

'He was driving on the limit,' said Brian Hart. 'He over-revved three times; it's the highest number of revs I've ever seen on the engine!'

Rather than being critical about Boutsen's apparent struggle, Hart was expressing relief that the V10 had withstood the punishment. But it didn't seem right that someone of Thierry Boutsen's class should be in such apparent trouble.

Was it the car? Or was it the driver? Those were not the sort of questions any self-respecting team should be asking at such a critical point in the season.

Chapter 18

The Million Dollar Mishap

All fenced out

'Eddie, you look very silly.'

Keke Rosberg, the 1982 World Champion, is not a man to mince his words. He was grinning from ear to ear as Eddie Jordan emerged, a touch self-consciously, from his motor home wearing flameproof overalls and carrying a crash helmet. To see a team boss behaving in this manner at a Grand Prix meeting is akin to a parent tucking into a birthday tea with a bunch of five-year-olds.

But Jordan was serious enough. Throughout the summer, Porsche had been staging a dramatic series of races for their 911 sports cars, many of the rounds coinciding with a Grand Prix. It was a promotional coup in front of an appreciative audience and, to add interest, a celebrity car was entered for each race. For this round at the French Grand Prix, Eddie Jordan was the 'celebrity'. He wore the mantel well.

In truth, Jordan had been apprehensive. He had not raced anything for several years and this was no place to make a fool of yourself. The trouble with the French Grand Prix was that, like the Canadian race three weeks before, it was a comparatively low-key affair. Apart from the usual routine work, there would be little to distract Jordan's colleagues. The danger was they might actually spare a moment to come and watch.

The vast tarmac paddock at Magny-Cours is a sterile place, devoid of atmosphere. James Hunt had hated it. The sport was still reeling from the news not long before that the 1976 World Champion had been found dead of a heart attack at the age of 45. Very much a jaunty part of the Formula 1 scene, Hunt's absence was keenly felt in all quarters.

'The trouble with this place,' he would say of Magny-Cours, 'is there's no crumpet; no anything, really.'

It was true. Magny-Cours, located more or less in the middle of France, had been upgraded at huge expense. The facilities were excellent but the atmosphere had been fenced out. And the track itself was nothing to write home about. Mind you, at the close of business on Saturday, 4 July, Sasol Jordan had few complaints; Rubens Barrichello was eighth on the grid; Thierry Boutsen, 20th.

Fruits of their labours

This was the pay-off for all that endeavour at Silverstone. A new front suspension configuration had been tried and the rear suspension geometry had been returned to the specification last used in Spain, two months before. The ride height control, as favoured by Barrichello in Canada, had been retained and, overall, he liked the feel of the car at this circuit, particularly in the high-speed corners.

Practice had been without serious dramas, the team getting through a schedule of work with both cars ready to run just when the track was at its best during qualifying. Unfortunately, though, Boutsen was still struggling, Thierry very unhappy with the nervous nature of his car.

But eighth place for Rubens was something else. It proved what Anderson had been saying all along; if time and money is devoted to serious testing it brings results. But what Gary was too modest to mention was the fact that Barrichello had also been helped by good management decisions about precisely when to send him out for a quick lap during qualifying.

Rubens would share the fourth row with Michael Schumacher's Benetton and start directly behind Jean Alesi's Ferrari. This was Jordan's best grid position of the season so far. Surely there had to be a couple of championship points in this for the team, just when they needed them most?

Trouble under foot

By eight o'clock on race morning, the sun was already having its effect. The perfect weather was in keeping with the upbeat mood around the Jordan motor home as breakfast got under way; fruit juice, cereal, a full fry, tea, toast. The perfect way to start the day. Now to see what the warm-up had in store.

At first it was routine; nothing untoward as both drivers became accustomed to the effects of a full load of fuel. Rubens returned to the pits. His car was pushed backwards into the garage in the usual way, a mechanic waiting by each wheel, ready to place an electric blanket around each tyre.

Earlier in the season, Geraldo Rodrigues had been something of a spare part on these occasions, particularly when his man was in the cockpit, going about his business. But now Geraldo was accepted and a fully integrated member of the team. He even had an official-looking shirt with his name embroidered on the front. As the car came to a halt, Rodrigues had the timing monitor ready for Barrichello to examine.

So far, there wasn't much to get excited about; Barrichello was near the bottom of the list. And, in any case, he wasn't looking at the screen;

something else was exercising his mind.

The routine check for leaks completed, tyre pressures and temperatures taken, the mechanics waited in silence as Anderson and Barrichello went through an apparent mime routine on the radio. Then a quiet instruction from Anderson – and immediate urgency all around.

The front brakes were running hot and the cooling ducts needed changing. Three men leapt to each front wheel and, as they did so, Anderson turned his back and walked towards the pit wall, confident that the job would be done – and done well – without the need for any supervision.

There were only 10 minutes remaining when Barrichello returned to the track. He managed no better than 13th fastest time. Boutsen was 11th. Reasonable. But not brilliant. And those brakes were a worry.

Meanwhile, the team's third racing driver was making his way to the pits. It was time for the Porsche Supercup event and, in the manner of a true celebrity, Eddie Jordan had walked into the pits, the only driver to have his machine brought to him; the rest of the competitors going through the mundane business of driving their cars from a distant paddock.

Since he had qualified near the back of the field, Jordan had to walk some way down the pit lane, his progress notable for the derisory remarks emanating from the Formula 1 garages.

That, perhaps, was expected. But there was a surprise in store as he climbed into the left-hand drive Porsche; a television camera had been mounted on the dashboard, ready to beam Jordan's every grimace – he had made the mistake of wearing an open-face helmet – on to a massive screen mounted conveniently within sight of the pit lane.

His race is best described as uneventful. He wasn't last but neither was he first. And, judging by the perspiration gathering on his flushed face, a considerable effort was required to maintain credibility in front of his peers. But at least he didn't make a fool of himself; it was a good effort. And, hopefully, he would have something more substantial to celebrate at the end of the day.

An ambassador comes to call

The air-conditioned hush of the motor home was in stark contrast to the heat and hurly-burly of the pit lane. Thierry Boutsen sat awkwardly, picking at a plate of pasta. In the room at the end, just visible beyond the sliding door, Rubens Barrichello was having his ration of carbohydrates while in conversation with Geraldo.

Boutsen was alone with his thoughts. Going through one of the quick corners the previous day, the sideways force – briefly measuring 3 G – had pulled a muscle in his back. Boutsen had received treatment from the masseur the previous evening and again this morning. But it had not been much help. And all of this compounded the main problem of discomfort in the cockpit.

'I have to sit in a kind of crouch position,' he said. 'If I sit up straight, my head gets in the way of the airbox, so I'm still not comfortable in the car. I don't have the confidence to throw the car about, to hang it out. It's very nervous in the fast corners – like it wants to spin. Rubens finds the same – our comments are similar – but he can cope with it much better than I can.'

(This would bring the retort from Anderson – now clearly tiring of Boutsen and his perceived troubles – that the car had been set up precisely the way Boutsen wanted it because, as a former Grand Prix winner, Boutsen knew best and Anderson was not about to argue. Besides, Gary confirmed that Barrichello liked the feel of the car at Magny-Cours – particularly in the fast corners. 'Confused – or what?' was Anderson's summary.)

Boutsen paused for another mouthful of spaghetti.

'I'm losing too much speed through the fast corners although I'm getting better all the time,' he went on. 'I like the car more and more but, to be honest, it feels aerodynamically unstable. You want to put your foot down and every time you do, it oversteers, tries to throw you off the road.'

Boutsen was interrupted by a gentleman wearing the jacket of his suit draped over his shoulders and asking for Eddie Jordan. The Irish Ambassador to France was paying a social call.

Jordan, wrapped in a towel, poked his head round the door of the shower room, introduced the ambassador to Boutsen, ordered coffee and, while continuing to dry himself, spoke enthusiastically about the team's chances for the day. The conversation between the two Irishmen flowed easily in such unusual circumstances. It was hard to believe that they had never met before.

Meanwhile, a telephone message had been received from a prospective sponsor; he had no passes and was waiting for collection at the helicopter pad.

'Great!' said Ian Phillips. 'Which one? There are two helicopter pads here.'

'Sorry, he didn't say.'

Phillips raised his eyes to the heavens. The McLaren marketing department would doubtless have covered such eventualities. But Jordan wasn't McLaren, and Phillips was still grateful for that. Nonetheless, the thought of leaving the paddock in such heat and doing battle with the chaos on the roads outside was not appealing. The lure of the dollar provided a suitable incentive. In any case, Phillips wanted to be back in time to see this race.

Damned Yankee

The start was perfect, Barrichello maintaining his place through the treacherous, sweeping first corner, Boutsen hanging on in 19th place, only to be overtaken by two cars in as many laps.

Boutsen's personal struggle became academic as Barrichello moved up to seventh. And then sixth. A Jordan in the points! Even the pit stop at the end of lap 26 went smoothly and Rubens maintained his place in the top six. So far, so good. Forty-six laps to go.

Ten laps later and Barrichello began to sense trouble. The brakes were becoming less and less effective, so much so that he was having to pump the pedal in order to achieve any kind of stopping power. On the back straight he was reaching 185 mph and he definitely needed his brakes when it came to dealing with the second gear hairpin which followed. It was not a pleasant thought each time he accelerated through the gears, not knowing if the middle pedal would work when he had urgent need of it in a few seconds time.

It became so bad that he had to resort to pumping the pedal with his left foot as he rushed down the straight. He did not have that luxury on the short straight leading to the fast curve after the pits. Here, he had to change down a gear in order to slow the car sufficiently. The nett result of all this was a gradual drop in performance. But he was still sixth.

Now the stop watches were on the gap to the Larrousse of Erik Comas in seventh place. With 30 laps to go, he was 10.4 seconds behind. Then it was 9.3. Then 8.6. Then 6.8.

With 10 laps remaining, it was 6.2 seconds. Rubens was holding his own; there was every chance he would have sixth place and that ever-so vital championship point.

But there was a new menace on the horizon. Michael Andretti had started from the back of the grid in his McLaren, the American in aggressive mood after being delayed by a technical problem. By half distance he had moved into eighth place and was closing rapidly on Comas. The Frenchman provided little resistance as the McLaren swept past on lap 65.

Andretti had just set his personal best lap of the race and it was more than one and a half seconds faster than anything poor Barrichello could manage as he pumped furiously at the brakes. The gap was 2.6 seconds with five laps to go.

Dear God, surely they were not about to lose that point at the eleventh hour? It was too much to bear. Jordan, Anderson and Phillips stared at the stop watch, utterly powerless to do anything to help.

Two laps to go. Andretti was a couple of car lengths behind. And closing. Then, to pour salt into the gaping wound, the McLaren overtook the Jordan within sight of the pits at the beginning of the last lap.

Shit!

Seventh place. What earthly good was that? Damn Michael Andretti. Damn McLaren bloody International.

Boutsen had managed to struggle home in 11th place. It may as well have been 111th. The team was devastated, just like at Donington.

But this was different. Donington had been early in the season and the performance there had been a harbinger of hope; there's always tomorrow; that sort of thing.

France was here and now; the final deadline. Fail to deliver today and you are out of the club, paying for your own travel. In blunt terms, it meant Jordan Grand Prix was going to miss out on $2 million in bonuses from the

Formula One Constructors' Association.

As the cars trickled into the pit lane, the Jordan mechanics went silently about their work, packing and tidying, keen to get away. Eddie Jordan emerged from the toilet beneath a concrete staircase at the back of the garage. The dent in the team's finances was written all over his ashen face. Two million dollars. Here one minute; gone the next. It was as if he had been mugged on the steps of the bank.

A tiny mistake

Gary Anderson was mystified. There were no clues of any kind; the brake pressure had simply disappeared with no good reason. Steve Bryan, the man from Automotive Products, was called in.

Anderson had explained the problem over the telephone, describing the little evidence there was available. As Bryan drove from Coventry to the Jordan factory, he ran through the symptoms in his mind. By the time he had reached Silverstone, Bryan was fairly sure he knew what the problem was.

If the basic design and manufacture of the brake caliper, pads and discs had been at fault, the trouble would probably have arisen earlier than it did, given the severe punishment dealt out from lap 1.

Barrichello had first noticed the problem not long after the pit stop, a point when the brakes come under the severest test. The calipers reach their highest temperatures of the day as the driver sits with his foot on the brake pedal – a necessary precaution to stop the wheels from turning while the tyre-change takes place – and there is no air rushing through the cooling ducts.

Brake fluid expands by 10 per cent for every 100° of temperature and the excess liquid is taken care of by a reservoir. The arrival of the fluid pushes air out of the reservoir and, under normal circumstances, when the system cools, the fluid should contract and return, drawing air back in through a breather in the reservoir cap.

The fact that Barrichello had to pump the brakes suggested that the fluid had not returned fully and done its job of pushing the pistons on to the pads. Which, in turn, pointed to the fact that the system was not properly pressurized. It seemed likely that the breather had become blocked and air had not been allowed to return.

When Bryan arrived at Jordan and walked over to the car, the first thing he asked Anderson to do was unscrew the top of the reservoir. As the movement was started, there came a soft hiss of air. It was exactly as Steve Bryan had feared.

A tiny copper tube had been used to act as the breather through the cap on the small plastic reservoir. The copper had attracted water and eventually caused corrosion within the tube. The subsequent plug of corroded copper, no wider than a hypodermic needle, had blocked the tube at precisely the wrong moment and cost Jordan Grand Prix $2 million.

'The *one* part which was not drawn up properly,' groaned Anderson, with typical honesty. 'It was done quickly and not a lot of thought given to it. That's a lesson for me.'

When the cars appeared a few days later in readiness for the British Grand Prix, the breather tubes were made of plastic. The modification had cost a matter of pence.

Chapter 19

A Broth of a Boy

The bookie and the banker

'I first met Eddie at a disco at Leopardstown. He was quite fat at the time. He had a beard and he was wearing a dickie bow. I thought he was, you might say, a bit unusual.'

Marie McCarthy was fairly extraordinary herself. For all the remarkable and frequently bizarre goings-on in Dublin, the city can boast few good-looking women with the mental agility to work as a settler in a bookmakers while, at the same time, playing basketball for Ireland. It was typical that Eddie Jordan should find one.

He was working for the Bank of Ireland in Camden Street; Marie was calculating the odds in Floods, a betting establishment treated by the locals with a reverence normally reserved for the chapel and the Guinness Brewery.

Whether by accident or design, Jordan found himself posted to a branch directly beneath Price Waterhouse not long after Marie's talents had been put to a more acceptable use – although the punters would seriously dispute that – by the firm of chartered accountants.

They became regular partners even though Marie was not remotely interested in motor racing. 'I went to Mondello Park once, got bored, and left after 20 minutes.'

She was even less impressed by the fact that her man was a driver of considerable note in local circles. When Eddie won the Irish Formula Atlantic title in 1978, it meant the end of his career in banking and the switch to an infinitely more exciting if less stable form of commerce as he moved to England to pursue a full-time motor racing career.

Shut your gob

This was not what his mother had envisaged when Edmund was born in the town of Bray, down the coast from Dublin, on 30 March 1948. A brief foray into the world of dentistry was forsaken for banking and simultaneous cost and management accountancy studies at the Dublin College of Commerce. That looked set to be his future and, ironically, it was only a serious breakdown in the Irish fiscal system which brought Eddie into contact with motor racing.

The bank strike of 1970 brought semi-paralysis to Ireland. It was a lengthy affair and, seeking alternative employment, Eddie moved to Jersey for the summer. A kart race at Bouley Bay was to have a more profound long-term effect than even the adventurous and idealizing Jordan could ever have imagined.

On his return to Dublin, he bought a kart and, within 18 months, won the Irish Championship. That done, the next step was a proper racing car and a move to Formula Ford, Eddie winning several races with the single-seater.

An excursion to Mallory Park in England brought disaster when he crashed heavily and missed most of the 1975 season as a result. But he was soon back, jaunty as ever, talking in grand terms about a talent which the motor racing world, in his opinion, could not afford to be without. Formula Atlantic, a series for powerful single-seaters, was the next step and his personal beliefs were bolstered by the securing of the Irish championship in 1978.

By which time, Marie McCarthy was about to become Mrs Eddie Jordan. They married in January 1979. On 8 February, they left the banks of the River Liffey for the bottom of a rainbow located near the Silverstone circuit in Northamptonshire.

While Eddie moved with moderate success into Formula 3 and then Formula 2, Marie was doing what she could by working in a factory to earn £40 per week as a packer, a bit of a change from the happy-go-lucky days of Floods and basketball.

Eddie got as far as testing a Formula 1 car for McLaren but this merely strengthened the conviction that he should run his own team. Eddie Jordan Racing was formed at the beginning of 1980. It sounded grand. The reality was quite different.

'It was hand-to-mouth for the first three years,' says Marie. 'But it was a lot of fun. Eddie would raise a bit of money by buying and selling, wheeling and dealing – you know what he's like!

'Zoe was born in 1980 and we all lived in a caravan – plus 'John Boy' Walton and another mechanic called Mal – while travelling to the European races.

'I remember we were at Monaco for the Formula 3 race supporting the Grand Prix. That was the big event of the year, obviously, and Eddie managed to get invited to the Marlboro dinner (nothing changes: it would be no different 13 years later!). I wore a second-hand gown which I got from Oxfam; we didn't have a care, it was wonderful.

'Eddie got the offer of a drive in a race the following week at Zandvoort. We drove from Monaco to Holland and there was enough money to allow us to stay in a hotel. I really thought we had it made!'

The Jordans bought a house – two up, two down, no central heating – near Silverstone. Eddie was beginning to realize that his talents would be better directed towards running the team and managing drivers rather than doing his bit in the cockpit. By the end of 1981, he had quietly retired and the income – or promise of it – had been enough to warrant a move to a five-bedroomed house in Silverstone village.

'After all we had been through,' recalls Marie, 'I thought this was it. We couldn't possibly want more than this. We could take in as many as four lodgers for bed, breakfast and an evening meal; they were mainly young racing drivers. I would do the washing and ironing; they would do the baby-sitting; Zoe was three and Michele had arrived. It was a perfect arrangement.'

Eddie Jordan Racing was established as a serious entrant in the Formula 3 scene in Europe, Martin Brundle finishing runner-up for EJR in the British series after a brilliant struggle with Ayrton Senna throughout 1983.

When Formula 3000 – a series for scaled down Grand Prix cars – came into being in 1985, Jordan moved up and moved out of the Silverstone hostel for homeless racing drivers. Westbury, a stone-built cottage in Buckinghamshire, had a pool and tennis court in the immaculate gardens. It was an idyllic retreat for Eddie and Marie; a perfect place for the family, now three-strong following the birth of Zak.

Enough to bring you out in spots

All the while, Eddie had his eye on Formula 1. It seemed something of a lofty ambition and Marie indulged Eddie in his dreams.

'But, in 1990, I suddenly realized he was *serious*,' she says, as if still shocked by the thought. 'He was putting together a plan to run a Grand Prix team in 1991 and this involved total commitment. That was to be the toughest time of all for us because we stood to lose everything – the house, the lot – if this didn't work.

'I never really thought I was the nervous type but my hands came out in spots, you know, thinking about selling the house, where to school the kids; things like that.

'Eddie's one of the world's great survivors and there was the thought that he was young enough and resilient enough to start rebuilding if things went wrong. But, even so, it was only natural that you should look at what we had achieved – and then wonder.

'But this was what he really wanted to do. It was driving him on. I knew there was no way it would be anything other than this.'

The £2.5 million venture was an outstanding success. For the first year at least. The Jordans had moved to a seven-bedroom period detached house in Oxford; there was a retreat in Spain where Marie would spend two months of the summer with the children, now four in number as Kyle made it two of each model. Life was good even though it was underpinned by Formula 1, the great gamble, the race without end.

Chapter 20

Can't get no Satisfaction

One for the boys

'EJ! Are ya going to win this, or wha'?'

The Irish brogue was pronounced and Eddie Jordan understood its full implication.

Silverstone, 1993. This would be the third British Grand Prix for Jordan, his home event in more ways than one. Apart from being across the road from the team's headquarters, it was the closest Formula 1 race for his friends and admirers in the 'Old Country'. The Irish were out in force. It was Cheltenham on wheels.

Eddie and Marie had made the tactical error of stopping in the circuit bar for a quick drink on the way home one evening.

'EJ! What'll ya have?'

They had scarcely got through the door before the cry went up and the boys were upon them. There was no turning back now. And when, they wanted to know, was EJ going to win a race?

Score a point more like. The British Grand Prix had not brought the team much luck, not even in the euphoria of 1991. Bertrand Gachot had squeaked home in sixth place but that race had resulted in one of the most spectacular crashes of the season as Andrea de Cesaris reduced the Jordan to component parts by ricocheting from Abbey Curve to the bridge at over 150 mph. A bolt in the rear suspension had broken.

1992 had been dismal, Mauricio Gugelmin and Stefano Modena both retiring with engine trouble; very much in keeping with the struggle elsewhere that year with the Yamaha V12.

But 1993 looked better. There had been the promise of Donington; the performance the previous week in France. Surely EJ would not let the boys down at home?

Much as he loved the company – the 'crack' as they say in Ireland, when describing the banter and the conversation - Eddie had to break free, make his excuses.

This was the most hectic weekend of all; pressure from all sides to produce a result. Besides, they would soon want him to go into detail about practice, explain why the Jordan-Harts were only 15th and 23rd on the grid.

'Jaysus Eddie. Aren't ya testing and practising here every day, wha? Why're you so slow?' He didn't need too many questions like that.

Sheepish behaviour

Practice had not been straightforward. Rain on Friday morning; faulty electronics affecting the front damper, and then gear selection problems in the afternoon. Rubens stuck out on the circuit with broken suspension on Saturday morning, the day's plans thoroughly disrupted as a result; handling problems (largely self-inflicted, according to Anderson) for Thierry and, when they were close to being put right, a broken exhaust pipe and the accompanying loss of engine power.

In short, nothing to write home about. And the weather was lousy for July. This weekend, supposedly the high point of the season for a British-based team, was turning out to be nothing but hassle and awkward questions.

By race morning, the sensible teams had employed the use of duck-boarding outside the motor homes. Silverstone's grass paddock was won-derful – very British – on a hot summer's day. But in the cloudy cool of Sunday 11 July, it was unbecoming to have to walk on tiptoe through the mud while conducting a multi-million dollar business.

Even so, Silverstone at Grand Prix time can conjure a unique atmosphere from the dregs of a bad day. A wartime airfield it may have been but the place has had tradition, right from the moment the first 'race' was held in 1947.

A group of motoring enthusiasts had arrived unannounced, slipped through the gate of the abandoned aerodrome and raced along a makeshift track of runways and the perimeter road. The only casualty was an unfortunate sheep, unaccustomed to being challenged to the right of way by an energetically driven Frazer Nash.

Silverstone was granted the very first round of the World Championship in 1950, an accolade which ensured that tweeds, brogues and Bentleys would become accepted as the hallmark of Britain's round of the world series. It was a hearty, outdoor sort of place, full of gung-ho and grass. If Wimbledon would become famous for its strawberries and cream, then Silverstone would be best remembered as it crackled to bacon and eggs just after dawn.

The tradition was maintained in the motor homes on race morning in 1993. Eddie Jordan, mug of tea and full fry in hand, attempted to join Marie at a table outside. It was a recipe for indigestion. Breakfast was interrupted by the need to get up and greet a steady flow of friends and acquaintances, accept their good wishes – and deal with the inevitable.

'EJ! Are ya going to win this one, or wha'?'

Racing nowhere

The already slim chances of Sasol Jordan Hart were halved before the start. Boutsen came to the grid, saying the car felt strange; it had been weaving unaccountably as he went down the straight. The mechanics checked it over but nothing could be found. Given Boutsen's unease with the Jordan at the best of times, this was hardly going to provide peace of mind on a circuit with a lap average in excess of 140 mph.

He pressed on bravely, but by the time the tyre change had been enacted at the end of lap 24 the car felt much worse. Boutsen trailed into the pits 21 laps later with a failed wheelbearing at the rear. His intuition had been right all along.

This was the last thing that the team had expected. After more than 15,000 miles of running, there had not been the slightest hint of trouble in this area. It had been the first such failure. And it would not be the last.

Barrichello, meanwhile, was in the thick of it. Right from the start, he had been embroiled in a battle, first with Fittipaldi's Minardi and then the Ferrari of Jean Alesi. It was tooth and nail, non-stop, for 190 miles.

'It was like we were on qualifying laps all the time,' said Barrichello as he walked back to the pits. 'It was a really good battle; really good. I learned a lot.' He was flushed, beaming from ear to ear, the adrenalin still pumping.

But, after all that, he had only finished 10th. It was one of those days when most of the cars in front had kept going. What can you do?

Eddie Jordan put a brave face on it when interviewed by BBC Radio 5 just after the race. Deep down, he knew that they simply were not quick enough. Fighting with a Ferrari was all very well, but the Italian team was having an even worse season than Jordan. It was good for Barrichello's confidence to hack it with a quick driver such as Alesi. But, overall, it proved nothing.

That made it nine races and no points. There were seven Grands Prix to go.

The song says it all

To hell with that. Let's forget about our troubles for a while. Come and have a drink.

With so many wives and girlfriends present, Silverstone presented the British teams with a unique opportunity to hold informal parties in the paddock when the weekend's business was done.

Typically, Eddie Jordan entered into the occasion with considerable enthusiasm. Draught Groslch beer and Guinness – fully piped and fettled; after all, his was a discerning guest list when it came to bibulous practices – were dispensed outside the motor home while the focal point was trundled into place. As helicopters continued to beat the retreat into the evening sky and barbecues began to sizzle, the platform of an articulated trailer on loan from Elite Truck & Car Rentals was made ready for music.

The temporary stage gradually filled with a motley collection of musicians, some average, some truly first class, but all performing and singing their hearts out as the appreciative audience released the tensions of the weekend.

Jordan beat the living daylights out of a set of drums. And Rubens Barrichello belted out 'Can't get no satisfaction'. He was still high on the heat of a clean fight. But the words had an apposite ring.

'EJ! Are ya going to win this one, or wha?'

Not today, my friend. And, at this rate of going, probably not tomorrow either.

Chapter 21

Staying Put

Leave my wee boy alone

The predators were circling, probing for weaknesses, hoping for Barrichello to drift from Jordan's embrace, waiting for their chance to sign him up.

But Eddie Jordan was wise to it. He had been down this road before. It had been a painful experience and his mind was still scoured by the memory of it all.

In one of the bravest and brightest moves, probably of the decade, Eddie Jordan had signed Michael Schumacher for the 1991 Belgian Grand Prix and, he thought, a season or two beyond.

The young German was relatively unknown but Jordan had been eyeing him for some time. The opportunity came when Eddie's regular driver, Bertrand Gachot, was imprisoned following a controversial altercation between the Belgian and a London cab driver over a piece of road outside Hyde Park. Schumacher was drafted into the team for Spa-Francorchamps, one of the most daunting circuits on the calendar.

Schumacher, calm as you like, had qualified seventh. It mattered little that his race lasted no further than the first corner because of a broken clutch. The youngster's future was assured and Jordan felt confident he would share a major part of it.

Two weeks later, Jordan was left holding the tatters of his so-called contract, a somewhat forlorn figure in the Monza paddock after his star turn had more or less been plundered overnight by Benetton, in collusion with Schumacher's personal advisers.

Jordan had, to the best of his knowledge, done everything right. But Formula 1 is no respecter of business etiquette. Any contract worthy of the name needs to be made of cast iron, set in stone, wrapped in barbed wire and protected by a beast with several heads. Even then, the entire box and dice is likely to be devoured by the enemy in the genuine belief that the need to win at all costs permits the abandonment of scruples. Fail to appreciate that and you are considered a wimp not worthy of this paddock.

Eddie Jordan's defences, on full alert, had positively bristled when he learned that Benetton, of all people, was circling overhead, eyeing his pride and joy. At the British Grand Prix, Sasol Jordan had issued a release, headed 'Barrichello confirms his future intentions' and containing a quote from Rubens saying he would be more than happy to see out the second year of his contract. The press release kept the inquisitive media quiet in the short term but, in the long term, the document was about as much use as the piece of paper waved by Chamberlain on his return from a visit to that nice Mr Hitler.

Rubens had a two-year unbreakable contract, with an option for 1995, and there was never any question of Barrichello breaching that agreement. But, as yet, he and Jordan had to fine tune the financial details for 1994. Eddie Jordan hoped to put that right two weeks later at Hockenheim in Germany.

Backed against the wall

On Friday afternoon, Rubens crashed. It was the first major accident he had suffered with Jordan and the first time he had seriously damaged his car. There were two ways of looking at this; either he was very good, or he had not been going fast enough up until now.

The Jordan had revised aerodynamics but, overall, the car was not much better. Indeed, on this occasion, they had been running with very little downforce in the interests of better straight-line speed. Rubens had been trying hard, following up a reasonable lap with one which, the split times showed, was half a second quicker at two-thirds distance.

Coming into the stadium – in which the majority of Hockenheim's corners are located, the rest of the banana-shaped track being a flat-out blind into the surrounding forest and back again – Rubens had felt the car show a reluctance to take the corner. But, since he knew he was on a quick lap, the racer within him refused to allow his right foot to come off the throttle. The car had other ideas and promptly hurled Barrichello into the wall. 'It was not,' he said, somewhat sheepishly, 'a small shunt'.

Barrichello was unhurt but damage to the front of the car was severe. He was credited with 16th fastest time from the previous lap; Boutsen was 24th, the morning having been lost while an alternator was changed. His luck would get no better on the second day when the gearbox gave trouble, Boutsen managing to improve his time but still remain in 24th place.

For Barrichello, it was even worse. He went quicker too, but not fast enough when compared with the improvements made by those around him. He qualified in 17th place, his lowest grid position yet.

Eddie Jordan was not deterred by that. He had his calculator at the ready and, later on Saturday afternoon, Rubens Barrichello agreed the finer points of his deal with Jordan Grand Prix for 1994.

Eddie was delighted. The negotiations had been conducted with Geraldo and Rubens Snr, the father having a mandate from Arisco, the comparatively young food manufacturing and distribution company which had bank-rolled the boy as their various careers expanded in unison.

The Barrichellos had been interested in the overtures from Benetton but it was felt that, at this stage in his career, Rubens would be better off without the pressures associated with a top team. Indeed, Rubens Snr's main concern was that Jordan would merely use his boy as a means of raising money by trading him on the driver market; Jordan was categoric that this would not be the case.

While this may seem to have been loaded in Jordan's favour, at the end of the day he was taking the risks associated with signing a young driver, paying for his excesses on the track, teaching him the trade – and then losing him to a big buck operation just as his talent was maturing into match-winning form.

Even so, Eddie Jordan was very pleased with the day's events in the motor home, if not on the race track. But none of this was helping solve the more immediate problem of earning some credibility and a place on the points table.

Another big zero

Thierry Boutsen finished 13th out of the 16 cars still running at the end of the 45-lap race. He was several miles behind the winner, Alain Prost. Barrichello, in 12th place at one stage, had retired with the second wheelbearing failure in as many weeks.

Now the alarm bells were ringing. Like the hydraulic seal problem earlier in the year, one failure is perhaps excusable. But the second is not acceptable. There were no answers so far. Anderson and his technical team was coming under pressure, Gary now totally frustrated by the restrictions imposed by a small organization working on a tight budget. Ten races down. Six to go. And still nothing to show.

Chapter 22

All Over in a Minute

Was that Rubens?

The picture on the television monitor was difficult to see thanks to the fierce reflections from the early afternoon sun. But the eyes of the mechanics, familiar with every millimetre of the Jordan-Hart, were not blind to the harsh reality played momentarily before them.

The Hungarian Grand Prix was less than a minute old. In the immediate aftermath of the sound and fury at the start, the team crowded round the portable televisions placed on the pit wall and in the garage entrance, anxious to see how their drivers were faring in the vital opening phase of this race.

The Hungaroring, a soulless venue dropped into the only piece of rolling countryside 20 miles north-east of Budapest, had little to commend it. Designed and built in 1986, this was a product of the recently arrived commercial era in which the demands of television outweighed the need to provide a track on which the drivers might actually enjoy racing.

The emphasis was on providing a succession of tight corners, the better to keep the cars bunched together, looking busy for the benefit of the cameras. The fact that there would be little overtaking was an irrelevance; at least no one would race into the distance and be seen lapping alone. Perish the thought that Grand Prix racing might appear to be boring.

So, if your driver lost ground at the start, the chances of making it up would be slim. Similarly, a spirited getaway could win a couple of places which the opposition might have difficulty in recovering.

Barrichello was starting from 16th place; Thierry Boutsen from the penultimate row. The morning warm-up had shown Barrichello to be 10th quickest. Clearly, in race trim, the Jordan was competitive although the track itself would militate against the Brazilian making the most of his advantage. An attacking opening lap would be his best bet.

Even before the start, Barrichello is one up as the pole position Williams of Alain Prost stalls at the beginning of the final parade lap and is forced to join the back of the grid. Now there are 14 cars ahead of Barrichello as the starter flicks the lights from red to green.

The television cameras focus on the leaders as the colourful train files through the chicane at the far side of the track.

Damon Hill is leading. There's Ayrton Senna in second place. Gerhard Berger – a brilliant start – is third. Who's fourth? Let's see ... it looks like – *what* the hell was that?

The ordered crawl through the corner is momentarily disrupted by a flash of movement and dust as one car shoots across the background at undiminished speed. Whoever he was, the driver made no attempt whatsoever to take the chicane. But it looked like he was driving a Jordan.

Seconds later, the camera confirms it. There is Barrichello, his right-front wheel torn from the chassis, tobogganing along the bone-dry grass on the edge of the track.

After the build-up, after 875 man-hours at the circuit – never mind the preparation at the factory beforehand – his race is over almost before it has started. Bloody hell! Whatever next?

A racing accident

Keen to make up whatever ground he could, Barrichello had tried to overtake Aguri Suzuki's Footwork as the Japanese driver applied more caution than Barrichello thought was necessary going into the chicane. Barrichello had darted to the right; Suzuki had moved to the right. Barrichello had gone to the left; Suzuki, at the last minute, did the same. Barrichello was committed; there was nowhere for him to go. The irony was, Suzuki's car survived more or less unscathed as the Jordan smashed into his left-rear wheel.

They called it a racing accident. But that euphemism for an infuriating sequence of events did little to alleviate the team's frustration. With Boutsen running steadily to finish an unspectacular ninth, Sasol Jordan was no nearer scoring their first points of the season. And now time was beginning to run out. Okay, there were five more races and anything could happen. Call it what you like; it was still bloody annoying.

Of course, they should have known the weekend would end like that. It had scarcely started on a positive note.

So, this is Hungary

Motor racing mechanics tire easily of well-intentioned remarks from their neighbours.

'Where's it this week?' is the usual question, pitched in mock boredom.

'Hungary. Budapest, actually.'

'Very nice. Lucky you. Need a helper for the weekend, do you? I'll be no trouble! Wish I had a job like yours, going to all these nice places.'

Mechanics do not see it that way. In fact, they get to see very little of anything. The usual routine is home-airport-racetrack-hotel-racetrack-hotel-racetrack-hotel-racetrack-airport-home. It never varies, except perhaps on a trip to a brace of trans-continental Grands Prix where there may be time off for sightseeing in between. But, otherwise, Heathrow and Gatwick are as familiar as Waterloo and Liverpool Street to the seasoned commuter. And the boredom factor is just as acute.

On Thursday, 12 August, it was Luton airport, an early start made worse by driving rain. There were supposed to be two planes waiting – a Boeing 737 and a Tupolev 154, chartered from Malev, the Hungarian state airline. The 737 landed safely but the pilot of the elderly TU154, without the benefit of ILS (Instrument Landing System), would not risk tackling the filthy conditions and chose instead to land at Heathrow.

Those booked on the 737 took off on schedule at 8.30 am. The rest – including the Jordan team – faced a journey by coach through the road works of the M25 to Heathrow. The aircraft finally departed at 12.15 pm. The weary passengers, most of whom had arisen before 5.30, reached Terminal 2 at Budapest's Ferihegy airport at 3.30 pm – only to discover that their hire cars and mini-buses were at Terminal 1. And, of course, that could not be reached on foot.

And now, instead of murk and rain, heat and humidity hung in the air, the insides of the waiting vehicles being almost too hot to touch. Green blazers, smart and businesslike at 8.00 am, were now a cumbersome appendage; once crisp white shirts were limp and damp; team ties hung loose at the neck.

With the day slipping into its final third, the priority was to be done with this seemingly endless routine and get to the race track to begin serious preparation.

So, this is Hungary. It may as well have been Hounslow. It was not the moment to suggest that foreign travel is a perk worth having.

Pure genius

Things looked up in the evening. Or, at least, it did for some. Marek Sobas, the mechanic specializing in dampers and hydraulics, had spotted an advert in the Malev in-flight magazine for a British-style pub serving genuine draught Guinness.

Forget local culture. When you've been working hard all day, known quantities are preferable to time wasted in uncharted gastronomic territory. And, by a stroke of good fortune, this watering hole, The Winston, was within walking distance of the hotel.

Surprise at finding a truly excellent Beef Wellington was exceeded by the standard of the Guinness, dispensed by a proper Irish pump (as opposed to the British version designed for quantity rather than quality) and served in proper mugs. The trials and tribulations of the day were quickly washed away. This was indeed an oasis.

While the mechanics were enjoying such sanctuary, the engineers and designers were somewhere else, struggling with the dubious pleasures of Hungarian cuisine. A visit to a nearby restaurant proved that, while Budapest may have changed immeasurably since the Grand Prix first came to town in 1986, the culinary arts had yet to satisfy the Western pallet.

The red wine was undrinkable. Brian Hart bravely worked through a bottle of white while the rest stuck to export beer. And, throughout this encounter, a collection of four men with equally elderly musical instruments attempted to prove without success that they were supposed to be the euphonious entertainment. They merely succeeded in accelerating the feeling of tiredness. Everyone was in bed by midnight, something as unexpected as – well, a decent pint of Guinness in Budapest.

Carpets and cobbles

The Beke Hotel is on Terez Korut, a broad thoroughfare carrying trams down its middle and assorted ramshackle cars and lorries on either side. It used to be known as Lenin Korut. But that was for times gone by. Just as the belching Trabants are slowly being superseded by more modern motor cars, the Beke Hotel has received an overhaul, the high-ceiling hall and revolving doors being the first signs of an expensive face lift within. It is indicative of a majestic city slowly recovering its dignity.

At seven in the morning, the bedroom doors click shut, the carpeted passageways carrying little sound as the Jordan mechanics make their way downstairs. John Walton and Paul Thompson have already joined the team uniforms of Williams and Dallara, gathered round the hall porter as the whereabouts of minibuses are discovered and ignition keys distributed.

A 7.15 am departure time has been set. One by one the mechanics emerge into the warm sunlight and blink as they look for the familiar Jordan colours. The team has rented two minibuses, driven by Thompson and Walton, to carry the 14 mechanics. By 7.14 everyone has appeared and you get the impression from those waiting that a minute early is actually too late. There is a job to be done – so let's get on with it.

The cobbled street along the side of the railway station is the final alarm call. The minibuses rumble and vibrate so much that conversation is almost impossible. Once onto the motorway, it is the scream of the engine being pressed to its limit which stints further discussion. The journey takes 25 minutes, the minibuses almost rushing the gates as the occupants show their permanent passes with the nonchalance of passengers at the Charing Cross barrier.

The paddock at the Hungaroring is on two levels. The pits, garages and transporters are on the upper, the motor homes on the lower; the two joined by a steep flight of steps. The minibuses draw up outside the Jordan motor home. The mechanics, ignoring the wafting smell of cooked bacon, sprint up the steps.

The upper level is strangely quiet, in keeping with a beautifully still morning as the rising sun begins to heat up the countryside beyond. The public address system is silent. The garages are uncharacteristically muted save for the sound of shutters being raised as teams open for business.

They work swiftly and methodically with hardly a word being spoken, each man intimate with his particular task. Equipment – stacks of tyres, spare wings, air bottles, jacks, portable generators – is rolled out and placed, ready for action. The cars are uncovered – a lingering tradition from the days of working in the open air – and the top bodywork removed, to be rested on stands erected outside the front of the garage.

By 7.50 am, the pit lane is a colourful line of graceful carbon fibre engine covers as the other 12 teams go through exactly the same procedure.

7.51 am, and the comparative stillness is shattered for the day as the Larrousse team coax a Lamborghini V12 into life. There seems to be no time to lose and yet practice is not due to start for another hour and a half.

Even breakfast is taken at a swift pace. Served at the motor home, the 16 traditional English fries have been consumed by the time Eddie Jordan, Ian Phillips and Louise Goodman arrive at 8.20 to start their day. Meanwhile, the engineers and Brian Hart's crew, who arrived shortly before, are half-way through their breakfast.

The drivers have appeared by 8.50 and, by then, the mechanics have everything ready in the garage. With 40 minutes to go, there is time to wander down the pit lane and exchange banter with their mates in the opposing teams.

Friends with the enemy

Mechanics, as with the media and team management, work for rival organizations but world travel promotes a camaraderie; a sense of being in it together. It is essentially a small business, everyone knowing everyone else's problems. Or most of them, anyway. Gossip is rife; the keeping of secrets an almost impossible task.

Formula 1 mechanics are generally chosen by reputation. Few are picked cold from a business outside racing. They need to know what Formula 1 is about, not simply because of the proficiency that will bring but because it means the mechanic will be aware of precisely what he is letting himself in for. This is not a nine to five job and the motor racing grapevine will let a team owner know whether or not his prospective employee can cope.

In the end, the good mechanics are good but the top mechanics are as skilled in their own right as the drivers who risk their lives in the mechanics' handiwork. It's just that one, the Superstar, gets the glory and the other, the so-called 'boltie', receives the brickbats on the rare occasions when things go wrong.

Mechanical failures are usually down to the supplier or the designer. But slack spanner-work is euphemistically referred to as 'finger trouble'. It is a polite way of saying a mechanic has screwed up – or not, as the case may be.

Either way, everyone in the team will know precisely who is at fault, each man having his own car to work on and certain tasks associated with it. And within 24 hours most of the mechanics in the pit lane will know the exact details concerning the spot of 'finger trouble' in the garage next door. Sympathy will not be in abundant supply but each mechanic will quietly and briefly dwell on the thought: 'There but for the grace of God ...' When life is at risk, mistakes cannot be tolerated.

Just as a driver does not invest much time in thinking deeply about the hazards of his profession, mechanics do not outwardly dwell on the consequences of finger trouble. But the thought is never far from the surface. And that encourages the bond between fellow members of the profession as they catch a moment or two of relaxation in the pit lane.

By 9.15, the Jordan mechanics are back in the garage, the soft music from the tannoy being blasted into oblivion as engines burst into life along the length of the pit lane. At 9.30 precisely, on-track activities for the 1993 Hungarian Grand Prix get under way. Already, the mechanics have worked for almost six hours at the track before the cars have turned a wheel.

Down to business

Now the regimented routine really gets into its stride.

At Jordan, each of the two race cars has three mechanics. Jim Vale, formerly with Benetton and now the Number 1 on Barrichello's car, is assisted by Phil Howell and Mick Shaw. Nick Burrows, in charge of Boutsen's car, works with Andy Stephenson and Chris Walker. The spare car is the concern of Tim Edwards and Dave Hudson, these two floating during practice on Friday and Saturday when the spare car is not in use.

Spares are taken care of by Simon Munger while the crews from the two ERF trucks – Rick Wiltshire, Gerard O'Reilly, Ian Webb and Micky Miller – look after fuel, wheels and tyres, Miller specializing in composites in the event of bodywork repairs being necessary. Marek Sobas, as mentioned before, is responsible for dampers, hydraulics and the unofficial divining of Guinness, and the entire crew is overseen by Paul Thompson who, in turn, reports to John Walton.

The major technical decisions are taken by Gary Anderson in consultation with either Brian Hart or engineers Mark Smith, Andrew Green and Tim Wright. At no stage during practice does Eddie Jordan or Ian Phillips play a part in the routine affairs in the pits.

Indeed, during this first practice session in Hungary, neither of them are seen in the garage as they work out the final details of a new sponsor announcement, due to be made the following day. The mechanics are completely oblivious to such matters; it is as though the team management is operating in a different world – which, in a manner of speaking, is true.

Barrichello has never seen the Hungaroring before – apart from a lap on a bicycle the previous day. In addition, because the circuit is rarely in use from one Grand Prix to the next, the track is invariably dusty and takes a whole day to 'clean up' as the cars begin to lay down rubber on the racing line.

Barrichello is 14th at the end of the free practice session.

Gerard 'Jabby' Crombac, a veteran French journalist gathering information for the FISA press bulletin, weaves his way around the cars and approaches Anderson at the back of the garage.

'Any problems?'

'Not really,' says Anderson. 'The balance of the car is okay but there is not enough grip at the moment.'

'It's the same for everyone,' observes Crombac.

Enmeshed in your own team, it is easy to forget that such a fundamental problem is not unique to your car as rivals also struggle with the circuit. Even so, there is still room for improvement. As the temperature nudges 30°C and activity slows down for two hours, there is time to realize this is thirsty work.

A floor-to-ceiling fridge in the back of one of the trucks supplies enough soft drinks to keep a small shop in business for a week. Coffee and tea have been brought up from the motor home.

Jordan and Phillips are in the back of the truck enjoying a coffee just as much as the ribbing they are dishing out to Walton over the team manager's extra-curricular activities in years gone by. Marie Jordan had once described Walton as having 'come to bed' eyes and there would seem to be a grain of truth in it if Eddie's outrageous stories are to be believed.

Two businessmen with shirts and ties arrive at the back steps and peer into the transporter. It's the new sponsor. Jordan and Phillips immediately switch from flippancy into business mode, inviting their guests into the truck to discuss how the launch will be handled.

It has been a last-minute deal, Jordan arranging sponsorship with Globalot, a Gibraltar-based lottery company whose identification will be on the car for just two races. Meanwhile the mechanics, still oblivious to all of this, continue their economic bustle in and around the garage.

Must do better

With neither car in need of repairs or major changes to the set-up, it is routine work; draining off the fuel, checking the car generally and examining the undertray for damage, cleaning out the radiator ducts and blowing dust and dirt away with an air line. Boutsen's ratios are being changed as a shorter third gear is fitted in order to help him make a quicker exit on to the all-important main straight. And, finally, a dust and polish with Unipart silicone spray.

Anderson is moderately happy although he feels that perhaps Barrichello is not tackling the final corner – a 180° right-hander taken in second gear – in the best way. Instead of braking at the last minute and almost throwing the car in, Barrichello is using the text book approach of arriving comparatively slowly and building up speed all the way through. It doesn't work here and promotes understeer which, in effect, costs speed at the exit.

It is a matter for careful discussion. Telling a driver how to do his job is not something to be treated in a cavalier fashion by someone standing on the sidelines.

First qualifying begins at 1.00 pm. The cars are ready, wheels mounted with the fresh tyres wrapped in blankets to keep the rubber at close to working temperature. With the number of laps limited to 12 for each driver, there is no point in wasting a lap by having to work the tyres hard simply to bring the rubber to optimum temperature.

Barrichello is standing at the back of the garage, chatting to Geraldo; Boutsen, helmet on, sits in his car and waits until he feels the moment is right. One or two cars scream past the pits and yet it is strangely calm. There are 12 people in the Jordan garage; they are standing absolutely still at the very moment you would expect furious activity. 1.09 pm. Now it's time to go. Barrichello is in the car and, on a nod from Jim Vale, a mechanic standing at each wheel removes a tyre cover. Barrichello signals to have the starter engaged at the back of the car, the Hart V10 bursting crisply into life.

Five minutes later and he's back, the bodywork coated with a thin layer of dust. The sidepod ducts are filled with gravel and grass; naughty Rubens has been off the road somewhere.

As the brake disc and tyre temperatures are checked as a matter of routine with measuring equipment, a more humble dust pan and brush (in Jordan blue, of course) is used to tidy away the debris extracted from the sidepods. There is not a hint of rebuke; everyone is entitled to a mistake.

After a brief consultation between Anderson and Barrichello on the headset, he returns to the track. Seven more laps. 15th fastest time. By 1.40 pm, he is back, the allocation of 12 laps used up.

As the temperature sensor prods the tacky black surface of the tyres once more, Barrichello climbs from the car, removes his helmet and pulls off his flame-proof balaclava, his fair hair standing on end. His face is flushed from the effort expended but his body language suggests disappointment with the lap time. Unrolling his overalls to the waist, he takes a swig of specially prepared light-green liquid and walks past Eddie Jordan as the team boss surveys the scene from the back of the garage.

There is not a flicker of communication between them simply because there is nothing to say. You can read Jordan's mind: 15th fastest; pretty average; could be better; *needs* to be better if we are to score these elusive points.

As the wheels are removed and fuel pumped from the car, Louise Goodman notes the drivers' comments and begins to prepare the daily press release. Not a great deal to write about this afternoon but, as ever, the bulletin will be upbeat and positive. Meanwhile, in the Minardi garage next door, the little Italian team is euphoric. Pierluigi Martini has just claimed fifth fastest time, an incredible achievement given their impoverished state. Typical of Jordan's luck that they have this of all teams at close quarters; the babble and laughter wafting across the partition tends to exaggerate the creeping mood of mediocrity at Sasol Jordan Hart. The arrival of sandwiches for lunch fortifies the enthusiasm; there's always tomorrow.

A delicate business

Before that, there is work to be done today. It is routine on a Friday; more checking, more cleaning, some minor modifications. The bulk of the work will be done on Saturday evening as the race preparation gets under way. That will involve rebuilding the gearbox, changing the engine, the brakes, the uprights, fuel filters, exhausts and various sundry items.

The £180 radiators, good enough for practice, will be replaced by versions which offer better cooling in a race during which much rubber and debris will accumulate in the cooling ducts. The fact that these replacement radiators cost £700 also has a bearing on the Saturday night switch. Winning may be the principal objective but the ubiquitous Bottom Line continues to comes a close second.

Winning seems a forlorn thought as the time sheets show Alain Prost's Williams, on overnight pole, to be 5.1 seconds ahead of Barrichello. Boutsen is down in 21st place, unhappy once again with the handling. But at least the Jordan mechanics have the consolation of two undamaged cars – which is more than can be said for most teams on a day when the slippery surface extracted its dues.

Underneath the calm facade, however, Paul Thompson is aware of a potential problem. Barrichello, having raced the spare car at Silverstone and used it during a test session at Pembrey in Wales in the week before Hungary, likes the feel of this chassis more than his race car. He wants to use it on Saturday. And, if his hunch is correct, then he will keep it for the rest of the weekend, his designated race car then becoming the spare.

Mechanics become attached to 'their' car. Having constructed it from the ground up, they know every nut and bolt, every little idiosyncrasy. Cars from one team may look the same but, to a mechanic, they are different in some subtle way not obvious to the untrained eye. Normally, if a driver switches, the mechanics stay with their particular car. But, when staff numbers are limited and the mechanics operating the back-up car do not have the experience of their counterparts, a change is necessary. Thompson realizes he has the delicate task of telling Tim Edwards and Dave Hudson that someone else is going to take over 'their' car.

Choosing his moment carefully, Thompson explains the position as Edwards and Hudson work silently without stopping. To their credit, they accept the facts without rancour. In the past, in other more celebrated teams, it has been known for such an occurrence to provoke angry scenes. Sasol Jordan is clearly without Superstar status from the top to the bottom.

By 6 pm, the majority of F1 personnel and the media have drifted back to town. Only the mechanics and engineers remain in full force, working their way through a routine which is roughly the same whether it is Barcelona or Budapest.

At 6.40 pm, Rubens Barrichello arrives on a moped to check progress in the Jordan garage. A visit by a driver is always welcome, if less common as he develops star status and his day is filled with media and sponsor obligations. But Barrichello is not yet at that stage in his career. His enthusiasm has not been tainted by familiarity with the job; he still relishes being involved with F1 and his mechanics love him for it. Besides, he has nothing else to do.

Dinner will be served at 7.00 pm. The work is nearly complete and the smell of carbolic soap begins to waft over Brian Hart and Andrew Green as they sit near the sink at the back of the garage, poring over their computers.

Out on the track, the late sun of a glorious evening throws a golden hue on to the grid. A team of lithe roller-skaters practise their pre-race routine for Sunday. The mechanics, welcoming the diversion, watch from the pit wall. About 40 spectators, dotted in the grandstand running the length of the main straight, make sure of extracting their money's worth. The tannoy plays dreamy piano music. The day is finally winding down.

The Jordan menu offers navarin of lamb, with potatoes and cauliflower, followed by pecan pie and cream. Chris and Henny have spent hours preparing it. Within 15 minutes, the meal has been wolfed down and the tables are empty. When it comes to chasing any free time available, racing mechanics will not let fine cuisine stand in their way.

There are still a few jobs to be done, such as placing the Globalot stickers on the cars. By 8.40 pm, the job lists are complete, the cars covered for the night.

Back to the motor home for a beer and a smoke. Then the ride towards a purple sunset, warm air still blowing through the air-vents as the minibuses blast down the motorway and into Budapest. A shower, quick change and a swift walk to The Winston. At least five pints of Guinness later and a slower return to the Beke and bed. The fact that the minibuses will be leaving again within six hours is the least of their worries. No hassle at the track; plenty of time for a drink; bed at 1.15 am. It's been a reasonable day.

Same again, please

Saturday turns out to be much the same. A seven o'clock start and a 9.30 pm finish; good going for a Formula 1 team on the eve of a race. Getting away before midnight is always a bonus.

In between, Barrichello had changed cars as planned. He felt more comfortable in the spare chassis. How much of it was fact and how much psychological no one could say but, if the driver is happier, then the rule is 'Just Do It'.

Driving a racing car quickly is as much about confidence and comfort as anything else, peace of mind in the cockpit promoting the self-assurance which allows the driver to take the car to the limit and find an extra couple of tenths of a second. Barrichello was quicker on Saturday afternoon – but, then, so was everyone else as the track improved. But he felt frustrated because 16th place was not indicative of what he could have achieved. Boutsen, meanwhile, was 24th out of 26. The team hid their disappointment well.

Crushed optimism

On race morning, Eddie Jordan sat in his den at the top of the motor home and thought about Boutsen. There was the suggestion that he might quit after the next race at Spa-Francorchamps, Boutsen's home Grand Prix. In which case, Jordan was mulling over the names of drivers available – and there weren't many capable of doing the job.

He talked about Heinz-Harald Frentzen and Eddie Irvine; F3000 drivers who had raced for Jordan in the past and were worth a try. The one thing sure was that Boutsen would not be staying for 1994 and Jordan was already thinking ahead and checking the list of likely candidates – Brundle, Herbert and Lehto being the favourites – assuming they would want to join Jordan's team.

They would need to be tempted by a few good results during these last few races. Almost absent-mindedly, Jordan flicked on the Olivetti monitor to check on the times being established in the warm-up.

'Good old Rubens – that's better,' he said, the relief palpable, as the Brazilian's name suddenly appeared in 10th place.

'Could be a good race,' mused Jordan. 'Pity overtaking is so difficult here.'

They were to be prophetic words.

Four hours later and Jordan would be stationed at the pit wall. He would be one of the first to recognize Barrichello's car as it three-wheeled its way into retirement. 875 man-hours and nothing to show. No points. No champagne. Just the packed flight home after a wasted weekend in Hungary.

'Been to Budapest, have you? Some people get all the luck.'

Chapter 23

Back Stage Drivers

Parking pretty

The men who drive the Formula 1 transporters must toe the line in every respect; it could hardly be otherwise for those responsible for taking £2 million of equipment back and forth across Europe.

When they finally arrive at the race track, the meticulous eye of Bernie Ecclestone, the FOCA supremo, demands that the trucks be parked inch-perfect in accordance with markings on the paddock surface. It is the equivalent of having the Cub Master check your finger nails for cleanliness.

In Ecclestone's ordered world, everything has its place, and that includes the two articulated transporters brought by each team, plus one from each leading engine manufacturer. The attitude seems to be: if we've got to have these things cluttering the place, then they must be in perfect formation.

By the Thursday morning of each Grand Prix weekend, you'll see the trucks parked side by side, backed up to the garages, each tractor unit and trailer immaculate. Toeing the line.

There are exceptions. At Monaco, the trucks have to be shoehorned either into the enclosure on the quayside or into a ridiculously tight multistorey car park in the back of beyond. At Spa-Francorchamps, the tapering paddock area means the last few transporters have to be parked without their tractor units attached.

It's untidy, but short of asking the Belgian authorities to shift the public roads bordering the paddock, there is no alternative – although some would say, half joking, half serious, it has probably crossed Ecclestone's mind to have a word with the Minister responsible for such matters.

In 1993, the Jordan team had drawn the short straw – or parking space, if you wish. In fact, it was their own fault. Garages are allocated, not on a first come, first served basis, but as a kind of league table. The most successful teams are usually at one end; the lesser lights at the other. With no points on the board, Sasol Jordan definitely belonged to the latter. The tractor units would have to be parked elsewhere. In a perfect line, of course.

Painting the floor grey

The two transporters edged their way into the paddock on Tuesday afternoon, a full five days before the race was due to start. Practice would not commence until 9.30 on Friday morning but, even so, there was much to be done in preparation for the arrival of the mechanics on Thursday.

As Rick Wiltshire and Gerard O'Reilly backed one truck into place, the sister vehicle was ready to follow suit in the hands of Ian Webb and Micky Miller. Given the close proximity of Belgium, the one-day trip from Silverstone had been comparatively brief, Wiltshire and his team usually allowing three days to reach far-flung venues such as Estoril in Portugal or Budapest in Hungary. But, wherever the location, the routine on arrival is always the same.

While two crew members wash the trucks, the other two apply Glasurit paint to the garage floor; the latter a recent innovation begun by McLaren and in line with the perceived need for Formula 1 to present a professional, polished image for the benefit of the sport in general and sponsors in particular. Once the light-grey gloss has dried, the team logo is sprayed on the thresholds of the front and rear doors. This is now officially Chez Sasol Jordan.

First, though, a spot more internal decoration. Gone are the days when the team simply threw open the garage doors, rolled out the cars, unloaded the red tool boxes, plugged in the kettle and called the place home. Corporate image is the thing and it is now necessary for the teams to screen off the breeze block walls and wire-mesh partitions with smart pvc backdrops which, handily enough, carry the sponsors' names.

This is not the work of a moment and it will take one man the best part of Wednesday morning to make the banners fit the space available without chopping off a sponsor's name or creating a blockage in the garage itself.

Meanwhile, another two crew members are working on the pieces of kit which require assembly, such as the tubular stand (with sun shade and, naturally, sponsors' names) used by the team management when operating at the pit wall. Then the so-called 'rolling items' are wheeled out of the trucks, the foremost being the three cars. These are followed by the Lista units which hold tools and equipment.

At first glance, these white cabinets seem part and parcel of the transporter, lining the floor along its length like large kitchen units. But, once unbolted, the chests of drawers can be wheeled easily into place in the garage, thus continuing to encourage the impression of efficiency while ultimately saving the mechanics the job of dashing back and forth to the truck for each item required during the course of the weekend. And, as an indication of attention to detail, 6 in high royal blue 'skirts' are hung around the bottom of each unit, the better to hide the wheels and add to the general stamp of tidiness.

Gone are the days of air and power lines snaking in dangerously haphazard fashion across the floor, supplies now coming from overhead, one set hanging between each car.

It is Rick Wiltshire's job to wire into the mains box in the corner of the garage and find a means of hanging the cables from the ceiling, a task which is easier said than done at somewhere like Imola where the pre-cast concrete roof, devoid of girders and ducting, requires an industrial gun to penetrate it with the necessary 'temporary' hooks. Power must also be supplied for the computers, which will be based on the engineers' tables set up at the back of the garage, and for the fabricator and the damper specialist. And the cable which will connect to the Olivetti/TAG-Heuer timing monitors must also be located.

By Thursday, the garage should be fully operational, Wiltshire and his crew carrying out final chores such as filling the fuel bowsers with Sasol and erecting a small tent to hold churns and other refuelling paraphernalia. Wheel rims will have been taken to Goodyear in preparation for fitting, and attention will turn to the trucks themselves, the cab windows receiving a polish (frequently the tap water available in the paddock is too dirty for such a job – although Spa, appropriately enough given the area's name, is a notable exception), the inside of the denuded transporters receiving a sweep out and clean.

'Then,' observes Wiltshire, 'we just wait for the mechanics to turn up and make a mess.'

He says it with a grin. Some truck crews possess neither his sense of humour nor such a respect for their colleagues. Indeed, it has been known for truck drivers to consider themselves a race apart; a cut above the 'bolties' with their spanners and grease. Some have even gone so far as to eat and drink alone, thus creating unnecessary tension in a tight community stretched at times to the limit of personal tolerance.

That is not the case at Sasol Jordan, the truck crews counting themselves as part of a compact fighting unit, everyone appreciating the *esprit de corps* which comes with mutual esteem. And they have a single goal this weekend; to open the championship score.

Frightened witless

There could be no better place to do it than Spa-Francorchamps. After the artificial constraints of Hungary, coming to this majestic place is, to quote the memorable line, like going from the ridiculous to the sublime.

Spa-Francorchamps is roughly triangular; a combination of broad, sweeping public roads on two sides linked by a magnificent purpose-built section utilizing the stunning topography of the Hautes Fanges region.

The pine trees, apart from bringing a sense of maturity which goes with the rich history of the circuit, act as an echo chamber, trapping and holding the sound of racing engines on full noise. It may seem an odd combination;

lush, mature trees and a man-made cacophony. But, to the motor racing enthusiast, the sound is as sweet and exciting as any orchestra operating in harmonious accord.

For the drivers, too, this place represents a motorized mecca. The satisfaction which comes with a quick, clean lap at Spa has no equal anywhere else in the world. You can see it by the look in their eyes, the quickness of the breathing, the animated conversation. Here is a circuit where the driver can extend himself, ask questions about his skill and get some pretty basic answers. He's either elated or frightened witless.

There are no half-measures at Spa-Francorchamps; no fudging with technical excuses; no ego protection of the kind afforded by the shorter circuits where a couple of tenths of a second can separate the good from the mediocre.

Spa measures 4.3 miles; the stop watch is unambiguous: you are either quick or you're not.

Deficiencies in the car are multiplied by the effect they have on a driver's confidence. And you need plenty of confidence at Spa. Even the bravest of the brave find their right foot involuntarily pulling back as they rush down the steep hill at 185 mph towards Eau Rouge.

Here, a row of metal barriers lies across the line of vision, the track jinking left before swinging violently right and climbing a wall of tarmac. The instant compression on the suspension is such that the driver is forced into the floor of the car, momentarily powerless to do anything. If he hasn't turned into the climbing right-hander with pin-point accuracy, it's too bad. He will run wide and, after that, who knows?

At the top of the rise, the car momentarily becomes light and skittish. Again, the driver is briefly a mere passenger before flicking the car into the left-hand curve which follows and the uphill climb beyond. Get all of this right and the surge of adrenalin lasts for the rest of the lap. Get it wrong and . . . well, the run-off area, where it exists, is merely cosmetic. So don't get it wrong.

The first practice session was 15 minutes old when Alessandro Zanardi got it wrong. The Lotus went out of control, pin-balling into the barrier on either side of the track, wheels, suspension and bodywork flung in all directions. Thankfully, the chassis remained intact and Zanardi was not seriously injured. But pictures later showed the first head-on impact had been severe enough to have his crash helmet hit the steering wheel. Normally, the driver should just be able to nod his head, forward movement rendered impossible by the six-point harness pinning his torso to the seat. The forces involved in this instance had been violent enough to stretch the shoulder belts by more than a foot. The stout metal crash barrier had actually been torn like soft plastic. He had been very lucky – even if the driving error was to do as much damage to his reputation as it did to the car. Zanardi did not race again for the rest of the season.

The severity of the accident was a reminder of the perils of Eau Rouge.

Drivers were generally appalled by the crash – but that did not seem to diminish the satisfaction of getting the corner right later in the day. Indeed, it may have subconsciously heightened the pleasure.

Best lap of my life

Certainly, Rubens Barrichello had a spring in his step at lunchtime on Friday; ninth fastest at Spa does wonders for a young driver's ego and he looked forward to first qualifying with relish.

The mechanics carried out their routine work, added to which was a change to a shorter top gear, the better to give more revs out of Eau Rouge. And, mused Brian Hart, make better use of his latest development engine.

According to Hart's computer, the V10 would be on full throttle for 13.5 seconds on the breathless climb from Eau Rouge to Les Combes. Similarly, on the return leg from Stavelot to the absurdly tight Bus Stop chicane, the engine would be at full chat for 20 seconds – assuming the driver kept his foot flat to the floor through the very fast left-hander at Blanchimont.

But the traces on the computer screen later showed that both Barrichello and Boutsen were lifting through there, the handling of the Jordan still on too much of a knife-edge. Neither driver had total confidence in the car and that was raised at the post-qualifying debriefing as a subdued Barrichello discussed his disappointing 14th place.

In return, it was pointed out that Rubens was perhaps not making best use of his second set of tyres, his inexperience failing to exploit the rubber when it was at its very best. This slightly strained exchange of views was the tip of the tensions beginning to surface as the end of the season appeared on the horizon. And still no points on the board.

Twenty-four hours later and all of that was momentarily forgotten. Barrichello positively glowed.

'I think that was one of the best laps of my life,' he beamed. 'After doing a 1m 53.2s yesterday, I thought maybe a 1m 52.0 was possible today. So, to do a 51.7 was unbelievable for me. It was just like I was setting a record through each corner!'

It was immaterial that his excellent effort had merely moved him one place further up the grid, every driver having improved in the warm conditions. At any other circuit, there would have been mild disappointment with the marginal improvement in grid position. At Spa, personal satisfaction is everything; Barrichello knew he could not have gone any faster and that was good enough.

Boutsen, meanwhile, was 20th; a desperately disappointing performance on his home circuit, the one place where he should have been a match for Barrichello's youthful vigour. He spoke quietly of feeling ill at ease in this car; talked once again about not feeling comfortable in the cockpit. In fact, he claimed at a press conference, the cockpit had never fitted him and he just could not drive the car as a result.

This was duly noted and printed in an official hand-out. The press release was shown by Ken Ryan, an Irish journalist, to a member of the Jordan team. The Jordan man was asked to comment.

'Bullshit,' he muttered quietly.

Speculation that this would be Boutsen's last Grand Prix quickly gathered momentum.

Moveable beast

Such matters were of passing concern to the truck crews. With practice now finished, the gradual reloading process could begin. Throughout the two days, they had taken care of tyres and fuel while always keeping the garage tidy, replenishing stocks of consumables such as aerosol sprays and paper rolls, and checking that batteries were always charged and the radios fully operational. But, once the mechanics begin to finish the pre-race preparations, items such as engine and gearbox trolleys can be cleaned and placed in one of the several under-chassis lockers in each truck.

At first glance, the two trailers seem identical. Bought second-hand from McLaren at the end of 1991 (at a total cost of £200,000), they are of differing specifications, largely because one is double-deck and the other single. The three race cars are carried in the former, the second truck filled entirely with most of the vast range of equipment necessary to do the job properly – and put on the necessary show.

The double-decker has full-length upper and lower wheel lockers, 11 Lista units, a workshop facility with a lathe, welder and grinder, full lighting and electric sockets powered by a 26 KVA generator (or a landline, if available) and hydrovane air compressor.

The second trailer is much the same except, with the higher floor, the under-chassis lockers run the full breadth with access from either side. In place of the workshop is the double-fridge stretching from floor to ceiling.

The layout of each trailer has been designed with a Formula 1 team in mind although, given a clean sheet of paper, Wiltshire and his mates would have done it slightly differently to suit their particular needs. And, besides, the impression is that the condition of the trailers was not all it might have been considering McLaren's reputation for excellence. One of the generators, for example, appeared to have received the minimum of maintenance and Jordan had payed the price in every sense.

Bearing up badly

By Sunday morning, the winding down gathers new momentum as soon as the warm-up has finished and final race preparations are completed. Drain trays, measures, oil and sundry items no longer required are gathered together, although loading is tempered by the thought that it is easier and more efficient to do most of the packing in one hit as soon as the race is finished.

Before that, however, while the mechanics and team management are engrossed in the race, the tyre men (who do not play a part in the pit-stop strategy) start to disassemble the temporary fixtures in the garage. This is done during the race because, once it is over, the tyre men are kept busy for at least an hour as they trundle trolley loads of tyres to Goodyear to have them stripped from their rims.

Rick Wiltshire, meanwhile, will be pumping any remaining fuel from the cars, once they have returned, the mechanics helping with the general gathering together of equipment. That, at least, is the theory, assuming both cars run the full distance.

At Spa-Francorchamps, the packing up process began early; good news for the truck crews in one respect but a bad sign for the team as a whole.

Boutsen raced all of half a mile before the car stopped.

'He melted the clutch on the uphill start,' noted Anderson. 'Inexperience, I suppose ...' Barrichello was holding 11th place when a wheelbearing failed. No one needed reminding that this was the third such failure.

The news did not go down well in the Jordan motor home. The pressure, building gently during the past six weeks, suddenly began to reach dangerous proportions. It is one thing to suffer an unexpected failure, have a driver make a mistake. Quite another to experience a fundamental problem for the third time. Questions were being asked and the answers were not immediately forthcoming.

(After Hungary, the rear uprights had been removed from Boutsen's car. They ran without any trouble for the equivalent of one and a half race distances during a test at Silverstone. Subsequent inspection revealed them to be perfect. Anderson thought, with justification, that the problem had been solved.)

Meanwhile, the area around the transporters was littered with blue tarpaulins and covers as the equipment was wrapped and packed. The two ERF tractor units had been backed into position – uniformity and straight lines didn't matter a damn now.

At 5.45 pm, the blue Jordan trucks were among the first to edge out of the paddock, gently weaving their way to the bottom gate at Eau Rouge before turning against the direction of what had been the race track a few hours before, the 12-speed semi-automatic gearbox helping the 4.2 litre Perkins engine haul 31 tons up the hill towards the village of Francorchamps.

By midnight they were parked outside the Novotel at Lille; by Monday afternoon, the unloading had begun back at the factory – ready for the process to start all over again almost immediately.

Twelve down; four to go. And still no points on the board.

Chapter 24

The Boy From Bologna

A gem of a job

Eddie Jordan is whispering out of the side of his mouth.

'People keep saying "Marco who ... ?" Well, fine. That's exactly what I want. The boy is quick, *quick*! He did a gem of a job in the car last Monday; I'm telling you, a *gem* of a job. This team needs some excitement. If you want my honest opinion, we didn't get much with Ivan Capelli and Thierry Boutsen.'

On the far side of the departure lounge at Heathrow, the choice of Marco Apicella as a replacement for Thierry Boutsen is being discussed by the *cognoscenti*.

'Eddie only chose Apicella because of the money,' said one. 'He's never won a Formula 3000 race; he's got no real track record. It's all about the dollars he can bring. That sums up Jordan at the moment. The year's a write-off, the team is short of money and Eddie's making what he can out of it.'

Jordan could read their thoughts.

'They can say what they like,' he muttered. 'We're actually in good shape financially; all our debts – well, most of them anyway – have been paid. I've no particular worries there. No, I've been watching Marco for some time. He's been quick in the Japanese F3000 series. He led at Sugo recently until the engine cover came off; I think these people are in for a bit of a surprise. I think *Rubens* is in for a surprise.

'Kenny Acheson (a personable Irish racing driver without the good luck to match his talent) knows him and has raced against him. As soon as he heard I'd signed Marco for Monza, Kenny went to the trouble of ringing me to say it's the right choice; Marco's good. Kenny was very enthusiastic about it. You wait.'

The news that Thierry Boutsen had retired barely caused a ripple. If his performance at Spa-Francorchamps had disappointed the team, it had frustrated the gracious Belgian more than he cared to admit. Spa was his home circuit, the place where he had made his Formula 1 debut 10 years before. He knew it well and loved racing there – providing the car was equal to the challenge.

In Boutsen's view, the Jordan was no match for such a serious test of a driver's commitment. It was too nervous; did not inspire confidence. And, if he could not do anything with it at Spa, then there was no point in continuing. (Gary Anderson's response to this broad statement is unprintable.) On the following Tuesday, Thierry had rung Jordan and asked to be released from his contract. The parting was entirely amicable.

It was Capelli all over again; a talented driver caught on the rack of self-doubt by a car which required the sort of bold resolution endemic in a 21-year-old with nothing to lose – just like Boutsen had been in his early days. Since then, he had experienced the comfort which comes with a good car. This was not the time to go back to risking everything, just as he had done with Ligier the previous year when struggling to move from 19th to 15th on the grid. What made it worse was that he was now trying to go from 24th to 19th. It didn't make sense; it was time to quit – for everyone's sake.

Made to measure

Jordan Grand Prix was immediately thrown into overdrive just as they were preparing for another busy race, the Italian sponsors due to come in force to their home Grand Prix.

The day after Boutsen's phone call, Ian Phillips had gone to Gatwick to collect his wife and children after a six week holiday for the family at the home of relatives in the USA. They were reunited for no more than a couple of hours, the first task for Merleen Phillips being the transportation of her husband along the M25 to catch a flight to Japan from Heathrow.

The irony was that Phillips had been bored out of his head in Hungary but things had picked up in Belgium. There had been discussions with Keke Rosberg about the possibility of his driver, J. J. Lehto, joining Jordan for 1994; there had been similar talks with the young Portuguese driver, Pedro Lamy, and the Scotsman, David Coulthard. And a long conversation with Johnny Herbert, currently with Lotus. Herbert had wanted $1 million for his services in 1994; the feeling was that he was quick but disorganized – and just about worth that fee for two years. But Herbert was well liked and knew Jordan well; at that point he was a strong candidate as negotiations for 1994 gathered strength.

Phillips thrived on the wheeling and dealing; loved every minute of the banter and heavy discussion. Things were hotting up and now he was off to Japan. For lunch!

The primary purpose of the trip was to oversee a promotion for Globalot in connection with the Jordan Grand Prix Supporters' Club, an association launched by Jordan in 1993 to provide a focus for the team's followers world-wide. Initially, it had seemed like a nice gesture; a fair amount of public relations work for the benefit of a few. But the team had been overwhelmed by the response, particularly in Japan, where Grand Prix racing is a major leisure interest.

According to Jordan, the fans were on to a good deal here, membership of the club costing $145, for which they would receive team paraphernalia, plus a free Globalot lottery ticket with a face value of $100. When Eddie Jordan spoke about the offer while wearing his sheepskin coat, Arthur Daley somehow sprang to mind. But it was genuine enough and, at the end of the day, there was always the chance that the Globalot ticket could bring the owner $1 million. Jordan himself could have done with a bit of that.

For the time being, however, Eddie was exercised by the need to find a replacement driver. Phillips was also charged with tracking down Eddie Irvine, yet another Irish driver, but one with a huge talent to match his self-confidence. Irvine was also racing in the Japanese F3000 championship, a lucrative series for young drivers on the way up.

Faxes flew to and fro between England and Japan but it soon became clear that Irvine was committed to an important test session just at the time when he would need to be in Italy, preparing for Monza. Besides, he had no sponsors interested in the Italian Grand Prix and, even though he was earning comfortably from his racing, he was not about to invest any of his personal funds in a one-off drive. His time would come in a major way two months later.

Jordan reviewed his short-list. It had two other names – Emanuele Naspetti and Marco Apicella – both of whom were, conveniently enough, Italian. As test driver, Naspetti appeared to be the logical choice but the deal with his sponsors did not go beyond testing. He – or, rather, the sponsors – was given the chance of taking Boutsen's place for the remaining races but nothing came of it, Naspetti surprising his backers and the team by turning down the offer.

Apicella jumped at the chance. At the age of 27, with a mediocre career in karts and single-seaters behind him, he might never get such an opportunity again. The team arranged to stop at Imola en route to Monza and give Apicella a test. Since he lived in Bologna and knew the circuit well, this was ideal. But, for the team, time was running out.

Apicella drove the car on the Tuesday before Monza. He completed 50 laps; the times were impressive, so much so that Barrichello, also running at Imola, phoned Eddie Jordan to say so.

Eddie smiled; this was turning out better than he had hoped. Not only was the lad quick but he was also giving Rubens something to think about for the first time this season.

John Walton, the team manager, had to finalize the deal as faxes and phone calls crammed the lines between Imola and Silverstone. The contract was signed at 2.50 pm on the Tuesday. There were 10 minutes remaining before the deadline with the Contracts Recognition Board in Lausanne. The fax went through to Switzerland with minutes to spare.

Then a call to Bruno Vaglienti at Sparco for another set of Sasol Jordan overalls. 'Who is it this time?' he joked. 'Ready in two days? That's easy. With Schumacher, I had just 24 hours.'

Whereas Schumacher had the lean but muscular build of the model racing driver, Apicella had the look of the man who had built Schumacher's car. Short, stocky and broad-shouldered, Marco had a cheeky round face with a crew cut on top. Doc Martins and a bag of spanners would not have been out of place. Instead, he had flame-proof driving boots, a crash helmet – and access to $60,000. A fine man by any standards.

No one at Jordan knew precisely where the money had come from. All they knew was that it came. And that Marco Apicella was a pretty quick driver – certainly by the standards they had reluctantly become accustomed to. But before he could exercise that talent, there were certain formalities which had to be attended to.

What did you do today, Marco?

It had been a long week for John Walton. But he was accustomed to that. Having been Eddie Jordan's mechanic in Formula 3 in 1979 and then moved into Formula 1 with the now-defunct Theodore team, followed by Toleman and Benetton, 'John Boy' knew all about the irregularities attached to motor sport, the sometimes extraordinary diversions along the way and the occasionally outlandish requests made in all innocence by Eddie Jordan.

To paraphrase the words of the distinguished sportswriter, Hugh McIlvanney, when discussing the pragmatic but sometimes insensitive demands of one particularly brilliant sports editor: 'It's as though he asks you to go to the corner shop to get him something – and then he says "Oh, and by the way, on your way back would you rob a bank?"'

Fortunately, Walton could take it. An easy-going Dubliner with a soft lilt and a twinkle in the eye, 'John Boy' knew the ways of his boss better than anyone. They spoke the same language in every sense.

The past few days had been typical; Walton finding himself in the role of team manager, mediator and negotiator. First, the diversion to Imola, then the test, then the finalizing of the contract. Now, here at Monza, Apicella had to be taken through the necessary induction procedures on Thursday as the teams prepared themselves for the weekend ahead.

First, try on the overalls and check his crash helmet, making sure there were no problematic personal sponsorship decals which might clash with the official team backers. Then, dressed in his fighting gear, on to the official weigh-in, where Apicella's weight was recorded and added to the computer.

With the cars having to conform to a certain minimum weight, the easiest and quickest way to conduct random checks was to stop cars as they entered the pit lane during qualifying. Rather than have the driver struggle from the cockpit each time, the car was rolled on to the scales and weighed gross, the computer then deducting the driver's weight.

Another regulation stated that the driver had to be capable of evacuating the cockpit of a Grand Prix car in five seconds, a rule which had been introduced to ensure that the pragmatism of the designers, in their quest for narrow, wind-cheating cars, did not allow the safety of the driver to be compromised in the event of fire or accident.

A FISA official duly presented himself, stop watch in hand, at the Jordan garage and solemnly watched as Apicella popped the seat harness buckle, threw his arms on to the top of the cockpit and wriggled free in the required time. No problem.

It was noticeable, too, that his lack of inches would not lead to problems of discomfort in the cockpit. If anything, he was too wide rather than too long.

Gathering the relevant paperwork together and checking it for the final time, Walton accompanied the new recruit to Race Control. Here, on the production of proof that he had competed and succeeded in the required number of races at international level, Apicella was granted the Superlicence necessary to proceed into Formula 1. In return, he had to pay the equivalent of 7,000 French Francs. Walton had made sure Apicella was in possession of his cheque-book; in all the excitement, drivers tend to overlook such mundane details.

Then a visit to Roland Bruynseraede, the race director and official starter, who welcomed the new boy to Formula 1 and gave a quiet but firm lecture on the standards that would be required of him on the race track. Apicella was familiar with most of the etiquette but, in Formula 1, any gaffes would be punished by the censure attached to fouling up in such a high profile arena.

On their return along the pit lane, Walton pointed out the position of the Penalty Box where Apicella would have to wait for 10 seconds if he had transgressed the law seriously enough to warrant a stop-go penalty during the race. Then a discussion with the team about the pit stop/tyre change routine, followed by a visit to the engineers to learn about the various ideas which were to be tried on the car during practice.

Hovering in the background, eyeing her watch, Louise Goodman was waiting to escort Apicella back to the motor home for a planned photocall and an interview with Murray Walker and BBC television. Then the Italian journalists wanted a word with the local man and, in between, Eddie Jordan would be keen to introduce Marco to Dr Dirk Mostert, Executive Director of Sasol Limited, and Russell Kennedy, a director on the board. There were also two technicians from Sasol Chemicals Europe, not to mention the host of Italian sponsors and their guests, babbling and smoking and making a major dent in the motor home coffee supply. Then there was local radio to take care of. And, no, you can't have any more passes, but don't forget to be here early because the traffic is horrendous on a Friday morning and, by the way, you will probably be required to attend an official press conference on Saturday afternoon, which reminds me, I must check that doesn't clash with any sponsor appearances we need you to make. Here's the list of what you will be doing and the people you will be meeting throughout the weekend and, no, we still don't have any more passes . . .

At about 7.30 pm, if he was lucky, Apicella might get the opportunity to call his Mum and his girlfriend Barbara to tell them how he was getting on.

'Must have been nice, today, dearie. Nothing to do but sit around and talk to your friends while waiting for everything to get going tomorrow. So exciting, eh?'

'Yes, Mum.'

Chapter 25

It Couldn't be Worse

Here's one I made earlier

Drivers had been the last thing on Gary Anderson's mind. For a man of his principles and dedication, the third wheelbearing failure had been like a knife through the heart. The need to find a fast and lasting cure had seen the Jordan technical department at full stretch, August Bank Holiday having been lost to the cause of revisions to the rear suspension.

The answer had been to abandon a ball type of bearing, introduced for 1993 in the interests of producing less drag than the tapered wheelbearings used previously. The ball bearing idea had been perfectly sound but the reality was that the need to have the wheel nuts – comparatively speaking – slightly less than 101 per cent tight (in the interests of a swift removal at tyre changes) meant that movement under load had allowed the ball bearing to overheat and break up. The tapered wheel bearing was not so critical in this area.

Nothing in motor racing is ever simple, not even a seemingly straightforward cure such as this. Because of the change, the uprights containing the bearing had to be returned to the 1992 specification – but these did not have pick-up points to suit the suspension geometry for the 1993 car.

The knock-on effect of one seemingly uncomplicated piece of remedial work lasted throughout the 12 days between the last race and the start of practice for the Italian Grand Prix. And, by the way, we've changed drivers again.

A pain in the grass

It was a bad start for Marco Apicella. Rain, lots of it, on Friday morning meant it was difficult to establish a base line of knowledge with the car at this circuit. For a while, he remained in the garage, sitting quietly in the car.

Photographers, anxious to add the new face to their stocks, gathered round the front of the Jordan. But they didn't crowd Apicella, and neither did they crowd each other, the lensmen operating silently by a sixth sense which told them exactly where their colleagues stood. And, throughout the impromptu photo shoot, the mechanics moved around the car as if the photographers did not exist.

Alongside, there was more intense industry as Barrichello sat there, concerned that the traction control had been switching on and off at random. The search for a cure continued through the break between free practice and qualifying, the team changing the electrics in the hope that the faulty component would be removed somewhere in the process.

Their efforts were in vain. As soon as Barrichello took to the track for his first lap of qualifying, he knew the problem remained, the staccato burst from the Hart reducing the power to the wheels at the most awkward moments. A button fitted to the dash panel would allow him to bypass the problem – but that was simply an additional function to think about at a time when he needed to put everything into his driving at this high-speed track.

The first and second Lesmo, a very fast pair of right-handers at the top of the pistol-shaped circuit, tax both the driver and the handling of his car. At the second Lesmo, Barrichello lost control and spun on his seventh lap.

Qualifying having ended prematurely, Barrichello was clearly disgruntled as he returned to the garage, threw down his helmet and automatically donned his Arisco baseball cap. Walking straight over to the timing monitor, his frustration was not helped by having to call up the second page of times, allocated to the slowest half dozen cars. And there he was; 25th.

'What about Apicella?' he asked no one in particular.

'That's interesting,' said Brian Hart. 'Normally he wouldn't ask about Boutsen's time until practice had been over for an hour or so.'

In recent weeks, Barrichello had become slightly tetchy; nothing serious but he was not his familiar sunny, willing self. Anderson found him more difficult to deal with than usual and it began to dawn on the team that he had perhaps been influenced unduly by comments from Boutsen as the old campaigner's jaundiced views surfaced in the privacy of the motor home.

The feeling was that Rubens needed to open his mind and make his own judgements. Apicella's potential speed was the perfect kick up the backside. Barrichello was on his toes now, annoyed about the spin and anxious to know how Apicella had fared.

In fact, there was nothing to say about Marco. His practice had been an even bigger disaster, and a self-inflicted one at that. On just his third lap of qualifying, and before he had established a quick time, Apicella had spun off – also at Lesmo.

Having both his cars parked on the same piece of grass did little for Eddie Jordan's humour. This was playing into the hands of critics who doubted his judgement of drivers. And having both cars at the bottom of the list of qualifiers was doing nothing for the team's reputation as the calendar wore relentlessly on. The tension within the garage was worse than it had ever been.

Actually, your car's not brilliant

Twenty four hours later, there had been little respite. Barrichello was 19th on the grid; Apicella, 23rd. It had been decided to switch Barrichello to the spare car for the day and, during free practice, when he was a more respectable 13th overall, Rubens felt he was beginning to come to terms with the circuit.

Then, on his first lap of qualifying, the car had developed an electrical problem. Since he had waited for several minutes while the track dried from an earlier shower, and by the time the trouble had been located and dealt with, there were only 10 minutes remaining.

He managed a time and, on the following lap (which, as always when a driver is relating a hard-luck tale, was potentially quicker), the engine in Lehto's Sauber blew up and covered Barrichello in hot oil.

Apicella's report after a trouble-free day might have said: 'Steady progress for a new boy; shows promise.' But of greater interest to the team were his comments about the car.

Apicella was quite categoric; the Jordan was nervous and did not seem to have enough rear downforce. The wheelbase, in his opinion, was too short.

'Huh!' snorted one of the engineers. 'Would you mind telling that to Gary?'

It was said with a smile. Sort of. The barbed note summed up the pressure the technical team had been under. Gary Anderson was not impervious to the criticism and Apicella's precise description of the car's behaviour was echoing up what Ivan Capelli and Thierry Boutsen had been saying all along. Indeed, plans were already at hand to increase the wheelbase, something which Anderson insists would have been tried and tested the previous March had finance permitted. Other team members refute that, saying they had suggested a long wheelbase some time before, but the idea had been rejected by Anderson. Either way, from this unexpected source would come the final confirmation which would eventually go some way towards changing the team's fortunes.

In the meantime, the Italian sponsors would be out in force, expecting a good result, not in a year's time or one month hence. But today, in the 1993 *Gran Premio D'Italia.*

Dropping in

Louise Goodman had made practical use of the scooter on loan to the team. It had been perfect for a swift reconnoitre on Saturday, Louise weaving her way through the noisy crowd drifting aimlessly outside the paddock. The purpose was to find the quickest and most accessible route to and from the Fiamm enclosure in anticipation of a visit by the drivers on Sunday morning. It was a necessary measure, the Italian fans being capable of mobbing a driver with amiable intent should he happen to get lost in their midst.

Louise was fortunate in that neither of her drivers were particularly well known; Barrichello having been able to ride, unnoticed, through the crowd the previous day. But both men, resplendent in their driving suits on race morning, might be a different matter. She could be had up for inciting a riot.

The expedition proper worked perfectly. Which was just as well since this was the first call on a whistle-stop tour. Exactly on target, the mini-cavalcade of scooters buzzed back into the paddock and headed for the next port of call, a room above the pits.

Inside, lunch for Italtabacchi guests was under way in glorious, rowdy fashion; pasta and china and silverware and glass and *vino* clattering and clinking in tune with the babble of conversation. The drivers, led by Louise and followed by Eddie Jordan, moved quickly up the stairs and made their entrance. Immediate and enthusiastic applause at first sight of the blue-green driving suits.

After a formal introduction in Italian by the man from Italtabacchi, Eddie Jordan stepped forward and spoke briefly about the rainy weather and how it reminded him of Ireland and since it bothered no one there it would be no trouble here because, despite the poor practice performances, hopes were high for at least a couple of places in the top ten and he hoped it would add to their enjoyment of the day and now here's Rubens to say a few words.

Barrichello spoke hesitantly in Italian and received great approval for his efforts, Apicella then adding the final touch by using his native tongue to communicate with great confidence and, judging by the smiles and laughter, subtle humour.

Then the family snap shots, guests moving forward, coyly at first, to have their pictures taken with the drivers. The babble gradually returned to its former level.

That's it. Goodbye everyone. Great to see you here; on behalf of everybody at Sasol Jordan, we hope you enjoy your day.

Seven minutes after scaling the stairs, the visitors are on the way down again and off to spend some time with the Sasol guests at the motor home. On the way, they bump into a similar party from Lotus, about to do their turn in an adjoining room on the first floor.

Immediately below the marble floor and the tables with the stiff white linen, the mood is totally different. There is a silence you could cut with a blunt knife in the Jordan transporter as rolls and tea are consumed with little enthusiasm.

The warm-up, a couple of hours earlier, had brought no respite from the misfortune of this miserable weekend. If the sponsors upstairs could have witnessed the scene, the guests' mood of anticipation would have been less pronounced. But not by much. This was Monza, the theatre of motor racing. There was always a good show here; something to talk about.

Indeed there would be. Unfortunately, the first act would also be the finale. As far as the Jordan team was concerned, the Italian Grand Prix would last no more than 30 seconds.

Knew that would happen

Marco Apicella knew all about the perils of the first corner at Monza. The original design of the circuit had allowed for a flat-out blind past the pits and into the very fast Curva Grande. Considered to be an unnecessary hazard with the advent of increased performance from the cars, the Monza authorities had reduced the potential danger of the corner by installing a tight chicane just before it.

The chicane achieved its aim but, paradoxically, the innovation also set the scene for unavoidable chaos each year as the field, bunched and accelerating hard from the wide starting grid, attempted to filter through the bottle-neck. Asking a driver to treat the approach to the chicane with circumspection while, at the same time, urging him to make the most of the start, was like telling a prop forward at Twickenham to keep his shorts looking nice for the second half.

Nonetheless, Apicella wanted to finish this race at all costs. As the field rushed headlong into the funnel, he backed off early. And, just as he did so, another car came from nowhere and thumped his right-front wheel. The Jordan spun, Apicella kept the engine running, but the damage had been done. He was out of the race.

As Apicella took his bearings, he noticed other cars abandoned in various states of disrepair. Among them was Barrichello's Jordan, the victim of an attack from behind by Philippe Alliot. There seemed no point in Marco telling Rubens that this sort of thing happened every time at Monza.

Sasol Jordan Hart had suffered major disappointments before but this was the last straw; the Italian Grand Prix had been a disaster from start to its premature finish.

And now there were just three races left. There was no need to talk about the absence of points any more. The big zero was burned into the team's collective conscience.

Chapter 26

Climbing Out of the Mire

Impossible odds

Gary Anderson had just about had enough. He sat outside the motor home, a big man slumped in a plastic chair. His demeanour, absently cradling a glass of beer and staring across the Estoril paddock, summed up the frustration burning within him.

It takes a lot to get the Ulster psyche into rage mode but, once there, the eruption is seismic and barely under control. Anderson is typical of the breed; reserved but amiable; shy but forceful; agreeable but bloody-minded when necessary.

Right now, he was not feeling agreeable to anything, particularly the hyperbole of his boss as Eddie Jordan smooth-talked some minor dignitary in the opposite corner. Not long before, Jordan had returned from a rambling and sometimes chaotic four-hour meeting with the heads of other teams. Jordan complained of having a 'massive headache'. He got little sympathy from the man whose headache had been running all season.

Anderson had been under enormous pressure and, with 13 races gone, he was entitled to crack a little. Many would have bowed to ego and flounced out months before. The past couple of seasons had subjected him to every conceivable emotion: the thrill and freedom associated with designing his first complete Formula 1 car; the anxiety before Jordan's first F1 year; the accolades and the awards at the end of it; the abrupt anti-climax of 1992; the hopes for a fresh start in 1993 – and the spiralling disasters and despair ever since.

Anderson had never worked harder – and that was now being recognized as part of the problem. As technical director at Jordan Grand Prix, the buck stopped at his desk if the results were not forthcoming. Eddie would put everything in place and then articulate the team's hopes with an intoxicating eloquence; Gary had to make it happen. It was too much for one man to cope with in these circumstances.

Anderson headed a team of seven; a small number by the standards of McLaren and Williams. Mark Smith's main concern was the transmission while Andrew Green took care of the suspension: quietly brilliant men and close associates of Anderson when it came to discussion of Gary's concept of the car as a whole.

Paul White handled the wind tunnel testing using a model based on Anderson's scheme for the car; John McQuillian looked after the composite stressing and chassis lay-ups, and Robert Stubbings could turn his hand to most things in the drawing office. The hiring of Tim Wright in April had been supposed to alleviate the strain but it hadn't worked out that way.

'Tim was going to be the resident race engineer,' said Anderson. 'We had hoped he would have time in between the races to devote to analysing and checking the data and just sitting at the computer, fathoming out what's going on. But that hasn't been the case and it hasn't helped us go forward. I haven't got time because I have been drawing the 1994 chassis.

'Mind you,' he goes on, 'it's been difficult for Tim because his driver has been changed every week. None of this has helped us in the situation we have been faced with this year. And Monza two weeks ago was probably the worst race meeting we've had in three years of Formula 1. Depression, which has been setting into the company for a while, finally arrived in a big way.'

Eddie Jordan, alert to the plummeting morale and the urgent need to turn things around, called a meeting on the Monday following Monza. It was a head-to-head in which no feelings were spared, emotions ran high – and the air was cleared.

It was agreed that a new chief designer should be brought in, allowing Gary Anderson to concentrate on engineering, a side he knew and liked best. He was relieved, and accepted the suggestion with equanimity. But, knowing Formula 1 as he did, Anderson was aware that others might not see it that way. He was once chief designer – and now he isn't. He had failed.

In fact, he had succeeded where others would have collapsed in a heap. His engineering team stood by him; the mechanics were loyal to a man. In other more lofty operations in the Formula 1 paddock, the range of failure endured by Jordan would have resulted in a coup at best and a football manager-type sacking at worst. Now, the problems facing Anderson had been acknowledged and the reorganization would benefit everyone.

In the meantime, this race without end was stopping for no one, least of all the team wallowing at the bottom of the league table.

The Portuguese Grand Prix would provide one last chance in Europe for Jordan to claim some points before the even more difficult task of tackling the final two races in Japan and Australia. It was simply another turn of the screw as a punishing season rushed towards its close.

'Yeah, I'm annoyed about the way things have turned out this year,' admitted Anderson. 'The package has great potential but we just haven't got a grasp of it. If we build a car that isn't reliable then the design team has to make it reliable and, while they're doing that, they can't be doing something else.

'We are a team that hasn't got a lot of money but we have adequate money to do a decent job and that decent job should have taken us into a top 10 qualifying position and a top six finish. Or, at least knocking on the door.

'But, while you are sorting out the problems we have had, you're not going forwards at a time when other teams are. It then seems that you are actually going backwards. So, I'm pissed about that. I know what people are thinking. And I don't care. But this doesn't reflect well on anybody.'

Then a pause.

'Anyway,' he said, draining his glass and brightening considerably, 'the wind tunnel model for the 1994 car is looking very good. Next year just can't be as bad as this. And we've got to see what the latest modifications do to the car in this race. After all, we've got another new driver! Got to keep looking on the bright side, y'know ... '

And, with that, he got up and walked off at a brisk pace, back to the familiar routine; back to his old self.

A few inches more

In the midst of the discussion post-Monza, a decision had been taken to lengthen the wheelbase of the car. It was a major alteration, not so much in physical terms when it came to adapting the car, but in the psychological warfare of the paddock; it said, in public 'I might have got this wrong originally.' Not that the team cared at this stage; with nothing to show for a season's work, anything was worth trying.

Anderson had taken care to warn everyone that there might not be a dramatic improvement in lap times during qualifying. The principal objective was to make the car kinder to the rear tyres in the races, thus doing away with the need for a pit stop. It would give Jordan the opportunity to make ground at the expense of those mid-field teams which had been forced to stop.

A quick glance at the starting grid for the Portuguese Grand Prix backed up Anderson's theory; the Jordans were 15th and 23rd. Not a lot appeared to have changed.

The drivers, on the other hand, were much happier, and had been from the moment the long wheelbase had first been tried during a test at Silverstone. The modifications had been made to the spare car. Barrichello had gone back to Brazil and the test work had been carried out by Emanuele Naspetti; not a particularly satisfactory state of affairs since they needed the regular driver to make the necessary comparison. Nonetheless, Naspetti had lapped within three-tenths of a second of Jordan's previous best on the Silverstone South Circuit – and this was with the car configured and prepared for Estoril. The signs were encouraging.

Barrichello backed that up as soon as he drove the car during first practice in Portugal. With Apicella committed to racing in Japan, Naspetti had been drafted into the team and the long wheel base was added to his car in time for the second day's practice. With a direct comparison now available between the two days, he said the Jordan felt more stable; easier to drive. But now the team was starting from scratch in some ways, learning about the car all over again.

Wired to the moon

BBC television wanted to know how the car felt and Murray Walker was dispatched to talk to Barrichello. Louise Goodman was horrified as she watched Rubens chat happily, his overalls rolled down to his waist and not a single sponsor's name – bar that of his friends from Arisco showing prominently on his tee-shirt – visible to the camera. Short of playing the high-handed matron – which she most certainly was not – and stopping Murray in full flight, there was nothing Louise could do but stand on the sidelines and fume. It had been that sort of weekend. No one was immune.

The test session at Silverstone had run until 5 pm on the Sunday, which meant the transporters were late leaving for Portugal. The cross-channel booking was changed at the last minute to another route in order to accommodate the revised schedule, Rick Wiltshire and his team reaching Portsmouth at the eleventh hour, the two transporters being the last to board the boat. One of them had a puncture and the wheel had to be changed in Le Havre docks at 6.30 am the following morning. But there was worse to come.

The trucks reached Lisbon safely enough but then a bolt sheared and the suspension holding one of the rear air bags collapsed. With one transporter immobile by the side of the road, the other continued the 20 miles to Estoril. By the time repairs had been carried out by a local dealer, a whole day had been lost before the stricken truck eventually reached the circuit. This transporter had the cars on board and Naspetti was waiting anxiously to try his cockpit for size.

Naspetti had paid $50,000 for the privilege of racing and, in return, he asked for passes for his father and his girlfriend. Ian Phillips tactfully explained that passes were in short supply (which was true, as was the belief that a young driver can be easily distracted by the well-meaning influence of his close family), only to discover that Eddie Jordan had grandly said everything would be fine, everyone would be welcome to visit his team; passes would not be a problem.

'Eddie's on a different planet at the moment,' said Marie Jordan, with a weary smile. 'You just can't talk to him. Well, you can – but he won't hear you.'

Apart from sorting out the problems within his team, dealing with the fast-moving politics surrounding the regulations for 1994, negotiating to have Eddie Irvine drive in Japan and Australia while keeping this information from Naspetti and the Italian sponsors, Jordan had been involved in discussions which had him salivating at the mouth.

Just before the Italian Grand Prix, Jordan and Phillips had been asked to fly to France to talk to Peugeot about a possible engine deal for 1994. Peugeot, having carried all before them in international rallying and then won Le Mans in sports cars, were interested in turning to Formula 1 as an engine supplier.

A link with a major manufacturer such as this could be the making of Jordan Grand Prix and Eddie did not need to be asked twice.

The original plan had been for Peugeot to make a low-key entrance with a team such as Jordan or the French-based Larrousse operation. Jordan felt they could do a much better job but that argument had been shot to pieces when both cars crashed at the first corner at Monza and a Larrousse went on to finish sixth. Nonetheless, Eddie was like a little terrier; harrying, talking, thinking, persuading, snapping at the big giant's heels.

At one point, the rumour in the Estoril paddock said the deal with Jordan had been done. But, before the weekend was out, Jordan knew that Ron Dennis was making a serious pitch on behalf of McLaren – in which case, the goalposts had moved yet again and were almost out of sight.

'Bloody Ron,' said Eddie, his weary voice tinged with respect. 'McLaren and Peugeot. That'll work well.'

He sat for a moment or two without speaking, perched high in his little office at the front of the motor home. Then he pushed back the sliding door and called down the stairs.

'Henny! Would you bring me a coffee please. And if you see Ron Dennis, tell him ... tell him he owes me a drink ... '

Chapter 27

Upstairs, Downstairs

Fast food

Henny Collins was accustomed to cheeky comments from upstairs. Her kitchen was directly below the boss's tiny office. She was at the hub of the team's affairs, overseeing the tables outside and vetting visitors at the door before allowing them up the narrow staircase leading to the main body of the motor home. Henny and her partner, Chris Leese, did not let much pass them by in every sense.

It was the same in the other mobile headquarters, parked close by in three neat rows on the lower level of the Estoril paddock. The catering staff knew just as much about the sport's dirty washing as they did about washing up in the aftermath of a busy lunchtime session. Prudence and tact were the watchwords; discretion downstairs as important to the team management upstairs as culinary expertise.

The so-called motor homers need to be jacks of all trades and master of most. The running of the purpose-built coach alone requires a combination of driving, electrical, plumbing, mechanical, cleaning, packing and, at border posts as well as the race track, diplomatic skills.

In common with many teams, Jordan Grand Prix runs a Van Hool Astral, the Belgian-built bus costing £300,000, a sum which is considered to be money well-spent. The motor home provides a smoked-glass workplace with telephones and fax, as well as offering a padded, air-conditioned haven in the middle of a hot and sweaty race track. But, above all, it is private; a rare commodity in such a public arena.

Jordan chose to divide the upper deck into three. Eddie Jordan's office, next door to the shower/toilet, sits on the ledge above the kitchen. The central conference area, lined on either side by settees, leads to an office on top of the driver's cab at the far end. Massive storage space fills the gap downstairs between the front of the bus and the kitchen at the rear.

The motor home is 12 metres long and 4.1 metres high, Chris Leese using skills learned as motor home driver with Goodyear and two other teams to negotiate the highways and byways of Europe. Usually, he will aim to arrive at the circuit on the Monday before race weekend, the first task being the removal of dust and grime picked up between, in this instance, Milan and Lisbon.

Most motor homes have usually arrived by Tuesday and each team is allocated a predetermined space. Then starts the scramble for power since most paddocks have insufficient outlets to cope with the needs of motor homes equipped with kitchens and offices, most of which are at full stretch from morning to night.

The bus must first be levelled with the aid of jacks and wooden chocks; a difficult task since this is no family saloon. It takes two full days to unload, set-up an awning along one side of the bus and generally make ready to receive the team management, followed soon after by however many sponsors and guests have been invited for the weekend.

Henny Collins will not be given precise numbers until Louise Goodman arrives on Thursday. It makes planning difficult since some of the shopping will have already been done, certainly as much as possible before the paddock begins to fill with sundry vehicles, making access and unloading even more awkward than it already is.

Heavy and bulky items will have been picked up at supermarkets en route to the circuit on Monday, but a hire car for additional visits to the shops is not usually available until Wednesday, by which time Henny will have decided on the menu for the mechanics' meals and, say, the pudding choice for guests. Cooking will commence on the same day.

'I've done a hotel management course,' says Henny. 'But, really, qualifications are not necessary. The main thing is being able to cook in a bizarre manner ... '

Cupboard cuisine

Henny's kitchen measures six feet by five feet. Budding Delia Smiths would be appalled. They would also be highly impressed by the quality and the quantity of food emerging daily from this compact working environment with its small sink, eight-ring domestic gas hob, large electric oven, 24-volt fridge, and gas fridge and freezer.

The first official meals are served on the Wednesday, the truck drivers receiving a decent lunch in return for the sausage, bacon and other disposables brought from the UK. Motor home crews soon learn that there are certain items which are unmatched outside Britain. When in some far-flung field, custard powder, gravy mix, Branston pickle, Marmite, tea bags, brown sauce and baked beans no longer seem mundane and commonplace. The transporter crews often find themselves engaged in a mini-mercy dash of a most serious kind ...

'Each country presents a different problem,' says Chris Leese. 'Here in

Portugal, fruit and veg are not that good. And daft, simple things like eggs; they are never that fresh. When we go to Japan, you need to bear in mind that everything is much smaller in every sense; even the can capacity is less than we are accustomed to, so you have to buy more in order to cope.'

A shopping expedition can run up a bill of £500, although £300 would not be considered excessive for one of the daily excursions to the supermarket. Monaco, despite the logistical problems presented to the rest of the team, is a favourite with the motor home people since an excellent market close by the paddock provides fresh produce daily.

In any case, if a catering crew happens to be caught short at the height of a busy day, their colleagues are always willing to help out with the proverbial cup of sugar. Certainly, in the event of some disaster with, say, an awning being blown from its moorings, neighbours will down tools and run to assist. Nowhere in the Formula 1 paddock is the camaraderie stronger than among the motor home crews as they battle against sometimes ridiculous odds.

'That's part of the fun, part of the challenge,' says Henny. 'It's not what you would call a regular job by any means. The pressure is worse at the start of the season because you don't know what's going to happen; there are new sponsors and different guests and it's a case of feeling your way initially. You get up in the morning and you honestly don't know what to expect.'

The crews sleep on board for convenience and cost, the only advantage offered by a hotel room being the luxury of stretching out in a bath: 'And I must admit,' says Henny, 'by Sunday night, you really feel you could do with one.'

Bed crumbs

Race day starts at 6 am. Chris gets up first and uses the bathroom, Henny rising half an hour later to take her turn in the tiny room not much bigger than a decent-sized closet. The beds are packed away, the room returned to the workplaces familiar to the management.

'There are two things you miss,' says Chris, 'and that is not being able to leave your personal effects lying around, and not being able to leave the bed as it is until you feel like making it up.'

As Henny sets to work with the Hoover, Chris fires up the massive Australian gas barbecue positioned outside, but under cover of the awning at the back of the bus. As tea and coffee are prepared in the kitchen, the aroma of bacon and eggs wafts through the door, the mechanics appearing at 8 am for their full breakfasts.

Chris and Henny grab theirs just as the management move on to the tea and toast at around 8.45 am. Then it's quickly into the clearing up routine before beginning the preparation of 60 sandwiches for the mechanics' lunch, taken on the move in the garage.

Meat cookery for a more sedate lunch at the motor home will have been prepared the previous day. Attention will turn to the preparation of a buffet before the two drivers appear in search of a light meal of pasta a few hours before the start of the race, which is usually at 2 pm.

For the sponsors and their guests, the build-up to the Grand Prix will centre around lunch, which is usually hot and always of a remarkably high standard. In Portugal, Henny and Chris served 40 race day guests with garlic king prawns, salad, pasta melazane, chocolate gateau, followed by cheese board and coffee, the food laid out buffet-style on a long table propped against the outside of the motor home.

The clearing away is done as swiftly and as subtly as possible since, given the limited financial resources at Jordan, Chris is needed for pit duties at race time. He is responsible for wheeling a generator and tyres on to the grid, his job during any pit stops being the brief but important role of reaching into one of the car's radiator ducts and removing any debris.

Henny will have ventured into the pits to watch the start – the only action she will see throughout the weekend – before returning to the motor home to commence the dismantling and packing. Usually they will aim to leave the circuit that night, park in a layby, or find a good restaurant and allow someone else to do the hard work.

'Some days,' says Henny, 'you don't get a break at all. The job has a momentum of its own although the setting up and the putting away can get to you after a while. But I don't even think about the washing up; it's there and has to be done.

'If that sort of thing worries you,' agrees Chris, 'then you shouldn't be doing this job – because there can be a lot of clearing up. Sometimes, the best bit is falling into bed at the end of the day!

'But it's nice to have a bit of a break for a day or two in between the races, if the travel schedule allows it and you've taken care of the laundry and things like that. For me, the highlight of the day at the race track is usually breakfast, particularly if the mechanics are on good form, which they usually are.

'That's the rewarding thing about this job,' he goes on. 'It's feeling you are part of the team and contributing to the team effort.'

'Yes,' agrees Henny. 'The team has to overcome all sorts of problems and we are tested in various ways as well. You are expected to get on with it and have everything ready when required. But above all, when you're cooking regularly for 30 hungry men, you need a sense of humour ... '

Chris and Henny required a sunny disposition as race day in Portugal drew to a close. Naspetti had retired after nine laps when the car caught fire (a bung had fallen out of the engine, allowing oil to pump on to the hot exhaust pipes) and Barrichello finished 13th, any chance of a decent result having been ruined by a puncture and a slow lap back to the pits for fresh tyres.

Fourteen races down; two to go; and don't even mention the other thing ...

Removal of the digit

The deal to race Eddie Irvine in Japan and Australia was completed quickly enough to have the Irishman drive the car when the team stayed behind at Estoril for a few days immediately after the Grand Prix.

It was a useful if frustrating time for Gary Anderson as the car set competitive times, Barrichello going better than he had managed in the race.

The faster times were put down to more ideal track conditions but Anderson pointed out that other teams had not managed to go faster than they had during the race. The quick lap times by the Jordan were due to serious work by the team and backed up Gary's continuous claim that this was precisely what Jordan should have been doing all season. There was also the fact that Rubens had become better acquainted with a very tricky race track and the new long wheelbase configuration.

Cynics – of which there are many in Formula 1 – noted that his times appeared to come when he was chasing his rival, Christian Fittipaldi, who happened to be out at the same time, testing for Footwork. It was, they said, an indication of precisely what Rubens was capable of – but only when goaded into action. That being the case, he was about to receive a metaphorical kick up the backside in Japan as he came face to face with the precocious talent of Eddie Irvine.

Chapter 28

Land of the Rising Son

Here's Eddie

Grand Prix people have mixed feelings about Japan. They like it because this is the penultimate race of a long and arduous season. And they like it because the Japanese race is different.

The culture, the people, the race track itself, the warm atmosphere generated by the gentle but totally besotted race fans; all of these things combine to make the Japanese Grand Prix – interesting. But nothing more.

Come Sunday night and most people have had enough of the place. The minuscule bedrooms, the inedible food (by Western standards), the chaos generated by the narrow roads, the language problems, all exacerbated by jet-lag and end of season weariness. The flight out of Japan is often the best part.

Only an Irishman could confess to actually liking the place. That, at least, was the paddock joke this time round.

Eddie Irvine was not the sort to pull his punches. He enjoyed living there, he said. But when you are footloose and earning $800,000 per year – twice as much as many Grand Prix drivers – you can put up with a lot.

This was Irvine's third year in Japan. It had been a brave move to abandon the European racing scene but Irvine felt he had no choice. His racing career had come to a halt. He had no financial backing and very few decent results; there was nothing to suggest he was worth taking on board as a Grand Prix driver. His only asset was a self-belief which bordered on arrogance.

Such a thing could be dangerous if let loose among the delicate egos prevalent in Formula 1. It would be perfect if he ever became a Grand Prix star, of course. But novices were supposed to know their place; pay due respect.

Such theories did not take into account Edmund Irvine, native of Conlig,

County Down, Northern Ireland. A staunch protestant, to boot. And not afraid to speak his mind.

Filed for the future

Eddie Jordan had been thinking about Irvine for some time. But any discussions were usually terminated by Irvine's refusal to even contemplate bringing the sort of money Jordan was looking for. Besides, he had no desperate desire to get into Formula 1. Sure, if offered a McLaren or a Williams or anything decent – plus a reasonable fee – he would jump at the chance. Who wouldn't? But there was no urgency about rushing into a mediocre seat, spending good money to do it, and then thrash around at the back of the field, motoring nowhere in every sense.

But Suzuka. That would be different. It was one of the longest and trickiest circuits on the 1993 calendar. It was difficult to learn. And Irvine knew it well. Three years in Japanese F3000 had taught him all about Suzuka's vices; told him where time could be made up; where time could be lost. Such knowledge could be worth a second a lap; maybe more. Irvine knew that. So did Eddie Jordan.

These two had raced together in 1990, Irvine driving Jordan's F3000 car in Europe, winning the support race at the German Grand Prix. You would think some people in F1 might have taken notice. But that's not the way it works.

To divert the gaze of F1 team managers beyond the boundary of their insular world, an aspiring Grand Prix driver needs to be dominating his particular game; taking it by storm; creating headlines in *Autosport* and *Motoring News*; becoming the flavour of the month in F1 conversational circles.

Irvine wasn't doing that because the F3000 chassis Jordan had bought – a Reynard – was no match for the Lola in 1990. Irvine's win at Hockenheim, therefore, had plenty of merit. But very few inside F1 knew that. Jordan, meanwhile, filed it away for future reference.

Political divide

The second drive with Sasol Jordan was available for Japan. Jordan could have stuck with Apicella or Naspetti but he had a gut feeling that Irvine would be the perfect candidate. Besides, on the emotional front, it would be nice to have an Irish driver on board – even if he was an Ulster protestant.

That was a joke. Jordan had to make sure he said it was a joke. People might take it the wrong way.

Jordan, in fact, couldn't care less, the contorted politics of the troubled North being no more than a source of deep sadness for him as the province was ravaged by a minority pursuing death and destruction in the name of some romantic notion. Eddie Jordan is as romantic as anyone when it comes to talking about the Emerald Isle. But, in common with most, he draws the line at gratuitous violence.

Jordan believes in looking on the bright side; poking fun at any Ulsterman who crosses his path, the insults being returned in humorous kind.

And so it was when the deal was signed to have Irvine join the team for the last two races. Jordan immediately issued a press release, saying how good it felt to have an Irish team with an Irish driver. Almost by return, a serious student of Anglo/Irish affairs pointed out that Irvine was not Irish, but British.

Louise Goodman contacted the Home Office. Where, exactly, should she say Eddie Irvine was from? Was he British?

Not really. He was a citizen of the United Kingdom of Great Britain and Northern Ireland. That's what it said on the front of Irvine's passport. Strictly speaking, he was from the UK. He was, in fact, Northern Irish. Using the phrase 'Ulsterman' was not acceptable because it had political connotations; a throwback to the provincial divide – Ulster, Munster, Leinster and Connaught – which quartered Ireland in the days before Northern Ireland came into being.

'Don't care how you slice it,' murmured one journalist, struggling with the political complexities. 'He's an Irishman. And that's all there is to it as far as my paper is concerned.'

One of Boutsen's driving suits had been tailored for Irvine. To counter any problems, two national flags had been stitched to the pocket; the green, white and gold of the Republic of Ireland, and the Union Flag. By strategic positioning, Irvine could stick his left hand in his pocket and have his index finger cover the flag of the Republic. He enjoyed doing that in Jordan's company. It was in jest. Well, almost.

More serious was the discovery that a Cosmo badge had been omitted from his overalls. Cosmo, a Japanese company in the oil and petroleum business, supported Irvine in F3000. They were paying for his F1 outing and, in return, Irvine would carry their emblem, high up on his overalls. To avoid any conflict with Sasol, the emblem would have Japanese writing.

Then, on Thursday, Irvine discovered that he had forgotten to have the badge sewn in place. It was typical of his disorganization when it came to such matters. Worse still, there was to be a photocall in the pit lane that afternoon to coincide with the winners of a Globalot-Jordan Grand Prix draw receiving a nose cone and VIP tickets.

Both drivers, complete with overalls, turned up. But photographers were puzzled by the reluctance of the normally gregarious Irvine to have his picture taken. And why, they wondered, had he a penchant for keeping his right hand in the region of his breast pocket? With the index finger of his left hand paying allegiance to his Protestant heritage, Irvine made a curious picture in every sense.

Motivating force

'Ha!' said the cynic as he flicked through the news pages of *Autosport*.

'Fittipaldi's not coming to Japan. That's bad news for Jordan.'

This was on board the British Airways flight to Nagoya. It was Wednesday, the day before *Autosport* was due to be published, but Martyn Elford, a staff photographer, had brought some advance copies on board the 747-400. The resident scoffer, in common with the many racing people on board the flight to Japan, had seized a copy as soon as he was given the chance.

Fittipaldi, a thorn in Jordan's side, had been replaced (for financial reasons) by a no-hope Frenchman. It should have been welcome news, but that was not the way it was perceived from Jordan's point of view. Fittipaldi kept Barrichello honest. That Estoril test had proved to some that if Fittipaldi was quick, then so was Rubens. Local honour was at stake here. Or, at least, it had been until *Autosport* published this latest development.

But it would turn out to be grossly irrelevant. A far greater motivational force than Christian Fittipaldi was waiting, languidly, in Japan.

Suzuka

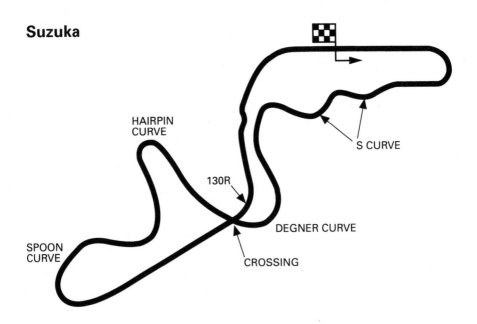

Chapter 29

Here we go, Here we go

Fifth fastest!

Eddie Irvine's influence on this weekend was felt immediately practice began. He was on the pace straightaway, comparing the Jordan 193 to other cars he had driven here. And the Jordan didn't shape up too well. Typically, Irvine was forthright when talking to Tim Wright on the radio.

'It's oversteering out of the second Degner (a medium-speed right-hander) and I've never had a car here that does that.'

This, of course, could have had much to do with the difference between a 450 bhp Formula 3000 car and a Formula 1 machine with in excess of 700 bhp.

They changed the rear dampers and talked about the front ride height. Then Irvine went out again. By the end of the session he was fifth.

A Jordan fifth! Unheard of. Irvine was totally unmoved.

'Look, I know how to lean on a car here,' he said to Wright as the Jordan rolled to a halt. 'I know what it should be doing because I've got the best car in F3000 at the minute. But this one is all over the place; it just doesn't handle.'

'Well, you're fifth,' said Wright.

'In that case,' said Irvine flatly, 'the rest must be bloody hopeless.'

In fact, Irvine was feeling the effect of having just 23 laps in a Formula 1 car compared to literally hundreds of laps spent testing at Suzuka in a Formula 3000 car. But it was good enough for the media, always in search of a decent story. As Irvine pulled off his balaclava and ran a hand through the shock of unruly hair, he was surrounded by a posse of journalists. The Jordan garage had not been graced with such a visitation since 1991. And this would be just the start of it.

Once free from his first serious meeting with the hacks, Irvine climbed on to a packing case at the back of the garage and filled out a questionnaire concerning the behaviour of the car at every corner. Fifth place in free practice was all very well; everyone knew it would be a different story when the chips were down during qualifying.

Nonetheless, the mood in the garage was definitely Up. The lads could sense something was going to happen.

Not satisfied

Irvine is in the car, ready to go. Qualifying has been under way for eight minutes.

'Can we go out?' he asks Wright.

'Wait a couple of minutes,' comes the reply.

Exactly two minutes pass.

'Think we should go,' says Irvine.

Five laps; 1m 42.046s.

There is little evidence of Irvine even breaking into a sweat. His voice is calm, without the laboured breathing normally associated with a quick lap.

'Not much grip,' he says. 'The car is sliding around a lot more.'

'The others seem to have picked up time,' notes Wright. 'Is there anything you want to do to the car?'

'Just leave it,' says Irvine. 'I'll have to try harder, that's all.' Then a pause. 'How many laps did I do there?'

'Five.'

'I got held up by Brundle. He never moved off line at all through three corners. Deliberately held me up. I don't think the track is going to get any quicker. Main thing is the traffic. Is there ever a lull?'

'Depends. It differs from circuit to circuit.'

'Then stick the fuel in, put on the fresh tyres – and let's go.'

Two laps; 1m 41.018s; P9.

Irvine is into an even quicker lap when the red flag appears. Jean Alesi has crashed.

'That's a pity,' says Irvine. 'On that quick lap before, I turned in a bit early at the 130R and understeered. The brakes were absolutely useless on the first lap; no braking at all. And the tyres seem to be gone after half a lap.'

'We'll tape up the front brake ducts a bit more; the rears are completely taped,' explains Wright.

Irvine waits for the green flag.

Five minutes later: 'Let's go, Tim.' Five laps; 1m 41.469s; no improvement.

Irvine returns, climbs from the car. Other drivers have beaten his previous best. Now he's 11th. And disappointed.

'The tyres were gone again halfway round. Had to lift off big time at the 130R. P11. Should be better than that.'

There is not a trace of confidence-boosting bravado. He means every word.

A marker for Rubens

Barrichello is in 19th place. Still learning the circuit, Rubens is building up speed. He says he expected Irvine, through his local knowledge, to be quicker.

'It's a difficult situation for me,' explains Rubens. 'I'm not unhappy with my time because Irvine knows Suzuka better than I know Interlagos. So, for me, this is normal. It doesn't matter. I don't care about it.'

And, the more he talks about it the more you realize he *does* care. Any self-respecting racing driver should.

Senna gets in the way on Saturday

Irvine stands behind the 4 ft high concrete wall protecting the rear of the signalling pits. He is leaning on the top of the concrete, a pose which sums up his *laissez-faire* attitude to Formula 1. Several photographers catch the moment. It is becoming apparent that this man's picture may be in demand by the time the weekend is out. But no one could ever guess the extent of the eventual clamour. In the meantime, Irvine is thinking about the car and how to improve it.

The second free session gets under way. Irvine puts together four laps. He's second quickest so far.

The mechanics grin. Irvine comes in. His mood is distinctly upbeat. He's talking faster now.

'Feels much better than it did yesterday. The car's almost got a bit of a balance ... ' The observation is delivered deadpan.

Wright laughs. 'A *bit* of a balance. Thanks Eddie!'

'Yeah,' says Irvine, momentarily oblivious to the sarcasm, his mind assessing the new situation. 'Got more traction out of the corners. Is that the circuit d'you think?'

'Don't know yet. It's hard to say. What about the brakes?'

'Much better. Fantastic.' Now we're getting somewhere.

More laps; more improvement.

'Yes,' confirms Irvine. 'Feels better; more grip; more understeer now.'

The rear wheels are removed and adjustments made to the suspension, Nick and Andy putting their respective sides together like a jigsaw they are entirely familiar with. The job is completed in seven minutes. Irvine sits patiently in the cockpit, watching the lap times fall as the opposition gets into its stride.

Irvine completes another two laps before further adjustments are made, this time to the camber of the front wheels.

Tim, having studied the read-outs, comes on the radio:

'You were losing time at Spoon. Was that because of the understeer?'

The reply stuns him momentarily.

'Nah, the two times I came to Spoon, I was right up Senna's chuff. He was costing me time.' Again, this is delivered, without malice or frustration, as a straightforward statement of fact.

Wright, unaccustomed to having his car compared favourably with a McLaren, pauses. A smile plays on his lips.

'Yeah, Eddie. Life's a bitch, right enough.'

Once again, the point is lost as Irvine mentally chases time around the 3.64 miles.

Another couple of laps.

'Big improvement to front-end grip.'

'Do you want to try anything else?' asks Wright.

'These tyres have gone, so we'll only go round in circles if we try something else with them. It seems pretty much there. Just give me the fresh set and we'll see how it goes.'

As the one hour mark approaches in this 90-minute free practice period, Irvine leaves the pits.

First flying lap! 1m 39.561s. Fastest of the day so far! Now Irvine is really talking the sort of language the team likes to hear.

'It's very, very good. The only problem is Spoon. It's pushing (understeering) a bit mid-corner. But that's reasonably normal. I can go in quick and just stand on it. No, it's fine. Just leave it.'

And, with that, he flicks off his belts and climbs out. The team is not accustomed to this. As the car is checked over, the mechanics keep glancing at the list of times on the Olivetti monitor. It's still there: 'P1. Car 15. E. Irvine.'

The point is not lost on Rubens Barrichello. Time had been wasted while the brakes were changed. There are 19 minutes remaining. Time to go for a quick lap. Rubens knows his reputation is coming under siege – even if he won't admit it.

Four laps; 1m 40.203s, P9.

'I tried taking Corner 6 flat-out in fourth – but I made a mistake, had to back off. Otherwise, the car is okay.'

He sounds confident enough. Final qualifying promises to be something else. The frustration and aggravation of the past few months seem to belong to another world. *This* is what we're here for. Let's give those other bastards some stick.

Yeeeeeessss!

The wind has picked up; it's turning cold. Mechanics don sweaters and jackets as Irvine saunters into the garage.

With 10 minutes to go before the pit lane opens, he is already in the car. Barrichello does likewise a few minutes later. You can tell something important is going on; Eddie Jordan is already standing at the pit wall. The sense of anticipation, absent all year, is palpable.

'I reckon,' says Brian Hart, 'we'll be 10th and 12th; something like that.'

It's a nice thought. But Hart is growing anxious. He has the 'development' engine in Barrichello's car and there's another one in a box, ready to race for the first time. But what happens if Irvine is the quicker of the two drivers? Who gets the better engine then?

'It's a decision I'm glad I don't have to make,' says Hart.

In the meantime, practice has started and Hart is perplexed. 'Look at that,' he murmurs. 'They sent them both out at the same time ... '

What Hart leaves unsaid is the question of team management. Having two cars running in close company is merely adding to the risk unnecessarily; increasing the problem of traffic for both drivers. Anderson disagrees. His argument is that, with the changing track conditions and the lap measuring more than three miles, sending both cars out at the same time is not the problem it might be elsewhere.

Such speculation becomes irrelevant when the red flag appears after four minutes; de Cesaris has crashed heavily at the 130R. Both Jordans return to the pits. Valuable laps may have been wasted.

Irvine: 'I'm okay. I couldn't get the tyres warm so I haven't used that set at all.'

Barrichello: 'I made a mistake braking into the chicane – but I still did a time. I've got that, so I'm happy now.'

Anderson: 'That's lucky, Rubens. You just got that in before the red flag. 1m 40.8s. That's good.'

Significantly, this is the first time all season that Barrichello has gone out and really stepped on it during his first flying lap. Irvine's influence can not be understated here.

Green flag.

Irvine goes out straight away. Barrichello waits. Irvine's first flying lap is 1m 40.5s. Then two slower laps – followed by 1m 40.481s. P13.

On the next lap, he runs out of fuel.

Fortunately, he can coast into the pits. Had he been on the far side of the circuit, that would have been it. His best lap would ultimately have been worth 17th place on the grid. The problem has been caused by Irvine doing two slow laps instead of one. Brian Hart remains tight-lipped. It doesn't take a genius to read his mind.

Barrichello does 1m 39.8s on his first flying lap. P10.

The track is getting quicker, the tempo is increasing dramatically.

With 15 minutes to go, Irvine leaves the pits with his second and final set of tyres in place. It's now or never.

Immediately, he is up to speed, crossing the line to begin his quick lap. The computer registers 173.05 mph across the start line. It's the fastest he's been through there all weekend. Team members brace themselves; management at the pit wall, mechanics staring at the screen, Andy and Nick mentally riding in the cockpit with their man.

One minute and 38.9 seconds later, Ian Phillips punches the air. The screens flicks up the new time; P7, car 15, E Irvine. A brilliant performance by any standards.

Seconds later, Barrichello does 1m 39.4s. P8. The team stare at the screen, almost in disbelief.

Barrichello completes two slow laps and then goes for another quick one. At the second corner, he runs wide slightly, gets on to the dust fringing the racing line – and spins off.

'Trying too hard,' he says. No one doubts it. The pressure is on, the gap between the two Jordan drivers exacerbated as Suzuki, Patrese and Lehto improve to force Barrichello down to 12th place. In isolation, that would have equalled his second-best performance of the season. But, today, it has been put in punishing perspective. The benefit of having a quick team-mate for Rubens is clear for all to see. And, it should be said, the team is finally realizing the true potential of Anderson's car. The fact is that this should have occurred at the beginning rather than at the end of the season.

Just follow me

Irvine, meanwhile, has been demoted to eighth by an excellent performance from Derek Warwick.

The two meet later that day on the steps of the Suzuka Circuit Hotel. Warwick, about to dine with team members, is dressed in neat, casual clothes in keeping with his well-groomed looks. Irvine wears well-used jeans, with a plain V-neck sweater over a tee-shirt. He is, at best, scruffy. But the only thing that bothers him is the fact that Warwick went faster.

'You beat me at golf the other day – now you're ahead of me on the grid,' says Irvine.

They exchange banter for a while; two streetwise guys talking the same language. Then Warwick has to go.

'Have a good race,' he shouts.

'Yeah,' grins Irvine over his shoulder as he walks into the foyer. 'Just follow me.'

By the time Warwick turns to reply, Irvine has gone. It is a suggestion which will have more serious implications 24 hours later when they meet under less jovial circumstances.

Orange and green

Eddie Jordan reads the press release and clutches his head.

'You said *that*!' he groans, stabbing his finger at the FIA press release. 'Yeah,' admits Irvine. 'But I didn't think they'd print it, you know, verbatim, like that.'

(At each Grand Prix in 1993, on the Saturday afternoon, six drivers were selected at random to attend a press conference to answer various questions, ranging from the serious to the off-beat and the banal. Irvine was chosen at Suzuka, the press office later releasing a transcript of the interviews.)

Jordan reads the press release aloud to the assembled company.

'Question. "Eddie, can you please explain the bright orange colour of your helmet?"'

'Answer (and Jordan is really hamming it with his best Ulster brogue)

"Well ... it's a bit political, really. I think I'll get shot for this ... No, it's Northern Ireland ... well, Ulster's colour is orange. You know? King Billy and all that history. Well, anyway, I am a Protestant, so ... we like the orange. And the green (also on the helmet) is to keep the IRA from shooting me!"'

Jordan raises his eyes to the heavens before exploding.

'Jaysus, Eddie! A bit political! That's the understatement of the weekend.'

Irvine shrugs and laughs.

At least it's a diversion from the tension building slowly but surely on race morning. Not that Irvine is showing any signs of anxiety.

The warm-up provides a first taste of the Jordan with more than 40 gallons of fuel on board. It feels a different car, the extra weight making the steering heavy and that, in turn, is aggravating his back and the discomfort associated with the poor seating position. In addition, the crutch strap is cutting off the blood supply to his right leg.

'Maybe it'll go numb and I won't feel anything,' says Irvine. It is difficult to decide whether or not he's joking. With Irvine, you never know.

But, with the Jordans only 18th and 20th at the end of the warm-up, it is clear they will have their work cut out over the course of the 53-lap race.

Waiting, waiting

Each team has a Portacabin, one of more than 20 stacked along the rear edge of the paddock. Jordan is on the ground level, abutting the Goodyear tyre compound and with Lotus and Sauber on either side. Inside, the cramped conditions add to the mounting nervousness as the morning wears on.

Chris and Henny are preparing sandwiches, the growing piles dominating the worktop thanks to the Japanese preference for absurdly thick slices of bread. Ian Phillips is sprawled, face down, on a nearby table, the physiotherapist yanking up Phillips's shirt and working below the belt line in order to massage a pulled back muscle. It is not a pretty sight.

Eddie Jordan is interviewed by a succession of media people. The talk is of one thing; the new wonder boy in car 15. The fax stutters into life and spews out a good luck note from some of Irvine's Irish fans in Dun Laoghaire. That's near Dublin. In the South. They obviously hadn't heard about the loyalist remarks emanating from their hero the day before.

Barrichello is on the telephone and, judging by the darting eyes and sweet murmurings, he's not talking business. Geraldo watches him from the door leading to a collection of tables and chairs in the busy passageway outside. Sitting there is Rubens's girlfriend, Danielle. Geraldo can see her from where he stands. He can also catch Rubens's eye if the need arises. A coincidence, surely.

Time rolls slowly by. It's a 1 pm start. Everything is ready.

Chapter 30

We did it! We did it!

Does the race start now?

Irvine is on the right-hand side of the track, on the inside of the fourth row. In theory, he ought to be pleased with that grid position because the first corner at the bottom of the hill is a right-hander. But Irvine's experience of Suzuka has told him that, while every one tends to cling to the favoured line on the inside, it is possible to run round the outside and overtake.

'No problem,' he says to Tim Wright. 'I'll just move across to the left as we go down the hill.' Bold words for a novice, but Wright has learned not to be surprised any more.

They discuss tyre changes. At least one stop is anticipated; probably two.

'If you're not getting anywhere and not making ground,' says Wright, 'sometimes it's best to be the first person to stop. You'll have to watch the Footworks; they're not running much wing.'

The inference is that Warwick and Suzuki will therefore have plenty of straightline speed at the expense of handling in the corners; which will be bad news if Irvine is stuck behind Warwick; he'll never be able to overtake. Better, then, to change tyres early and see if he can take advantage of the Footworks that way.

In the event, the gathering rain clouds on the horizon will render such tactical play irrelevant.

Irvine says very little. He climbs from the car, walks across the grid and sits with his back to the pit wall. The build-up is reaching its pulsating crescendo now; loudspeakers blaring, mechanics dashing, poseurs ambling. There is a frisson of expectation. After two days of intense preparation, this is the point of it all. Conversations are short and usually animated; everyone is on a high. But the drivers say very little.

Eddie Jordan hunkers down beside Irvine and calls upon his experience as team owner and former racing driver to offer some advice.

'First couple of corners – go for it. Then see where you are. Try and look after your tyres. And if you think you can score points then just go for it. Don't think about the guy behind; just go for the one in front. If you're hurting or you're tired, don't freeze. Just relax.'

Then Jordan pauses before stating the obvious: 'Eighth on the grid in your first Grand Prix; it's your big opportunity. You have a great chance of scoring a point here and making a bit of history.'

He fails to add: 'while pulling my team out of the mire.'

Irvine nods. Then he gets up and walks over to the car. Ear plugs in place, the balaclava is pulled on, followed by the now-famous orange helmet. Into the cockpit; belts fastened by the mechanics.

Signal to start engines.

Irvine gets on the radio.

'Pull me back a bit. I want to lay some rubber down.'

(It's a common tactic, the resulting tyre marks giving the base for extra grip when the cars return to the grid for the start proper.)

'Don't be too hard on the clutch, Eddie,' warns Wright.

He may as well have addressed the pit wall. With a healthy number of revs stoked up by his right foot, Irvine slips the clutch, the rear wheels spinning and leaving blue smoke swirling above black streaks on the road beneath. Wright shakes his head and smiles.

And there's more. As the field slowly makes its way down the back straight towards the biggest moment of Irvine's racing career, he comes on the radio again.

'Is this the actual start now?' he asks, as if discussing a matter of little consequence.

Wright, in the midst of the tension and apprehension running the length and breadth of the pit lane, clutches his head set, scarcely able to take it on board.

'Yes, Eddie,' he says with resignation, 'this is the start. This is the start.'

'Okay.'

Take 'em on the outside

The cars are hidden by the high pit wall. The entire Jordan team gathers in the garage entrance (management personnel are not permitted to stand by the wall until the cars have safely left the grid), necks craned, watching the television monitors hanging overhead.

The crescendo from beyond the wall seems to shake the foundations and fill the garage to bursting. The television camera at the first corner catches the furious activity as cars fan out, drivers ducking and weaving down the hill. Already, you notice Irvine's orange helmet moving to his left-hand side of the track in preparation for the demon move.

The cameraman follows the leader, Ayrton Senna, through the corner. But in the background, you can clearly see one car out of line, almost up on the kerb, as it runs round the outside. The car, viewed from a distance, is difficult to recognize. But the Jordan team have no doubts about who it is.

'Christ! Look at Eddie!' someone shouts.

'He's done it!' grins 'John-Boy'.

Tim Wright just smiles. Absolutely nothing surprises him now.

Having passed the likes of Damon Hill and Michael Schumacher – big names who are supposed to be in with a chance of winning this race – Eddie Irvine is lying fifth. A Jordan has never been that far up the field at the exit of the first corner. The management personnel sprint across to the pit wall with noticeable enthusiasm.

Schumacher uses the superior power of the Benetton-Ford to overtake Irvine on lap three. It takes Hill another three laps to do likewise. Then Suzuki, spurred on by the home crowd, demotes the Jordan to eighth.

He gains a place when Schumacher runs into the back of Hill and tears a front wheel off the Benetton. Then Alesi's Ferrari blows up and Suzuki spins off. Lap 15 and Irvine is now fifth.

Barrichello, meanwhile, has been running steadily. Fifteenth at the end of lap seven, he is in ninth place. And rain is beginning to fall.

It's pissing down!

Senna, the leader, has already stopped to change to a fresh set of slick tyres but it is becoming apparent that the thing to do is wait and see if the rain becomes serious, and then make one change to wet tyres. As things stand, Senna will have to make a second visit to switch to wet tyres and lose a valuable 20 seconds or so.

'Do you want wets?' Tim Wright asks Irvine. The response is immediate.

'No, not yet.' The Jordan crew notes that Irvine does not have his rear red light illuminated; a punishable offence in these conditions.

'Put your light on,' shouts Wright. There is a pause.

'Where is it?' asks Irvine, referring to the on/off switch.

'Under the ignition. Under the ignition.'

A minute or so later, the rain really begins to fall. At the end of lap 21, there is a flurry of activity as the first three cars come in for wet tyres.

'Coming in!' shouts Irvine as he accelerates away from Spoon corner, plumes of spray flying from his glistening slick tyres.

'Eddie – stay out!' shouts Wright. 'Stay out for another lap.' Again, the response is immediate.

'You're crazy! It's pissing down!'

'Stay out! Rubens is coming in.'

Barrichello arrives and Irvine then gets the all clear – just as he is passing the entrance to the pit lane.

(With hindsight, Irvine was the architect of his own downfall. By refusing first call, Irvine had ensured that the pit stop was set up for Barrichello. By the time Irvine had decided he was ready for wet tyres, Barrichello's pit stop routine was already in motion.)

Irvine now faces another 3.64 treacherous miles on tyres with no treads.

He is not best pleased. It requires consummate skill to keep the car on the track without losing too much ground.

It takes 20.4 seconds for Irvine to cross the entrance to the pit lane, change tyres and reach the pit exit. Barrichello took 21.6 seconds. By comparison, Hill, the fastest of them all, took 16.4 seconds. The painfully slow lap has cost Irvine even more time and he rejoins in 10th place. Barrichello is seventh. But all is not lost.

There is little to choose between the Jordan drivers' lap times as they fight their way through the spray. By lap 34, Barrichello is fifth: Irvine seventh. The rain is easing. And Hill, who was running in fourth place, has already changed back to slick tyres.

Anxious to avoid more confusion at this next pit stop, Wright gets on the radio to Irvine. Irvine knows Suzuka well enough to realize that the water takes time to disperse. Slick tyres will not necessarily be an advantage straight away.

'Come in now,' orders Wright.

'No way!' says Irvine. 'It's still wet.'

'Rubens has got to come in yet; so come in *this* lap.'

'No, I want to do three more laps.'

Apart from prompting a swift change of plan to bring Barrichello in immediately, Irvine's tactic is about to set in motion a sequence of events which will propel a hitherto unknown driver into the headline news.

Closing fast, still leading the race, is Ayrton Senna, about to lap Irvine for the first time. Or so he thinks.

Senna gets in the way on Sunday

Irvine has caught Hill (on slicks, remember) just as the circuit is on the turn from the point of view of grip. Wet tyres still have an advantage in places; slicks are better in others. But Irvine knows all the right places and he's anxious to get ahead of the Williams while he can and put as much space between himself and Hill before taking his turn to call at the Jordan pit for slicks.

Senna laps Irvine and then has one go at doing the same to Hill. He nearly comes to grief as Hill slithers on the greasy surface. Senna decides that, in the tricky conditions, discretion is the sensible course. After all, he is under no pressure from Prost's second-place Williams.

But Irvine can't afford to waste a single second. Frustrated by Senna's apparent dalliance, Irvine retakes the McLaren.

Senna has never experienced such a precocious act before. And he's not happy about it. Senna then has a grandstand view as Irvine pulls a daring move to overtake Hill going into the chicane. But the superior traction of the Williams allows Hill to repass Irvine on the way out of the corner, Irvine then running round the outside of the Williams at the bottom of the hill.

They pass and pass again, two drivers thoroughly enjoying the cut and thrust of battle. The press room is on its feet. The cheers in the Jordan garage almost drown the racket from the track. It is racing in its purest form; forget tactics, just go for it.

Senna does not see it that way, the race leader feeling that he is being put unnecessarily at risk by the antics of these two. Eventually he passes them both for good and all.

On lap 39, Irvine comes in for slicks. Senna does likewise two laps later.

In the points

Now the Jordan team is on tenterhooks. A controlled and intelligent drive by Barrichello has moved the Brazilian into fifth place. Irvine is seventh and catching Warwick.

By lap 47, with six to go, he is right with the Footwork. Irvine knows as well as anyone that Warwick is a wily old campaigner. He is difficult to pass at the best of times. On this track – where the approach to the chicane represents the only reasonable place – he will be impossible to overtake.

Going into the chicane on lap 49, Irvine taps the back of the Footwork and they both spin. The problem for Warwick is that he has spun right off the track and is stuck fast in the gravel.

Irvine is also stationary – but still on the tarmac.

Has he stalled? No, he hasn't. The Jordan rejoins.

All of this has taken place out of sight of the pits and the first hint the Jordan garage receives is when a television picture shows Warwick at a standstill.

A cheer goes up. It's an automatic reaction. Warwick is one of the most popular men in the pit lane. But, in the heat of battle, business is business. The fact is that Irvine is now sixth and en route to one championship point. Who would have believed that?

Warwick is furious. He claims he was shoved off by Irvine. Irvine will say later that he was caught by surprise when Warwick braked early for the chicane.

Observers familiar with Suzuka note that it is not uncommon to see one driver, frustrated at being unable to pass, remove the man in front with a gentle nudge from behind at the chicane. And Irvine is very familiar with overcoming the problems presented by racing at Suzuka. 'Anyway,' he says later, 'you didn't see what Derek did to me when I tried to get by a few moments before.'

But, right now, he is still in the race. The Jordan-Harts are fifth and sixth. Not just one car in the points – but two!

The next five laps are purgatory. Brian Hart, pale as the concrete beneath his Rockport shoes, doesn't know what to do with himself as he paces around the garage. Both engines are running perfectly. He knows all about the stresses and strains inside the engine blocks. But he will never forgive himself if one of them gives up now – with less than 20 miles to go.

The rising excitement in the garage is gagged by the worry that so much could still go wrong. There's a harsh note coming from the exhaust on

Rubens's car. The team can hear it. So can Rubens. All he can think about is a similar noise at Donington and the disappointment which came there.

Everyone knows how fickle such a highly-tuned piece of equipment can be. The Sasol Jordan team has had their fair share of that. But, please, not now. Not at the very moment when the first points of the season are there for the taking. Not when these points have been earned on merit rather than through the default of others.

As they blast past the pits to start the final lap, all conversation stops. Silent prayers are offered. Sod's Law dictates that Suzuka is one of the longest circuits on the calendar. It will take more than a minute and three-quarters for them to appear again.

With the threat of a last-minute pit stop gone, the mechanics break ranks and join the rest of the team running to the pit wall, everyone leaning over the concrete, squinting up the hill to their left, watching the man with the chequered flag on the gantry some distance away.

To make matters worse, Irvine had unlapped himself again – this time in less controversial circumstances – so that he crossed the line to start his last lap seconds before Senna took the flag. In fact, this has been a sound piece of management by the team. If any of the cars in front of Irvine stop on the final lap, he will pick up another place. Had he not unlapped himself, such an opportunity would be denied. But the net result is that Irvine will be the last to finish on the road.

Prost comes through, followed by Hakkinen, third for McLaren, and then Hill, fourth for Williams.

Twelve seconds later, and Barrichello accelerates into view. The sight of the Jordan sweeping beneath the chequered flag is too much to take. The release of bottled-up tension brings an emotional scene as the Jordan burbles down the hill, Barrichello off the throttle, an arm in the air, the team crazy with delight as he goes by.

Gary Anderson, with apparent sang-froid, stands quietly in the midst of the bedlam erupting around him. But he is completely choked. Calmly, ever so calmly, he comes on the radio.

'Fifth place ... Thank you, Rubens.'

The reply is barely coherent from the man who has just scored his first world championship points.

'We did it! We did it!' And then a babble of Portuguese mixed with sobs of pure, uncut emotion.

Then it's eyes left again, waiting for this memorable day to be completed in the best possible way. Irvine finishes his first Grand Prix in sixth place. And the delirium by the pit wall simply accelerates.

Mechanics embrace and shake each other's hands. Anderson accepts congratulations from rival team managers. Everyone beams from ear to ear. Two cars in the points. It is the first time one Jordan – never mind two – has completed a full Grand Prix distance this season. Brilliant job! What a race!

Chapter 31

In the Green Corner

Never satisfied

John Walton and Gary Anderson head towards *parc fermé* at the top of the pit road. The way is blocked by a crowd gathered beneath the rostrum. Barrichello, surrounded by Brazilian journalists and television people, makes his way through. Congratulations all round. He's thrilled to bits.

Then Irvine appears. Alone. His face is flushed; the adrenalin is still pumping. He's not smiling.

'Congratulations Eddie,' says someone.

'Yeah, thanks.' Then the briefest of pauses before giving vent to frustration which has obviously been burning him up for the past hour.

'What the fuck was going on?' he asks no one in particular. 'That tyre stop ... They called me in just as I was passing the pit entrance. No way I could stop. That next lap must have cost me, I dunno, 20 seconds. Jesus! I mean ...'

His voice tails away as he thinks about what might have been. Sixth place? Very nice. But it could have been fifth. Or higher. Typical racing driver. Never satisfied.

'How's your back?' asks a journalist as Irvine walks down the almost deserted pit road.

'What?' says Irvine, shaken from his thoughts. 'Pretty bad. The rain definitely saved me; boy, was I glad to see it. If it had remained dry, I couldn't have gone on at that pace. No way.'

Now he and Barrichello have reached the Jordan garage to tremendous applause from within. Grinning broadly, Irvine immediately forgets his problems and begins to let the weight of his achievement sink in. But not for long.

A hint of trouble

'Mr. Irvine, driver of car 15. Please come immediately to the third floor of the control tower.'

There is a momentary lull in the celebrations. The public address call can mean only one thing: a stewards' enquiry – and possible exclusion. But for what? Overtaking Senna? The incident with Warwick? An inadvertent contravention of the rules somewhere else? With Eddie, you never know.

Irvine reports to the third floor, there to discover that Warwick has protested his driving tactics. After a lengthy discussion and replaying of the video, the objection is overruled. The results stand. No mention is made of Senna.

On with the celebrations.

Driving like a lunatic

Ayrton Senna is speaking at the winner's press conference.

'The back-markers were driving very unprofessionally. I came up to some guys who were fighting each other and didn't care about anybody else. They were hitting each other and spinning off in front of you. In fact, I had to go off the circuit to avoid some of them. Then I managed to squeeze past one or two guys when they were banging wheels.

'Suddenly I got disturbed by another car again; the guy behind me came like a lunatic. It was as though he was fighting for position. If he is a back-marker he should respect someone who is one lap in front. It was dangerous because those guys were going to hit each other and that could have cost me something.'

Throughout his typically unsmiling monologue, Senna does not name Irvine. But it is clear who he means.

Word is passed to Irvine as he sits in the Jordan Portacabin with the team.

'Senna says you were driving like a lunatic.'

Irvine's reply is casually dismissive. It is, in fact, a typical response which is not meant to be a carefully chosen insult. It says he doesn't really care much what Senna thinks.

His words are duly relayed to Senna who, at this stage, has no inclination to take the matter further despite being annoyed by Irvine's behaviour on the track. But that soon changes.

A drop of the hard stuff

Gerhard Berger is relaxing in the Camel office, enjoying a glass of schnapps with Karl-Heinz Zimmermann, a brilliant Austrian chef with a mischievous sense of humour matched only by Berger's. In walks Senna and it does not take much to persuade him to have a glass of strong refreshment.

Being almost teetotal, and having worked hard for close to two hours, the effect of the schnapps is immediate and exaggerated beyond normal bounds.

Senna is talking about Irvine's behaviour in the race and, throughout, Berger is agreeing with him.

'You should do something about it,' says Gerhard, as he manages to disguise his devilish intent. So, suitably fortified by Karl-Heinz's hospitality, Senna takes Berger's advice.

His first port of call is the control tower. There, Senna gets a sympathetic hearing from Sir John Rogers, Chairman of the RAC Motor Sports Association and one of the stewards still present at the track. Senna is informed that Irvine has already been spoken to but perhaps the best solution would be for both drivers to have a quiet chat. Senna agrees and, chased by two personnel from the McLaren team, heads for the Jordan Portacabin.

Inside, several members of the Jordan team are enjoying the meagre share of a single bottle of champagne. Irvine is sitting on a table. Nearby is Adam Cooper, Japanese correspondent for *Autosport* magazine and a close friend of Irvine. Cooper has his tape recorder at hand when the door opens and Senna marches in.

Senna looks around the room. He does not appear to know who Irvine is. Sensing there may be a story about to break in the biggest possible way, Cooper switches on his tape recorder.

Irvine raises his hand.

'Here!' calls Irvine.

Senna walks over and gets straight to the point.

Senna: 'What the fuck do you think you were doing?'

Irvine: 'I was racing.'

Senna: 'You were racing? Do you know the rule that you're supposed to let the leaders come by when you're a back marker?'

Irvine: 'If you were going fast enough, it was no problem.'

Senna: 'I overtook you! And you went three times off in front of me, at the same place, like a fucking idiot, where there was oil. And you were throwing stones and all the things in front of me for three laps. When I took you, you realized I was ahead of you. And when I came up behind Hill, because he was on slicks and in difficulties, you should have stayed behind me. You took a very big risk, to put me out of the race.'

Irvine: 'Where did I put you in any danger?'

Senna: 'You didn't put me in any danger.'

Irvine: 'Did I touch you? Did I touch you once?'

Senna: 'No, but you were that much from touching me, and I happened to be the fucking leader. I HAPPENED TO BE THE FUCKING LEADER!'

Irvine: 'A miss is as good as a mile.'

Senna: 'I tell you something, if you don't behave properly in the next event, you can just rethink what you do. I can guarantee you that.'

Irvine: 'The stewards said "No problem. Nothing was wrong." '

Senna: 'Yeah? You wait till Australia, mate. You wait till Australia and the stewards will talk to you. Then you tell me if they tell you this.'

Irvine: 'Hey, I'm out there to do the best I can for me.'

Senna: 'This is not correct. You want to do well. I understand, because I've been there, I understand. But it's very unprofessional. If you are a backmarker because you happen to be lapped ... '

Irvine: 'But I would have followed you if you'd overtaken Hill!'

Senna: 'You should let the leader go by ... '

Irvine: 'I understand that fully!'

Senna: '... and not come and do the things you did. You nearly hit Hill in front of me three times, because I saw and I could have collected you and him as a result, and that's not the way to do that.'

Irvine: 'But I'm racing! I'm racing! You just happen to ...'

Senna: 'You're not racing! You're driving like a fucking idiot. You're not a racing driver, you're a fucking idiot.'

Irvine: 'You talk, you talk. You were in the wrong place at the wrong time.'

Senna: 'I was in the wrong place at the wrong time?'

Irvine: 'Yes. I was battling with Hill.'

Senna: 'Really? Really? Just tell me one thing. Who is supposed to have the call? You, or the leader of the race who comes through to lap you?'

Irvine: 'The leader of the race.'

Senna: 'So what have you done?'

Irvine: 'You, you were too slow, and I had to overtake you to try and get at Hill.'

Senna: 'Really? How did I lap you if I was too slow?'

Irvine: 'Rain. Because on slicks you were quicker than me, on wets you weren't.'

Senna: 'Really? Really? How did I come and overtake you on wets?'

Irvine: 'Huh?'

Senna: 'How come I overtook you on wets?'

Irvine: 'I can't remember that. I don't actually remember the race.'

Senna: 'Exactly. Because you are not competent enough to remember. That's how it goes, you know.'

Irvine: 'Fair enough. Fair enough. That's what you think.'

Senna: 'You be careful, guy.'

Irvine: 'I will. I'll watch out for you.'

Senna: 'You're gonna have problems not with me only, but with lots of other guys, and also the FIA.'

Irvine: 'Yeah?'

Senna: 'You bet.'

Irvine: 'Yeah? Good.'

Senna: 'Yeah? It's good to know that.'

Irvine: 'See you out there.'

Senna goes to leave but catches everyone by surprise as he suddenly turns back and swings his left hand, hitting Irvine on the right side of the head, sending him to the floor.

Senna is restrained and removed from the room, shouting as he goes: 'You gotta learn respect where you're going wrong!'

There is a momentary pause. Then Irvine, dusting himself down, jokes about making an insurance claim. Everyone laughs.

Is there no end to this extraordinary day?

Over the top

Ian Phillips goes to the control tower and quietly makes officials aware of what happened. Meanwhile, word of the altercation has reached the press room and journalists, with the time difference to Europe working in their favour, are able to stop what they are doing and return to the Jordan office. If Eddie Irvine wasn't a celebrity before, he certainly is now. The trouble is that no amount of retelling can do justice to the mood of the moment. Senna did not have the slightest intention of striking Irvine when he arrived but he was clearly outraged by the novice's casual response.

The use of sarcasm is a familiar tool during verbal swordplay in Northern Ireland and Irvine made full use of it. Senna, having been humiliated (in his eyes) on the track, and unfamiliar with such devastating deliveries with the tongue, was an easy target. He simply could not cope with the lack of contrition any more than Irvine was prepared to accept a lecture from a driver whose record was scarcely a model of rectitude. And here of all places.

Three years before, Senna had driven into the back of Alain Prost's Ferrari as the field swept at 150 mph into the first corner at Suzuka. With both drivers out of the race, the championship automatically went to Senna. He said he had to do it that way and was perplexed when few people accepted his reasoning. Gamesmanship in Formula 1 had taken on a sinister meaning from that moment on.

Adam Cooper, meanwhile, is pounding away at his typewriter, the transcript of the conversation being the journalist's equivalent of the scoop photograph. The Jordan team fall upon the first copy from the printer and begin to play-act the interview with appropriate flourishes and exaggeration – not that it needs much embellishment.

On a more serious note, Ian Phillips gives the team's official comment.

'It's a real shame when the best driver the sport has ever known does something like this,' he says simply. That seems as good a summary as any.

Gary Anderson has already left to catch a flight to London. (This is a critical period when it comes to finalizing the design of the 1994 car and he needs to work in the office even though the time difference will militate against him for the duration of his short stay before flying out to Australia.)

As the rest of the management walk back to the Suzuka Circuit Hotel to celebrate the success achieved in such a worthy fashion on the race track, the mechanics finish packing the crates and boxes, ready for shipment to Australia. With a limited number of rooms available in the circuit hotel, the mechanics are lodged in Yokkaichi City, a sprawling nondescript place about 20 miles away.

They make it back just before McDonalds closes at 10 pm. It's hardly a trip to Paris. But, at the end of a day such as this, a Big Mac and a Coke never tasted so good.

Chapter 32

Down and Out

One for my boy

'I had dinner with Ayrton a few nights ago,' said Barrichello. 'At one stage, I got up to go to the bathroom. I left my cap on the table and, when I came back, Ayrton had signed it for me. I said I would give him a present one day.'

Droll as ever, Gary Anderson murmurs, 'Yeah, but did you ask for an autograph for Eddie? I'm sure he'd like one, y'know ...'

Tipple effect

Eleven days after the Suzuka incident, the story was refusing to die. Eddie Irvine had been mobbed for the first time in his life as he arrived at Adelaide airport. He had been staying in his girlfriend's flat in Macau ever since the Japanese Grand Prix and, typical Irvine, the apartment did not have a telephone. This was his first major appearance since the now infamous left hook.

The story had made headlines worldwide. *The Daily Telegraph* in London had run the report by Tim Collings on the front page, partly because of its straight news value and partly because all of the main stories that night were desperately gloomy and the front page was in need of a lift. It was that sort of news item; unconscious humour with serious undertones.

Eddie Jordan had been to Port Douglas on the Barrier Reef. Having made a swift exit from Japan, he had missed the altercation and, therefore, the immediate publicity, the television interviews and the issuing of statements. He bore the disappointment well.

His policy on arrival in Australia was to say nothing and consign the matter to history.

Unfortunately, Ayrton Senna changed all that by implying at a press conference that the Jordan team members had been drunk when he arrived to interview Irvine. It was a dangerous allegation to make, given Ayrton's preoccupation with a glass or two of schnapps not long before invading the Jordan office.

Eddie was deeply offended. His employees may have been very happy – but drunk they most certainly were not and he made that point perfectly clear to anyone who asked.

In any case, Irvine and Jordan had plenty of sympathy, particularly after Senna had scored another own-goal by accusing the British press of being incompetent and knowing nothing about motor racing. It was not a move which endeared him to scribes, most of whom took their jobs almost as seriously as he did – even to the point, it is rumoured, of enjoying the odd tipple at the end of a hard day.

In Australia itself, the advice to Irvine had been unequivocal from the outset: 'Mate; you should've hit him back.'

A slow sort of day

Senna got his own back in the best possible way by dominating practice for this final race of the season. It had been a difficult year for the Brazilian as the McLaren-Ford swung between bouts of average competitiveness and runs of occasional excellence. In Adelaide, the McLaren was working better than ever before and Senna was making good use of it on a street circuit which suited his committed, dramatic style.

Life at Jordan had slipped back a notch or two after the excitement of Japan. Within an hour of practice beginning, it was evident that the cars were struggling to find grip on the bumpy roads of the city suburb but, as far as Irvine was concerned, he simply wanted to beat Barrichello and perpetuate the legend born two weeks before in Japan.

A faulty electronics control box put paid to that during first qualifying, a misfire preventing Irvine from extending either himself or the car. For the first time since they started working together, Barrichello was faster than Irvine in an official practice session, 13th place being a good performance considering Rubens was suffering from an upset stomach.

'Must have been that dinner you had with Senna,' quipped Irvine.

Certainly, Senna had been having an influence. An examination of the speed trap times showed Barrichello to be high in the order with 182 mph on the back straight. Senna, by comparison, was 6 mph slower. But he was on provisional pole position.

Senna called Barrichello down to the McLaren garage and quietly advised his fellow-countryman that straightline speed is not everything at Adelaide; better to compromise speed on the straight by running more downforce and being faster elsewhere. It was a generous gesture which indicated that he liked Barrichello, didn't see him as a threat – and perhaps felt moderately guilty about his previous accusations over a lack of sobriety at Jordan Grand Prix.

Rubens never got the chance to put the advice to good use. Free practice on Saturday had shown him to be ninth fastest in the session and therefore poised to improve during final qualifying. But, by a geographical and climatic quirk, the track was actually slower in the afternoon than it had been, either in the morning or on the day before.

Thus Barrichello was still 13th at the end of it all but Irvine was affected more seriously since he could only struggle from 22nd to 19th even though the car was running without any problems. The electrical trouble the previous day had hobbled him in the long-term and he would never recover from it.

Keeping the customers satisfied

Cosmo were sponsoring Irvine for these two races to the tune of $150,000. Naturally, they wanted their money's worth and there was a fair amount of oriental consternation from their representative in Adelaide when Jordan number 15 appeared without the company logo on the nose wings. As a matter of post-race routine in Japan, the team had removed the stickers. When it came to decorating the car in Adelaide, it was discovered that Cosmo stickers were in short supply. In fact, there were none at all since the Cosmo representative in Suzuka was believed to have sold them to the race-mad fans.

This was aggravation Phillips did not need. One hour after arriving direct from Japan, he had launched into a meeting with a prospective sponsor. For five days, he was never out of his suit as he visited local companies interested in supporting the team for this race.

The success of his endeavours could be measured by the increased identification on the car, a motley variety of names which, while not being at the forefront of international business, were nevertheless delighted to be paying for the privilege of a brief association with Formula 1. And each had different ideas about how to utilize this exciting alliance.

Mecc Alte, an Italian firm manufacturing alternators and generators, bought grandstand seats for 135 guests and dressed them in Sasol Jordan gear; Tip Top cleaners had Irvine drop by in front of the cameras and leave his overalls for cleaning; Fasta Pasta became the team's official supplier of food; the local Casino adopted the team and used the occasion to launch a one-armed bandit poker machine by having Barrichello drive the Formula 1 car along the street and park outside. Meanwhile, inside, Eddie Jordan was entertaining the team's main sponsors in a function room and thanking them for their support throughout the year.

It frequently seemed this was the sole purpose of the weekend; an end-of-term social occasion in a gracious city where the Grand Prix was almost incidental.

Chris Leese, a prime mover in the Grand Prix Hackers Golf Club, had arranged a tournament on the local fairways where the priority was to have a beer trolley follow the 30 'players' as they meandered through the idyllic surroundings. Phil Howell, (Barrichello's Number 2) had won the mechanics' go-kart race.

Generally, the lads enjoyed the relaxed atmosphere as they prepared the cars in the agreeable climate while posing for pictures for the enthusiastic local press. Adelaide ranked highly as a race venue thanks to the excellent facilities, the fact that this was the last Grand Prix and the discovery some time before that the Australians have the art of partying worked down to a fine art.

On race morning, Jordan joined the popular habit of having everyone gather in the pit lane and pose for a team photograph. The tension and furtiveness of races gone by had completely disappeared; what you didn't know about the competition now wasn't worth knowing. Only the curiously sweet but rancid smell – reminiscent of old socks – as racing fuel was pumped into the cars served as a reminder of the true business of the weekend. For all the jocularity and apparent laid-back mood, there was still a race to be won.

The way we were

Jordan did not hold out much hope of that but the lingering euphoria of Suzuka prompted the vague thought that another point or two seemed possible. The harsh reality was to be hammered home before the race had even started.

Irvine misjudged his position on the grid and stopped too far forward. Not knowing what to do, he stalled the engine. His reasoning was that the subsequent handicap of starting from the back of the grid would be better than receiving a 60-second penalty for jumping the start. He never recovered from that and, on the 12th lap, locked his brakes and slid unceremoniously into a tyre barrier, damaging the Jordan beyond immediate repair. As he limped slowly back to the pits, there could not have been a more stark contrast with his exuberant progress in Japan a fortnight before.

Barrichello was not faring much better, trouble with the traction control ruling out any chance of a serious dispute with those around him in the mid-field. Then he spun, found himself with no one to fight with and drove home to a slightly dispirited 11th place, three laps behind his friend and eventual winner, Ayrton Senna.

The mood afterwards was anticlimactic; certainly quiet and subdued compared to the heady pleasures of Japan. That's it; no more races; no more chances; no more 'well, never mind, we'll do better in a fortnight's time'; no more opportunities to score points.

There were just three on the board to the credit of Jordan Grand Prix. The fact that it was three times as many as the previous year was no consolation at all. Williams, with 168 to their name and the championship long since wrapped up, were operating in a different world.

The priority now was to pack up quickly and head for the party hosted by Camel, get some Fosters down your neck and say goodbye to 1993.

'Well,' said Eddie Jordan in the weary way of a host after his last guest has just left, 'it was hard work, this year. And it was pretty chronic at times, I have to admit. For a while it looked as if we would *never* score any points.

'The car was very difficult to drive, I admit that. But that was an excellent test session we had at Estoril after the race. We sorted out a lot of the problems and the mood has been upbeat since then. But there is no doubt that we need to increase the tempo even further. The level we're at is just not acceptable. Not acceptable at all.'

Then a pause

'Right, who's for a beer?'

The party's over

Breakfast on Monday was either late or not at all. The last check-in of the season was characterized by muted conversation, thick tongues and faint aroma of garlic and stale alcohol.

Outside Adelaide airport, a multitude of boxes containing bits of the Formula 1 circus were already being stacked, ready for loading into a freighter for the flight back to Europe. The hundred or so weary and dishevelled racers barely gave the pile of packhorses and cars a sideways glance as they boarded the Quantas and Singapore Airlines 747s waiting to carry them home.

The route took them to Singapore and on across northern India, Azerbaijan, the Black Sea, and then close by Budapest, Hockenheim and Spa-Francorchamps, places they had visited in this race without end.

That seemed like a long time ago. In fact, it was only a matter of months. And it would only be a matter of days before they would talk about doing it all over again.

Chapter 33

One Year's Work
in an Afternoon

This time it's different

'Never before have we built a car with the potential of the Sasol Jordan Hart 194. We're positive. We're very enthusiastic.'

Yes, yes Eddie. We've heard it all before. Twelve months ago, almost to the day. You said then that the Jordan 193 was the best car your team had ever built. And look what happened to that. Why should this car be any different?

The assembled media shuffled in their plastic seats. The customary benevolence accorded to Eddie and his wondrous works was not so plentiful on 11 January 1994. This was the third year in succession that the same upbeat speech had been delivered. Forgetting 1991, Jordan Grand Prix had four points to show for two seasons' work. Eddie's credibility was beginning to wear thin.

And yet it could not be denied that there was a positive edge to the day's proceedings. Jordan had dispensed with the hit and miss idea of unveiling the new car in the draughty garages of the Silverstone circuit. Instead, the factory itself was being put to full use, a slick ceremony would have a more authoritative and congenial air.

Coffee had been served in the pleasurable expanse of the reception area, the polished marble floor crunching with biscuit crumbs as the press – another impressive turn-out – then made their way into the main body of the factory. Space had been cleared and screened for a stage, with the car out of sight to the left.

On a given signal, the audience inserted ear plugs and Rubens Barrichello fired the Hart V10, the new car rolling into view through clouds of artificial smoke. Quick as a flash, Eddie Jordan pointed out that the blue haze was part of the act and not an imminent engine failure. Brian Hart smiled bravely. It was the only element of show-biz to be seen and it had been incorporated for good reason.

The choice of a driver to partner Barrichello was still under negotiation and the favourites – according to the media – were Eddie Irvine, Mark Blundell and Jos Verstappen. Only *Motoring News* mentioned in passing that Martin Brundle might be in the running.

In fact, discussions between Brundle and Jordan had been intense, so much so that there was hope of a deal being struck just before the launch. In which case, having the new car, with Brundle in the cockpit, appear through the smoke would have produced a dramatic news story indeed.

In the event, agreement was not reached and Jordan had to launch the 194 without knowing the identity of their second driver. Brundle eventually chose to gamble on waiting to see whether or not Alain Prost would accept a drive with McLaren-Peugeot, Blundell opted for Tyrrell and Verstappen was snapped up by Benetton. Which left Eddie Irvine – who had been the favourite for the job in the first place.

The team was pleased because they knew all about Irvine's promise. But, more important, his presence would not destabilize the maturing relationship with Barrichello.

But what about the car? Was the choice of driver academic and entirely dependent on the competitiveness of the Sasol Jordan Hart, the best car the boss's team had ever built? Certainly, it looked the part, a logical development of the long-wheelbase 193. But, underneath the skin, a huge amount of development had taken place as the technical team refined the many good points of the 1993 car.

This had largely been the inspiration of Gary Anderson even though, in the light of end-of-season reforms designed to ease Anderson's workload, Steve Nichols had been brought in as chief designer. Nichols, formerly with McLaren, Ferrari and, briefly, Sauber, had arrived too late to have a significant influence on the design of the 194. Besides, as he pointed out, there was nothing he would have wanted to change in any case, Anderson's small team having produced a first class scheme which belied the restrictions of manpower and budget.

As Nichols, a laid-back American, quietly stood in the background at the launch of the 194, the more intriguing question was one of personalities and how the revamped technical department would gel as the season got into its stride. Anderson seemed happy enough as the world waited to see what Nichols had to offer.

Yet more steam

Brian Hart's team had also been hard at work, major revisions to the V10 allowing the engine and gearbox to be mounted closer to the ground, thus lowering the car's centre of gravity. Hart, in connection with intensive work by Sasol on the fuel, had been producing a three per cent increase in power. It was a significant gain – but barely in keeping with advances made by the larger, well-heeled engine manufacturers and their associated fuel companies.

Fuel, in fact, would be a major talking point. With the advent of refuelling, the races would be more of a sprint than an economy run. In other words, Sasol and Hart could concentrate on producing out and out power without having to worry about the need to keep the fuel load, and hence the weight, to a minimum at the start of the race. Consumption figures were still important – but not half as significant as the power beneath the driver's right foot and its ease of delivery to the rear wheels.

And that was another thing. A ban had been placed on so-called driver aids. In 1994, items such as active suspension and traction control would be forbidden in the interests of returning the influence of the driver, containing costs and reducing the technical gap between the haves and the have-nots. It was plausible enough and would suit the likes of Sasol Jordan Hart, although the argument remained that the big budget teams would still be able to exploit the latest rule changes better than anyone else.

In the meantime, the Jordan 194 was ready to run for the first time.

Straight out of the box

Barrichello had come out with the usual new car platitudes. The 194, he said, felt very good. No one paid much attention since such enthusiasm was part of the staple diet at any new car launch. The driver was hardly going to come out and say the car had the stability of a failed soufflé, even if that was exactly how it felt.

But the media sat up and took notice when the Jordan-Hart began posting competitive times wherever it went. This was a far cry from the previous January when the 193 was two or three seconds off the pace at Estoril. To use a popular motor sporting aphorism, the 194 felt good 'straight out of the box'. When Barrichello went back to Estoril and matched the best time established by Ayrton Senna and Williams-Renault – the clear pre-season favourites – Louise Goodman's press release machine went into overdrive with justifiable optimism.

Of course, there was always the thought that Senna had been in the 1993 car and probably sand-bagging – holding back, not wanting to show his hand – but that did not detract from the plain fact that Gary Anderson's car was working well.

Anderson had pushed hard for a busy test schedule. 'There's absolutely no substitute for miles,' he would frequently say. 'We need to develop the product but, unfortunately, this costs money and we haven't got enough.'

Anderson had mapped out a plan of what he wanted to achieve. He got little satisfaction from the management but at least it was agreed that 24 days of testing should be schemed into the closed season.

'That was then cut to 18 and we actually succeeded in only doing 12 days,' said Anderson ruefully as the team prepared for the first race in Brazil. 'In terms of lessons learned in 1993, have we gone forward?'

It was a rhetorical question. The answer came when the team ran into unexpected technical problems during practice at Interlagos, became sidetracked and then had to make do with a disappointing 14th and 16th on the grid when rain fell half-way through the final qualifying session. Before practice began, Barrichello had spoken confidently about easing into the top six and there had been no reason to doubt his optimism. But the race would be a different story, one of enterprise, strong team-work, near-disaster and splendid success. Barrichello and Irvine both made excellent starts, each driver gaining four places on the first lap, Irvine then becoming embroiled in a mid-field battle which was eventually resolved in the worst possible way.

The trouble started when the flywheel on Brundle's McLaren-Peugeot parted company with the engine, the centrifugal forces flinging the wheel through the transmission casing and wedging it between the bottom of the car and the track. Eric Bernard, following in his Ligier, was as surprised as Brundle when the Mclaren began to slow and then weave unaccountably at a point where the cars should have been reaching 195 mph.

Catching them both came Irvine, with Jos Verstappen drawing alongside, the Benetton driver unaware of the mechanical mayhem erupting in the back of the McLaren but keen to trap Irvine behind the Ligier.

When Bernard suddenly slowed 120 metres before the anticipated braking area, Irvine was faced with a stark choice as he covered the ground at the rate of 285 ft every second: either dart right and on to the grass and into the crash barrier, slam into the back of the Ligier, or move left towards Verstappen and the vacant track beyond the Benetton. In the time available, and at the closing speed in question, hitting the brakes was never an option.

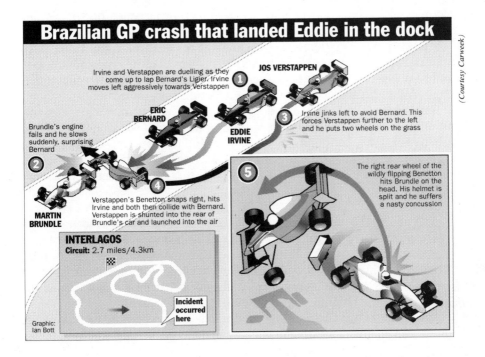

Brazilian GP crash that landed Eddie in the dock

(Courtesy Carweek)

Irvine and Verstappen are duelling as they come up to lap Bernard's Ligier. Irvine moves left aggressively towards Verstappen ①

JOS VERSTAPPEN

ERIC BERNARD

EDDIE IRVINE

Brundle's engine fails and he slows suddenly, surprising Bernard ②

Irvine jinks left to avoid Bernard. This forces Verstappen further to the left and he puts two wheels on the grass ③

MARTIN BRUNDLE

Verstappen's Benetton snaps right, hits Irvine and both then collide with Bernard. Verstappen is shunted into the rear of Brundle's car and launched into the air ④

⑤ The right rear wheel of the wildly flipping Benetton hits Brundle on the head. His helmet is split and he suffers a nasty concussion

INTERLAGOS
Circuit: 2.7 miles/4.3km

Incident occurred here

Graphic:
Ian Bott

His natural instinct was to swerve to the left even though it brought the risk of touching Verstappen.

Anxious not to lose ground, Verstappen keep his foot to the floor, even while jinking to the left to avoid Irvine. When the left-rear wheel of the Benetton got on to the grass, Verstappen was pitched sideways, straight across the front of the Jordan. In the ensuing chaos, the Benetton hit the back of the McLaren and began a terrifying barrel-roll, a rear wheel on Verstappen's car fetching Brundle a wicked blow to the head and splitting the Englishman's helmet.

All four drivers were lucky to emerge without serious injury. But in the hysterical aftermath – and given the seemingly damning evidence of head-on television pictures showing the Jordan apparently shoving Verstappen towards the edge of the track – Irvine was subsequently fined $10,000 and suspended from the next race in Japan.

The team subsequently lodged an appeal. Given the weight of evidence available, it seemed this would be a formality, so much so that Ian Phillips and Eddie Jordan paid scant attention to finding a replacement driver for the Pacific Grand Prix in 10 days' time.

Irvine was accompanied by Steve Nichols (complete with telemetry read-outs and other proof of Irvine's predicament in Brazil) and Ian Titchmarsh (a lawyer with a thorough knowledge and understanding of motor sport) on the trip to Paris on 6 April.

When a subdued Irvine duly reported back to base, Phillips could not believe what he was hearing. Not only had the appeal been rejected, Irvine's ban had been extended from one race to three. The fact that the $10,000 fine had been rescinded was almost an insult. The entire affair was unprecedented.

The team was shattered by the news. The flood of calls, apart from offering sympathy, wanted to know precisely why such heavy-handed action had been taken. There were no obvious answers – other than to suggest that the FIA had been out to teach Irvine a lesson, come what may.

Barrichello, meanwhile, had driven a flawless race at Interlagos. The two pit stops for refuelling had gone without a hitch and, at the end of 70 laps for the Brazilian, he found himself in fourth place. The car, as he had said from the outset, was perfect. In 97 minutes, Jordan Grand Prix had scored the same number of points it had taken eight months to achieve in 1993.

Nip and tuck

The Irvine affair soured everything as the team set about finding a replacement at such short notice. Jordan had just signed Kelvin Burt as a test driver but the reigning British Formula 3 Champion, for all his youthful promise, would be out of his depth in Japan without so much as having sat in the car. In the event, they may as well have taken the Englishman on the long haul to the Orient.

Aguri Suzuki was chosen to fill the breach, the Japanese driver having the benefit of actually being on hand and available – not to mention $250,000 in sponsorship to support his application for the vacancy. The actual figure was not circulated at the time but it was clear that money would have changed hands since Suzuki's reputation was not brilliant. Even so, Eddie Jordan became indignant when the Italian press suggested Suzuki had been selected purely for financial gain; Jordan genuinely believed that the Japanese driver could put up a good show. When Suzuki qualified 20th, 1.5 seconds behind Barrichello in eighth place, such expectations seemed naive and merely exacerbated the denials of fiscal opportunism. In any case, Eddie Jordan was now focused entirely on Barrichello and the need to have a good result to help heal the wounds inflicted by the FIA.

Motorway madness

Even though Irvine was absent, the story refused to go away. With very few exceptions, the paddock expressed shock at the nature of the punishment and the FIA's standing received a further knock when its president, Max Mosley, fatuously compared the Brazilian incident with a motorway accident.

The Jordan team had already been perplexed by Mosley's behaviour following his off-the-record encouragement to go ahead and appeal while, at the same time, telling others that Irvine was in need of a sharp lesson. Eddie Jordan was mystified by Mosley's attitude. And now, the teams were wondering why they had been dragged all the way to Honshu Island and then transported into a mountainous region where the access was so restricted that only the chosen few could travel by car. Even worse was the fact that the new circuit, designed by a wealthy motor racing enthusiast, Hajime Tanaka, scarcely made the trip worthwhile.

Eddie Jordan and the drivers stayed in the only hotel nearby. Life was so dull that Eddie was in bed by nine each night. But at least he was saved the inconvenience imposed on the rest of the team on race morning when they left their respective hotels at 5 am in order to beat the 900 coaches – or most of them, anyway – aiming for the narrow road leading to the circuit. Still, there was the prospect of a reasonable race although, in truth, no one genuinely expected a repeat of Brazil. Eighty-three laps round this place threatened to be very demanding.

On the podium

The retirement list opened at the first corner when Ayrton Senna and Nicola Larini's Ferrari spun off. Rubens, having made another good start, grabbed his chance and finished the first lap in fifth place.

He never looked back. Driving brilliantly throughout, and never letting up for a second, he was perfectly placed when others made mistakes or suffered mechanical failure. The only heart-stopping moment came at the second pit stop when the engine cut out as he came to a halt. For an instant it seemed that the hot V10 might not fire. But it did, and Barrichello rejoined the fray, having slipped from second to fourth. Then the McLaren of Martin Brundle dropped out.

With 15 laps to go, Barrichello was third. The prospect of finishing on the podium for the first time brought a return of the apprehension which had filled the team the previous October when a few hundred miles down the road at Suzuka. Now fifth place would be a major disappointment. How things had changed in the space of six months.

As the 194 accelerated into view for the last time, the entire team lined the wall, Eddie Jordan and Brian Hart embracing each other as they balanced precariously on a railing at the back of the frenzied, blue-shirted throng. They had come a long way, these two. Now the names Jordan and Hart were third in the Constructors' Championship – ahead of the reigning champions, Williams-Renault. Eddie and Brian were fit to burst.

As for Gary Anderson and his technical team, this had been a wonderful reward for the struggle in 1993. But as the champagne popped, Anderson, Steve Nichols, Mark Smith and Andrew Green sat down to examine the data produced during this landmark event.

They knew as well as anyone that the Pacific Grand Prix had merely been an opening skirmish in the 1994 championship. Within a couple of weeks it would be history. Another 14 Grands Prix beckoned in this race without end. And then it would be time for Eddie Jordan to stand up again and say the 1995 car was one of the best his team had ever made . . .

Index